GREAT KINGDOMS
OF AFRICA

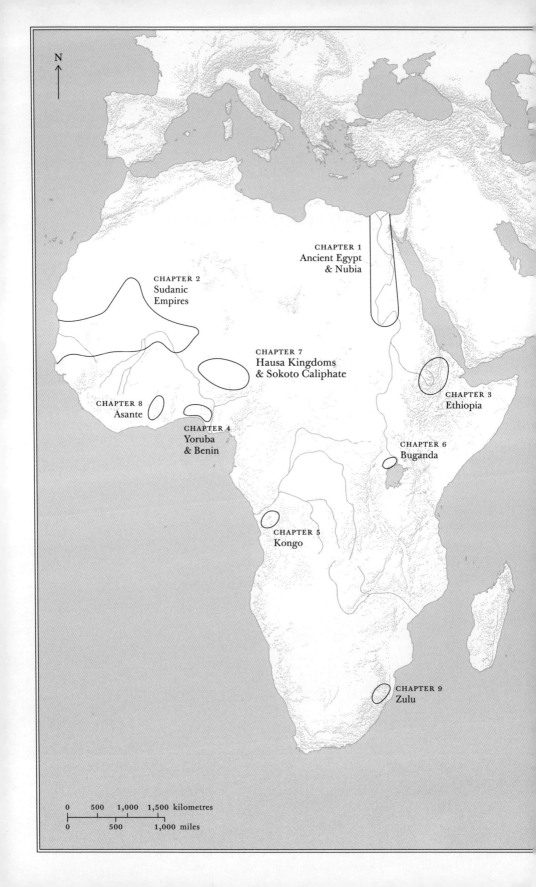

N

CHAPTER 1
Ancient Egypt
& Nubia

CHAPTER 2
Sudanic
Empires

CHAPTER 7
Hausa Kingdoms
& Sokoto Caliphate

CHAPTER 3
Ethiopia

CHAPTER 8
Asante

CHAPTER 4
Yoruba
& Benin

CHAPTER 6
Buganda

CHAPTER 5
Kongo

CHAPTER 9
Zulu

| 0 | 500 | 1,000 | 1,500 kilometres |

| 0 | 500 | 1,000 miles |

GREAT KINGDOMS
OF AFRICA

Edited by John Parker

Foreword by David Adjaye

Endpapers: Woman's rayon *kente* cloth with fine silk details woven at
Bonwire village, Ghana. Photo James Austin. From *African Textiles: Colour
and Creativity Across a Continent* by John Gillow, Thames & Hudson Ltd.

First published in the United Kingdom in 2023 by Thames & Hudson Ltd,
181A High Holborn, London WC1V 7QX

Great Kingdoms of Africa © 2023 Thames & Hudson Ltd, London
Foreword © 2023 David Adjaye
Introduction © John Parker
Text edited by John Parker

Designed by Matthew Young
Maps on pp. 2, 28, 56, 86, 114, 142, 168, 198, 224 and 252 by Matthew Young

British Library Cataloguing-in-Publication Data
A catalogue record for this book is available from the British Library

ISBN 978-0-500-25252-9

Printed by Shenzhen Reliance Printing Co. Ltd

Be the first to know about our new releases,
exclusive content and author events by visiting
thamesandhudson.com
thamesandhudsonusa.com
thamesandhudson.com.au

CONTENTS

RECLAIMING ANCESTRAL NARRATIVES

Sir David Adjaye OBE

While Ghana is my ancestral homeland, growing up in various locations across Africa and becoming attuned to its rich diversity of cultures and histories gave me a distinctively pan-African view of the continent. After this formative experience, I went on to document all fifty-four African capital cities during a ten-year period spent investigating the role of architecture in the making of urban space. This became a study less about the construction of symbolic urban objects than about the synthesis of cultures going back over several centuries. I came to see the city as an inclusive conglomerate of shared identity rather than a series of free-standing architectural icons. A similar ethos drives this book, which seeks to understand African kingdoms not by the usual historical periods, but on their own unique evolutionary terms.

Through my research, it became clear to me that the political map of Africa has distorted our capacity to recognize the diversity of its cultures and the critical role of geography in shaping its histories. I developed a different kind of map of the continent, which became the basis for classifying its capital cities according to their position in one of six geographic terrains. These distinct terrains – the Maghrib, the Desert, the Sahel, the Savanna and Grassland, the Forest, and the Mountain and Highveld – portray the continent as a place of shared geographical inflections and identities. It is this range of terrains that has enabled such diverse kingdoms to emerge and mutate within a single continental plate.

The map of the African kingdoms in this book can also be seen as a redrawing of the colonial diagram. The edges of these kingdoms appear deliberately imprecise. Like geographies, they are flexible and constantly shifting forces. Applying my geographical methodology to the kingdoms, ancient Egypt and Nubia would fall under the category of Desert; the Sudanic empires between Desert and Sahel; Ethiopia predominantly Mountain and Highveld; the Hausa kingdoms and Sokoto Caliphate Savanna and Grassland; and Zulu between Grassland and Mountain and Highveld. The other four kingdoms could all be considered as falling within Forest territory: Yoruba and Benin, Buganda, Kongo and Asante. This reflects the contemporary situation, where the Forest region has the largest number of capitals, many of which are port cities. While the forest itself has often been cleared, the combination of heat and moisture and consequent settlement patterns still determine the character of these places.

This book offers a critical reclaiming of African kingdoms. It looks anew at these historic regions and understands systematically the relationships between them. Their identities are intertwined physically with features such as rivers and lakes; spatially with urbanization, temples and tombs; and materially with things such as gold and art. A key part of this process of reclaiming narratives is to understand the long histories and ongoing trajectories of these kingdoms.

For as long as I have practised architecture, I have been fascinated by indigenous civilizations. I am interested in the root essence of places. My work is developed out of a particular set of circumstances and an interrogation of contexts. I think of architecture as constructed narratives, by which I mean making buildings in deep dialogue with both time and place. This entails constructing buildings that acknowledge their histories, while creating something entirely new to serve communities into the future. Two of my projects in particular engage directly with the narratives of African kingdoms:

the National Museum of African American History and Culture in Washington, D.C. (completed in 2016), and the Edo Museum of West African Art in Benin City, Nigeria (ongoing). In my mind, they have a dialectical relationship: the former is about a reconciliation of our present, the latter speaks to a recovery of our past.

The National Museum of African American History and Culture addresses this present condition and the evolution of the African diaspora. It occupies what was the last vacant site in Washington's National Mall, a symbolic place and a charged landscape. Celebrating the importance of the Black community in the social fabric of American life, I designed the 'corona' structure – an inverted pyramid form – taking inspiration from a triple-tiered crowned sculpture created by the famous Yoruba craftsman Olowe of Ise (*c.* 1873–*c.* 1938). This silhouette has since become the primary register for the building, which relates the diaspora so profoundly to their origins in Africa. In contrast to its neighbours made of stone and marble, it is also the National Mall's only metal building, which is in part a reference to the bronze and copper traditions of Benin. In so many ways, the museum brings a certain tangibility to the remarkable contribution of the African American community.

The Edo Museum of West African Art is a key element in a project aimed at the restoration of Benin City, the capital of one of the continent's most ancient kingdoms. To be situated adjacent to the Oba's palace, the epicentre of the kingdom of Benin, the museum will house repatriated artefacts and art seized during the British colonial conquest of 1897. Given the significance of this project, the museum is envisaged as part of a larger masterplan that will excavate, preserve and restore Benin City's extensive system of earthwork walls punctuated by moats and gates. I designed the new museum to connect to the city's extraordinary earthen landscape, its orthogonal (or right-angled) walls and its courtyard networks. The museum will be a set of elevated pavilions, taking their form from the very fragments of these historic compounds. I want Benin City to regain its position as an artefact in and of itself. I see the Edo Museum as a re-teaching tool – a place for recalling lost collective memories and to instil an understanding of the cultural foundations of Africa.

From my Accra office, I am now involved in the making of other civic buildings across Africa, which I approach in a similar way to the Edo Museum: using architecture to illuminate history and form collective identities. On a personal level, I have also returned to my ancestral land in the Akuapem hills of Ghana and constructed a country home for myself in my father's village. To be rooted locally, I designed it using rammed earth and it has been constructed organically. I am entirely preoccupied with thinking about the elemental quality of earth, our co-relationship with nature and the origins of Black architecture. Like this book, I believe my return is a process of going back to the past to reconstruct the future.

KINGS, KINGSHIP AND KINGDOMS IN AFRICAN HISTORY

John Parker

In 2018, King Mswati III of Swaziland decided to mark his country's fiftieth anniversary of independence by changing its name to Eswatini. Wedged between South Africa and Mozambique and with an area of just 6,704 sq. miles (10,789 sq. km) and a population of 1.1 million, Eswatini is one of Africa's smallest nations. It is also the continent's last absolute monarchy. Emerging as a distinct state in the mid-eighteenth century and consolidating its position a century later under the forceful leadership of Mswati II, the kingdom of the Swazi people, or *Umboso weSwatini*, was one of the few in Africa to survive European colonial rule and emerge intact as a modern nation in the era of renewed sovereignty in the 1960s. Indeed, Sobhuza II, who became king at the age of four months in 1899 and who oversaw that transition, is one of the longest-reigning monarchs in world history; after a brief experiment with democracy following independence from Britain, he suspended the Westminster-style constitution and ruled by royal decree until his death in 1982. Today, Mswati III, on the throne since 1986, continues to govern as king or *Ngwenyama* ('the lion'), in consultation with his queen mother or *Ndlovukati* ('the she-elephant'). Together they preside over the hallowed annual rituals of *ncwala* and *umhlanga* – the latter emerging in recent years as a matter of concern for women's rights activists, as it was then that each year the king was presented with a young bride to add to his retinue of wives.

Eswatini remains one of just a handful of absolute monarchies – systems of government in which a hereditary ruler holds or dominates executive power – left in today's world. So-called constitutional monarchies, such as the United Kingdom or Japan, are more common: in these, kings or queens continue to symbolize or embody the nation as 'head of state', but real authority has been devolved to representative bodies like parliaments. Yet the decline of royal power is a relatively recent phenomenon in world history: dynastic kings emerged as the rulers of the earliest centralized states in the Middle East, Africa, Asia, Europe and the Americas, and continued generally to hold sway for thousands of years until the idea of absolute monarchy began to come under attack from the seventeenth century. In Africa, as elsewhere, kingship went into terminal decline only in the twentieth century and in some cases this is an ongoing process: in Morocco, which following independence in 1956 saw the restoration of the long-established Alaouite dynasty, it was as recently as 2011 that King Mohammed VI agreed to a reduction in his autocratic power in an effort to placate popular protest associated with the Arab Spring. The current direction of those reforms, however, is unclear. Throughout much of the rest of the continent, moreover, 'traditional' kingship continues to function within modern nation-states. Shorn of most of its political sovereignty, it remains a focus for older and more localized forms of identity, culture and sacred power. This is not to say that centralized kingdoms dominated Africa's varied political landscapes throughout history: as we will see, the ability of many of the continent's peoples to govern themselves without recourse to kings may be just as important as the state-building efforts of would-be dynastic rulers. Yet from the ancient Nile Valley to the savannas of medieval West Africa, the highlands of Ethiopia and on to the forests and grasslands stretching away to the south, African civilizations have given rise to some of the world's most impressive kingdoms. The history of these kingdoms and the nature of royal power at their core is the subject of this book.

Over the course of some five thousand years of recorded history, Africa has witnessed the rise and decline of hundreds of kingdoms, great and small. These have been ruled by countless kings: the great majority of them have been men, but queens too have played a role in the African past, as have powerful 'queen mothers' like the *Ndlovukati* of Eswatini. No one book can consider all of them, so what this one does is to focus on nine key regions where centralized states and expansive empires emerged at different times to dominate the political landscape. Some of the nine chapters look at the history of a single famous kingdom, while others trace a broader and longer political tradition that gave rise to a sequence of states. Perhaps the best-known of these regional trajectories is the succession of three great empires in medieval West Africa: Ghana, Mali and Songhay, examined in chapter 2 by Rahmane Idrissa. The first chapter, by David Wengrow, also explores a wider regional context by shifting the history of the emergence of Africa's earliest kingdoms away from its established focus on pharaonic Egypt to a dialogue along the Nile Valley, between Egypt to the north and Nubia to the south. This analysis sets the tone for the chapters that follow: their aim is not simply to offer chronological narratives or reiterate received wisdoms, but to consider fresh insights into the role of kingdoms and kingship in African history. Understandings of this key aspect of Africa's past have changed in significant ways since the history of the continent emerged as a subject of sustained academic study in the mid-twentieth century. Over that time, much has been achieved in recovering and interpreting histories of state-building in Africa: no longer is the continent's deep past an indistinct realm of 'lost kingdoms'. Yet the African past does remain poorly integrated with that of the rest of the world – a marginalization, as Michael A. Gomez argues in his recent study of empire in West Africa, that has only been underlined with the recent emergence of the field of 'global' history.[1] This book seeks to contribute to the task of rectifying that marginalization by presenting to a general readership some of the most exciting recent developments in the understanding of states and societies in the African past.

CHANGING PERCEPTIONS
OF KINGSHIP IN AFRICA

What exactly is a king and what distinguishes him from ordinary people? Do kings – and queens – forge their own power as autonomous historical actors, or are they created by wider social structures and processes? Are they predators or peacemakers, and do the systems of dynastic rule they preside over function by coercion or by consent? How, in the words of one study of the rituals of royalty, 'are people persuaded to acquiesce to a polity where the distribution of power is manifestly unequal and unjust, as it invariably is?'[2] Africa's diverse peoples have long had their own debates about these questions. As everywhere, the nature of political power has been gradually worked out, experimented with, modified and contested over time. Africans also developed their own ways of recording and celebrating – and sometimes critiquing – the history of dynastic states and the kings who ruled over them. As we will see in the chapters that follow, recovering and interpreting these political traditions remains a key task for the continent's present-day historians. To begin to make sense of Africa's bewildering variety of historical experience, however, we need first to think about how scholarly perceptions of African kingship more broadly have taken shape. What factors, in other words, have shaped what can be called the 'production of knowledge' about Africa in the modern world?

The first point to make is that the production of knowledge about Africa and its peoples took place in a particular historical context: the increasingly unequal encounter between the continent and the world beyond it in the age of European imperialism. This culminated in the violence and dispossession of the European conquest and partition of Africa in the late nineteenth and early twentieth centuries – from which only the ancient kingdom of Ethiopia emerged as an independent state. In the opening phase of globalized interaction, European slave traders, explorers, missionaries, envoys and, ultimately, conquerors were all drawn to Africa's royal courts – that is, to recognized authority figures with whom they could negotiate or do business. Like earlier Arabic accounts of Africa south of the Sahara Desert, the records of these contacts therefore tend to stress the prominence of powerful kings – 'savage' or 'barbaric' kings in the ugly racialized language of the time, but the rulers of centralized kingdoms, nonetheless. As the age of European exploration and commercial penetration gave way to that of conquest, it was the same kings and their associated ruling elites who were often best placed to negotiate the terms of colonial rule. Despite having lost much of their authority, they used what remained to try to control knowledge of the past and of their own role in it. Kings, that is to argue, were clearly of great historical importance – but in some cases they might not have been quite as important as outside observers or they themselves sought to demonstrate.

In some parts of the continent, such as ancient Egypt, Ethiopia, Islamic North Africa and the so-called Sudanic zone of West Africa, the development of literate cultures gave rise to the production of royal chronicles and other written documents from which dynastic histories can be recovered. Elsewhere, it was often the imposition of colonial rule that led to the writing down of what had long been orally transmitted traditions of kingship. Some of this innovative textual production was by European missionaries and officials, but much of the most important was by newly literate African elites or 'cultural brokers'. One famous example of the latter from British-ruled Uganda, examined in chapter 6, is *Basekabaka be Buganda*, a history of the kings of Buganda first published in 1901 by the kingdom's prime minister and leading intellectual, Apolo Kaggwa. Other, non-elite views of the past were often drowned out and are only now beginning to be recovered.[3] Yet the production of knowledge in colonial Africa was dominated not by the discipline of history but by that of anthropology. It was anthropologists – whose research focused not on the past but on the contemporary 'ethnographic present' – who sought to understand how African societies continued to govern themselves within the framework of colonial overrule. Initial findings from those regions under British rule were drawn together in 1940 in a landmark volume edited by M. Fortes and E. E. Evans-Pritchard. *African Political Systems* divided societies into two broad groups: one characterized by the presence of royal authority, administrative machinery and judicial institutions, that is, by states; the other by the absence of centralized rule – so-called stateless or 'segmentary' societies. This picture of a polarized political landscape is now regarded as too simplistic and too static. A significant revision was soon suggested by the anthropologist Aidan Southall, who, based on his research among the Alur people of northern Uganda, argued that between kingdoms and non-centralized societies there existed a third structure of governance he called 'segmentary states'. Southall defined these as states in which the reach of political sovereignty and ritual authority did not exactly coincide: direct political control was confined to a central, core domain, while ritual authority extended beyond that core 'towards a flexible, changing periphery'.[4] What a given kingdom looked like could depend on the position one viewed it from.

These colonial-era models of political systems are just that: models. It would take the advent of historical research in Africa's new universities and beyond in the era of decolonization and independence to flesh them out by looking back in time and considering the circumstances in which individual kingdoms emerged, expanded and in turn declined. Yet pioneering anthropologists made a crucial observation about African kings, one that has contributed to an understanding of the nature of kingship in other parts of the world as well. Royal power, that is, was fundamentally underpinned by ritual authority. 'An African ruler is not to his people merely a person who can enforce his will on them', Fortes and Evans-Pritchard argued; 'his credentials are mystical'. The 'mystical values' of kingship typically referred to the preservation of fertility, health, prosperity, peace and justice, and were symbolically dramatized in great public ceremonies that expressed 'the privileges and the obligations of political office'.[5] A classic example of such an annual ritual drama was the *ncwala* of the Swazi kingdom. *Ncwala*, depending on which of many interpretations of the ceremony one favours, served to renew the identity of the king as an agent of fertility, as a heroic warrior and as a sacred 'stranger'.[6] As interpretations of 'the king's two bodies' and the curative powers of the 'royal touch' in medieval and early modern Europe have shown, the entanglement of political and ritual authority has not been limited to Africa.[7] Indeed, in a recent re-examination of the ritual aspects of kingship, the historical anthropologists David Graeber and Marshall Sahlins argue that claims to divine power 'have been the raison d'être of political power throughout the greater part of human history'.[8]

The understanding of kingship in Africa took a new turn as historians began to examine the continent's past. If anthropology developed as a 'colonial science' (despite anthropologists often taking a dim view of the damaging impact of European rule on the people they studied), then African history as a discipline took shape in the era of anti-colonial nationalism and the liberation struggles of the 1950s and 1960s. The imperative for many of this first generation of historians was to reject the denigrating colonialist view that Africans had no history worth studying by recovering a 'usable past' of achievement in state-building and governance. The succession of powerful Islamic dynasties in North Africa could hardly be denied, but it was in these years that attention turned to the forging of kingdoms and empires by civilizations south of the Sahara. The long history of connectivity across the desert also began to emerge, most prominently the role of Islam and long-distance trade in the emergence of the great empires of what medieval Arab geographers called the *bilad al-Sudan*, 'the land of the Blacks'. More controversially, trans-Saharan connections took shape in the idea that a distinctive 'Sudanic civilization' may have been influenced by the diffusion of rituals of divine kingship from pharaonic Egypt. There was in fact little evidence to support the notion of ancient Egypt as the font of African statecraft – an argument that had uncomfortable echoes of the

colonial-era Hamitic Hypothesis, the racist myth that any sophistication in African civilization could only have been the result of conquest
by waves of light-skinned 'Hamitic' invaders from the north.[9]

The phase of history writing focused on the heroic achievement
of African kingdoms as an exemplar for modern nation-building,
however, was short-lived. As early as the 1970s, more radical scholars
influenced by Marxist thought were inclined to portray states –
whether precolonial, colonial or postcolonial – less as mechanisms
of good governance than as engines of exploitation. While nationalist
historians looked to the political logic of states, Marxist scholars
looked to their productive logic; the dispute between them, an early
survey of these divergent interpretations pointed out, 'was really
over the evolutionist assumption that it is "better" to live in states'.[10]
For those non-centralized African peoples who struggled to preserve
their independence from would-be state-builders, this assumption
was surely wrong. For many who came under the rule of kings, too,
dynastic power was something to be wary about: for the Nyoro
people of Uganda, for example, the concept of 'rule' was synonymous with 'oppression'.[11] Yet there was a great deal of other evidence
to suggest that many African communities did think that it was more
civilized to live under the rule of kings – despite the trouble they
could sometimes cause. Much of this evidence is embedded in oral
traditions, which would emerge as such a crucial source for the
continent's historians. Those traditions preserving the origins or the
'founding charters' of states often tell stories of the borrowing of
the institution of kingship from more sophisticated neighbours.
Olatunji Ojo examines one famous example in chapter 4: that of
the kingdom of Benin in present-day Nigeria, whose elders appealed
to the ruler of Ile-Ife, the 'cosmic metropolis' of the nearby Yoruba-
speaking peoples, to send them a divine prince. Others tell stories
of roving immigrants, heroic 'strangers' from beyond the established
cultural order who usurped power from autocratic tyrants and instituted just and sacred kingship. Those left without kings were often
dismissed as either unfortunate or uncouth by those who had them:

as the immigrant Suku peoples sang of the Mbale in what is now the Democratic Republic of the Congo: 'They are *bahika* (slaves) because they have no king'.[12] Likewise, the upstart city of Ibadan in nineteenth-century Yorubaland was denounced by its more ancient rivals as being 'without a king or even a constitution'.[13]

More recent historical research has moved beyond the analysis of African kingdoms as either triumphs of effective governance, on the one hand, or as engines of predation, on the other. There is now a greater focus on the nature of political cultures and the ongoing relationship between states and the societies from which they arose. These approaches have been shaped by an increasing interest in the continent's social history – the challenge for which was to seek out new sources of information beyond the authorized dynastic tradi-tions, which kings since the time of the Egyptian pharaohs had used to impose an 'official' view of the past and thereby consolidate their own rule. A new generation of Egyptologists, for example, looked to the written records left by communities of working people and to the dynamics of the religious realm in order 'to liberate ancient Egypt's complexity from the weight of its official ideology'.[14] South of the Sahara, too, the discovery of new historical sources and the reinterpretation of old ones have offered fresh perspectives on the process of state-building. One recent example is the work of Paulo de Moraes Farias on medieval Arabic epigraphy (i.e. inscriptions on stone) in present-day Mali, which challenges some key aspects of the 'imperial tradition' as enshrined in chronicles produced in seventeenth-century Timbuktu (see chapter 2).[15] Another is the anal-ysis by Neil Kodesh of political identity and well-being in Buganda, which offers a perspective on the history of the kingdom quite dif-ferent from that of Apolo Kaggwa's dynastic narrative, *Basekabaka be Buganda*. In his tellingly titled book, *Beyond the Royal Gaze*, Kodesh considers how Buganda might have looked not from its royal court but from its peripheries, where older traditions of public healing and belonging that focused on sacred sites continued to shape clan identities after the accumulation of centralized power from the seventeenth century. As we will see in chapter 6, this revisionist view of Buganda suggests the importance for the history of the Great Lakes region of East Africa and for the continent more broadly of 'diffuse forms of power, as well as ritual and other types of knowledge, in achieving political complexity'.[16]

RITUAL POWER AND POLITICAL COMPLEXITY

These and other studies demonstrate an emerging tendency on the part of historians, anthropologists and archaeologists to return to the earlier idea that kingship in Africa was originally – and in many ways remained – an essentially sacred institution. The same argument has been made for many other parts of the world, from the so-called theatre state of nineteenth-century Bali to the 'galactic' or 'cosmic' polities elsewhere in Southeast and South Asia and on to the pre-Columbian empires of the Americas and the chiefdoms of Polynesia. It is the central contention of Graeber and Sahlins's recent book, *On Kings*. Understanding the sacred logic of power is crucial, Graeber writes of Merina and other highland states of the island of Madagascar, because these kingdoms were organized essentially on ritual terms. 'This is not to deny that they were not also vast forms of labor extraction', he cautions; 'rather, it is to suggest that within them no clear distinction between what we call "work" and what we call "ritual" could be made'.[17] Neither is it to deny that many African kingdoms used wealth generated from agricultural production, from trade or from tribute to develop sophisticated mechanisms of governance, supported and extended by military technology. Indeed, there is no doubt that state formation was closely shaped by the successful exploitation of different environmental niches, by the exchange of commodities across ecological zones and, in some cases, by military violence. Yet it is a mistake, as Graeber suggests, to separate these bases of real or 'rational' power from an imaginary realm of mystical power, as African peoples themselves never drew such a distinction.

Another set of terms that scholars have used to describe these contrasting realms is 'instrumental' power and 'creative' power. 'Unlike political leadership in Europe, realized in imperative control backed by armed forces', Wyatt MacGaffey argues, 'African and especially Central African leadership depended on manifesting the kind of power that Europeans think of as supernatural, although "the supernatural" did not exist in traditional African thought'. 'The "religion" of Kongo', MacGaffey writes, '*was* its political theory'.[18]

Understanding the historical development of African political theories and of the creativity of power at their heart is beginning to supersede an older and often futile search for the origins of states and of kingship.[19] Jan Vansina's insightful book on the deep past of Angola, *How Societies Are Born* (2004) suggests that 'origins' have not completely disappeared over the academic horizon. As chapter 1 on Egypt and Nubia's earliest kingdoms demonstrates, archaeologists too will certainly have more to say on the matter. Yet there is a growing recognition on the part of historians that although hallowed oral traditions are crucial to an understanding of kingship, such myths of origin tell us more about how power was conceptualized and mobilized by those who held it than about what 'really' happened at the dawn of remembered time. Rather than being disinterested repositories of historical knowledge, in other words, traditions of origins functioned more as self-serving and malleable commentaries on the nature of sacred royal power. This shift in interpretation is perhaps most apparent in the study of the dramatic origin myths of the Bantu-speaking savanna kingdoms of the present-day Democratic Republic of the Congo, Angola and Zambia, which share stories of founding culture heroes, who, crossing rivers from the east, insinuated themselves into societies ruled over by corrupt, violent and infertile despots and then sired warrior sons who overthrew the anarchic order and instituted sacred kingship (see chapter 5). It can be seen too in new approaches to the great Mande epic of Sunjata, the heroic thirteenth-century founder of the West African kingdom of Mali, whose exploits are preserved in the song cycles of the famous *griots*.[20] And it is there in an emerging understanding of the rise of kingdoms in the Great Lakes region of East Africa, where history begins with the first men and women sent down from heaven to earth followed by dynasties of spirits that came to be reconceptualized as kings, or of kings who after death became spirits.

Enshrined in many of these dynastic myths of origin is the fundamental idea of the king as a stranger, not only originating from beyond society but also situated above it. It encapsulates the ambivalent nature of kingship: as the source of order, fertility and well-being, but also a thing apart – volatile, capricious and potentially dangerous. This widespread notion of the king as a sort of sacred monster emerges too from rituals of royal succession and from the great annual festivals like the *ncwala* of the Swazi or the *odwira* of Asante. In many arid regions of eastern and southern Africa, the king was also a rainmaker; there and elsewhere, he presided over the ceremonial advent of the new harvest as the guarantor of human prosperity. Yet typically embedded within these ceremonies were more threatening reminders that kingship transcended the normal rules and constraints of society: dramatizations of royal incest, or, as in Asante and Dahomey, the all too real ritual killing of sacrificial victims. At these dramatic moments in the annual ritual cycle, power was on public display for all to see and revel in. Yet at other, normal times it was often hidden away. The fringed beaded crowns that covered the faces of Yoruba kings (see pl. x), for example, signified the concealed nature of royal power. In the Bulozi kingdom of Zambia, the secluded king was known as the 'hidden hippopotamus' – a reminder that, as with the king of Eswatini's praise name of *Ngwenyama*, 'the lion', the power of kings was often symbolically equated with that of volatile and potentially dangerous wild animals.[21]

Yet ideologies of kingship in Africa were unlikely to have been forged by the marvellous, transformative actions of mystical culture heroes so often preserved in traditions of origin. Rather, archaeological and linguistic evidence suggests that 'pathways to complexity' – meaning the emergence of states – tended to unfold over many generations or even centuries, as the gradual development of production, trade, wealth and, ultimately, inequality, gave rise to a perceived need for centralized institutions and 'territorial' leadership that transcended older bonds of kinship and community.[22] The Swazi kingdom took definitive shape in the eighteenth and nineteenth centuries, for example, but in 1894 the royal house could recite forty-one generations of kings going back deep into the past.[23] Nor, as Vansina has shown for west Central Africa, was there ever 'a single inherent program that automatically forced people to expand the scale of their societies' or to wrest power from villages 'in order to concentrate it in a single capital'.[24] Rather, he argues, people debated and made choices about how to solve problems of governance – choices shaped by local environments and by collective imagination. As the role of chiefs became more permanent, people speculated about the sacred wellsprings of power and developed new political vocabularies with which to speak about them. In northern Angola by 1600, for example, the key political concept was *ulamba*, 'authority' or 'majesty'; to the south among the emergent Ndongo kingdom, it was *ngola* (from which early Portuguese colonists derived the name Angola); and far to the east in what would emerge as the Luba kingdom, it was *bulopwe*. It is likely that it was the gradual spread and localized elaboration of these vernacular concepts of sacred power and the practices of dynastic governance associated with them that came to be personified in traditions recounting the exploits of founding heroes like Kalala Ilunga of the Luba and Cibinda Ilunga of the Lunda.

In Central Africa and elsewhere in the continent, then, the emergence and evolution of kingdoms is now looking somewhat different than it did to earlier generations of historians. State-builders faced very real limits to their ambitions: in a continent with vast expanses of land, open frontiers and historically low population densities, local communities fiercely protective of their autonomy could often simply move away from those who sought to rule them. In time, the development of new forms of military technology and new sources of wealth accumulation – including those generated by participation in the overseas slave trade – enabled warrior kings to impose their will on surrounding peoples through conquest. Yet conquest and coercion are now seen as probably less important in the history of kingship in Africa than creativity and consent. As often as not, dynastic power sought legitimacy by rooting itself within deep-seated understandings of the world and cosmos, and by positioning the king as the arbiter of sacred authority and the protector of culture. If these notions were encapsulated in the language of power, then they were also projected via ritual and through material culture and art. As we will see in Cécile Fromont's chapter on Kongo, art historians are making an increasingly important contribution to an understanding of royal power.[25] The shape and nature of the resulting kingdoms, too, often look very different: more like the old model of segmentary states, characterized by a core region surrounded by a periphery linked to the royal court through various mechanisms of reciprocity and exchange. Kingdoms such as Luba and Lunda, once viewed as expansive 'empires', for example, now look more like loose confederations or commonwealths, where office-holders in outlying areas exchanged allegiance to the centre for the civilizing benefits conferred by its courtly culture.[26]

AFRICAN KINGDOMS ACROSS TIME AND SPACE

Great Kingdoms of Africa seeks to explore processes of dynastic state-building and understandings of the nature of kingship in the period before the European colonial conquest. The chapters that follow contribute to an emerging picture, which stresses the creative nature of political power, the ongoing dialogue between that power and the broader culture from which it emerged, and the coexistence of political hierarchies with other sources of authority. None of this means that Africa's kingdoms are any less 'great'. It means that African kingdoms need to be considered on their own terms. Indeed, their greatness might be seen to reside less in an ability to dominate and coerce than in their inventiveness in forging forms of statecraft able to secure legitimacy by more inclusive means. Neither is it to say that heroic histories of warrior kings, in which dynamic leaders emerge from the underlying structures of society to seize the political initiative, are nothing but invented traditions. There is ample evidence to demonstrate that dynastic politics – rather than generalized notions of 'political culture' – reshaped the destiny of African kingdoms and the peoples they sought to rule. Dynastic power, moreover, did not emerge and operate in a vacuum: if one of the faults of early anthropology was to consider African societies as self-contained 'tribal' communities, it is equally misleading to view the continent's history in isolation from the broader global forces with which it interacted. The role of trans-Saharan connectivity in the rise and decline of medieval Sudanic empires is a crucial case in point. From the sixteenth century, globalized interactions increasingly included those with slave traders and other agents of an expansionist western Europe, whose arrival on the coasts of Africa disrupted existing economic circuits and shifted the dynamics of political power.

The application of the successive historical periods of ancient, medieval and modern to Africa has not been without controversy. Originally devised for European history, these terms have been criticized for failing to reflect African realities – although alternatives such as a sort of medieval 'African Iron Age' have been no more successful in capturing the continent's complexity. Historical processes unfolded in different ways across Africa's diverse regions, so such a simple division of time is never going to fit everything or everywhere – and has been questioned on this score for Europe as well.[27] In terms of the enlargement of social scale, increase in political complexity and emergence of centralized kingdoms, however, it is possible to discern a broad sequence of development. Africa's earliest states in Egypt and Nubia together with Roman North Africa, the Ethiopian kingdom of Aksum and the urban centre of Jenne-jeno in present-day Mali (founded in the third century BCE) all belong unambiguously in the realm of antiquity; developments in eastern and southern Africa before 400 CE have also been described as an African 'Classical Age'.[28] Although the advent of a subsequent era turns to some extent upon the perceptions of outsiders, Arabic-language sources dating from the ninth century CE, which first record the existence of the kingdoms of Ghana and Gao in the Sahel or southern 'shore' of the Sahara, can be taken to mark the start of a distinctive African Middle Ages. If this era continues to be most clearly associated with the 'imperial tradition' of Sudanic West Africa, the first half of the second millennium CE also saw the development of long-distance trade and centralized states in a variety of other regions as well: the West African forest, Hausaland, the Zimbabwe Plateau and west Central Africa.[29]

The series of transformations taking shape across much of Africa from the late sixteenth century points to another broad turning point in the continent's history. Not all of these were associated with increasing interaction with Europe: the Battle of Tondibi in 1591, which saw a gun-bearing army dispatched across the Sahara by Sultan Ahmad al-Mansur of Morocco defeat Songhay and bring an end to the eight-hundred-year imperial tradition, has been identified as marking the end of West Africa's medieval period. By 1600, too, centralized kingdoms were beginning to take shape in the savanna to the south of the Congo rainforest and in the Great Lakes region of East Africa. Yet it was expansion of the Atlantic slave trade and the consequent upsurge in predation and violence that acted as a catalyst for a new form of state-building. Some existing kingdoms, such as Jolof in the Senegambian region, were destabilized and fatally weakened by the trade in enslaved people. Elsewhere, firearms, enslavement and new sources of wealth underpinned the rise of expansionist West African kingdoms such as Oyo, Asante, Dahomey and Segu: so-called fiscal-military states that departed to some extent from the model of a more consensual sacred kingship.[30] As we will see, militarized state-building continued into the nineteenth century: in the forging in Hausaland and beyond of the vast Sokoto Caliphate; in the reinvigoration of imperial rule in Christian Ethiopia; and, perhaps most emblematically, in the dramatic emergence in southern Africa of the Zulu kingdom.

It was in the second half of the nineteenth century that these and other ongoing state-building projects came up against a new and increasingly aggressive rival: European imperialism. The result was a series of bitter and often violent regional struggles for power, which have been subsumed under the term 'the Scramble for Africa'. Except for imperial Ethiopia, which in 1896 secured its independence by routing an invading Italian army, these were struggles that African kingdoms lost. For the following half-century or more, the continent was partitioned between seven – and then six – European colonial powers (Germany's colonies were confiscated following its defeat in the First World War). The history of Africa's great kingdoms, however, did not end there. The era of colonial rule was transformative, ending in most cases not with a return to old sovereignties, but with the creation of modern nations based on the frontiers created by colonial rulers. But it was also short and characterized by much continuity from the past. Indeed, many historians are now uncomfortable with another common way of dividing up Africa's history: that is, between its 'precolonial', 'colonial' and 'postcolonial' periods, as if the brief interlude of European domination was the key hinge on which everything else turned. It was not, and it is no longer appropriate to collapse African history before 1900 into an undifferentiated precolonial period. As we will see in this book, the legacy of African kingdoms shaped the continent's history throughout the twentieth century and continues to be felt today.

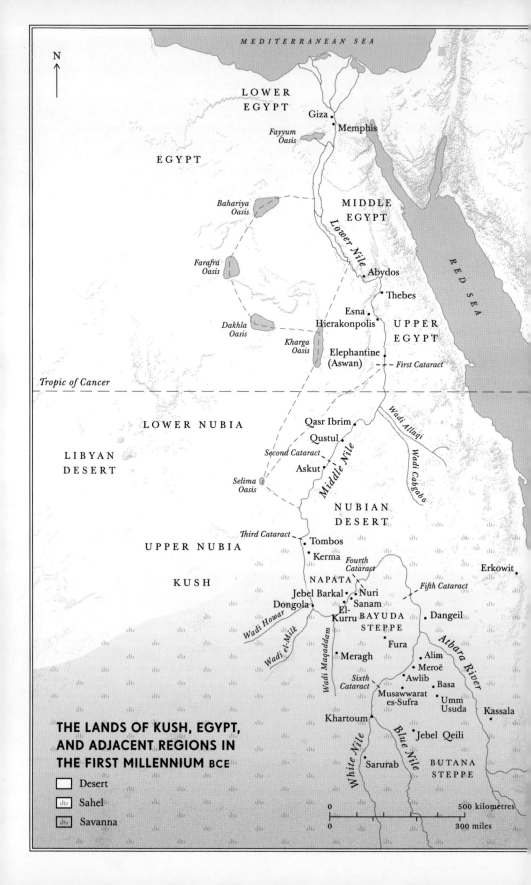

N

MEDITERRANEAN SEA

LOWER
EGYPT

Giza
Memphis

Fayyum
Oasis

EGYPT

MIDDLE
EGYPT

Bahariya
Oasis

Lower Nile

Farafra
Oasis

Abydos

Thebes

Esna
Hierakonpolis

Dakhla
Oasis

UPPER
EGYPT

RED SEA

Kharga
Oasis

Elephantine
(Aswan)

First Cataract

Tropic of Cancer

LOWER NUBIA

Qasr Ibrim

Qustul

Wadi Allaqi

LIBYAN
DESERT

Second Cataract

Askut

Middle Nile

Wadi Gabgaba

Selima
Oasis

NUBIAN
DESERT

Third Cataract

Tombos

UPPER NUBIA

Kerma

Fourth
Cataract

Erkowit

KUSH

NAPATA

Jebel Barkal   Nuri

Fifth Cataract

Dongola   Sanam
El-   Dangeil
Kurru BAYUDA
STEPPE

Wadi Howar

Fura

Wadi el-Milk

Meragh   Alim
Meroë
Awlib

Wadi Maqaddam

Sixth
Cataract

Basa
Musawwarat   Umm
es-Sufra   Usuda   Kassala

Khartoum

Atbara River

THE LANDS OF KUSH, EGYPT,
AND ADJACENT REGIONS IN
THE FIRST MILLENNIUM BCE

White Nile

Blue Nile

Jebel Qeili

Desert

Sarurab

BUTANA
STEPPE

Sahel

Savanna

0   500 kilometres

0   300 miles

CHAPTER 1

ANCIENT EGYPT AND NUBIA
KINGS OF FLOOD AND KINGS OF RAIN

David Wengrow

'Do not become entangled with the Nubians!
... beware of their people, and their conjurors.'

From a letter sent by the Egyptian king Amenhotep II
to User-Satet, Viceroy of Kush, fifteenth century BCE.[1]

History is often written as a story of the rise and fall of kings, but
the history of kingship in Africa, as elsewhere, is shaped as much by
the people kings governed as by the varied nature of kingship itself.
This is as true of the Nile Basin, where Africa's earliest known kingdoms arose, as it is for other parts of the continent. Throughout
history, institutions of monarchy in this region have been a way of
extending personal authority, but also of containing it, by obliging
the incumbents of royal office to perform sacred roles and observe
customary duties to their people. Nilotic kingship could be a stranglehold on power as much as its vehicle, and up until relatively recent
times, certain kings met their ends through suffocation or other
violent means at the hands of their subjects, for failing to fulfil their
ordained roles as protectors of life, fonts of prosperity and bringers
of rain.[2] Which way the pendulum has swung through the centuries
depended no less on the personalities of royal individuals than on
the collective will of their subjects and the extent to which they were

able to refuse commands or, when faced with arbitrary violence, to move away to other pastures. Viewed in such terms, the ancient past of Egypt and Nubia poses intriguing questions for the history of African kingship and politics, which this chapter sets out to introduce.

A VIEW FROM THE KINGDOM OF KUSH

Let us begin by considering the phase of history from 747 to 664 BCE, when Egypt was ruled by a succession of Kushite kings, including Taharqo and Shabaqo, whose royal line originated in the land of Nubia on the Middle Nile, far to the south in what is now central Sudan. Historians have often viewed this episode – the 25th Dynasty of Egypt's pharaonic chronology – as something of a puzzle.[3] Unlike the Persians and Ptolemies who ruled Egypt after them, the kings of Kush assumed control of Egypt's imposing state bureaucracy, as well as much of its military apparatus and extensive royal and temple estates, without first having developed a stable apparatus of government in their own lands. From their temple-towns and royal residences at Napata and Meroë, these Kushite kings claimed control over a greater part of the Sudanese Nile Valley, some 600 miles (1,000 km) in length, while simultaneously governing the whole of the Nile Valley (so-called Upper Egypt) and the Delta (Lower Egypt) as far north as the Mediterranean.

The nature of Kushite rule is often simpler to ascertain in Egypt than it is in the Kushitic half of this 'double kingdom' itself. Partly that is a result of scholarly bias towards Egypt, but there are other reasons. Within its Sudanese territories, from Egypt's southern border at Aswan to Sennar on the Blue Nile, the Kushite (or 'Meroitic') state is often considered an example of 'Sudanic' (as opposed to 'Pharaonic') kingship.[4] In terms of the religious and ceremonial aspects of kingship, the distinction is moot: rulers in both lands derived sovereignty from the gods, notably through the cult of Amun, whose temples were ubiquitous in Egypt and Sudan. Both Egyptian and Kushite kings, moreover, were expected to devote a substantial part of their time to the observance of royal rituals, ancestor cults, festive journeys and the consultation of oracles. The real difference lies in the economic and logistical underpinnings of monarchy in these early Sudanic kingdoms, where population densities were generally far lower, and mobility much greater, than in Egypt.

Meroitic temples, unlike their Egyptian counterparts, were not supported by grand estates, as the alluvial floodplain of the Middle Nile could not foster agrarian production on such a scale. A network of palaces oversaw the collection, storage and distribution of valuable materials acquired through raiding and long-distance trade, which connected the Nile corridor with the Red Sea to the east and the African grasslands to the south. A rich inventory of tropical and savanna products – ivory, gold, ebony, rhinoceros horn, exotic animal skins and pelts, ostrich feathers, as well as goods less visible to the archaeologist, such as spices and resins – passed through them. Palaces were also centres of skilled manufacture, probably including glass and faience production and, at Meroë, a sophisticated iron industry.[5] Yet there is little evidence to suggest that they housed a complex administrative apparatus, or that their ruling elites managed significant surpluses of staple foods or exerted day-to-day control over territories far beyond the immediate ambit of the royal court.[6]

In the absence of territorial sovereignty (which was claimed, but hardly enacted) and without a civil bureaucracy, it is difficult to define what sort of a 'state' ancient Kush really was. Moreover, the ability of Kushitic rulers to undertake political projects was, at least theoretically, limited by their requirement to follow a demanding schedule of religious duties. Kushite coronation ceremonies were carefully staged and repeated at not one, but a series of locations scattered across the country between the Second and Fifth Cataracts of the Nile. Along with the royal household, the new Kushite ruler was then obliged – again, at least in theory – to perform an annual circuit of the country and its many temples for the duration of his reign, in accordance with a fixed ceremonial calendar (a pattern of 'ambulatory kingship').[7] Such demands were not uncommon in Egypt, too, but in ancient Nubia they seem to have formed the substance of kingship to a greater degree, effectively confining the ruler's capacity to act outside the constraints of a traditional pattern.

Ambitious Kushite rulers like Piye, Shabaqo and Taharqo broke through this sacred stranglehold on the expansion of power in spectacular fashion by invading and taking over Egypt to the north. The consequences were profound. In their newly conquered territories – and especially in the ceremonial landscape of Memphis, located at the juncture of the Nile Valley and the Delta – Kushite rulers found an ancient repository of knowledge that was in some respects recognizable, resonating with their own political and theological notions, but in others was foreign and arresting, especially in its technical execution. A striking feature of Kushite hegemony in the eighth and seventh centuries BCE is the care lavished by Kushite rulers on revitalizing, nurturing and conserving the myths, rituals, arts, crafts and architectural skills of earlier Egyptian dynasties, extending back to the 'Pyramid Age' of the third millennium BCE. This care was further reflected in the transfer of cultural forms and practices to their homelands, most strikingly seen in the iconic pyramid fields and temples of El-Kurru, Nuri and Jebel Barkal (see pl. 1).[8]

In terms of governance, perhaps the most significant innovation of the Kushitic 'double kingdom' – from an Egyptian perspective, at least – was the sustained elevation of women to pre-eminent positions in the state and a corresponding development of the female (mothering) role in the theology of Egyptian kingship. In the Kushitic homelands, the political freedom of women and the powerful status of queens and queen-mothers appears to have been an enduring feature of society. Centuries later, this would attract the attention of Greco-Roman and early Christian observers.[9] To the more patriarchal world of the Egyptian pharaohs, it came as something of a novelty. At Thebes, in Upper Egypt, wives and daughters of the high priest of Amun had long held important religious offices, but between 754 (just before the onset of Kushitic rule) and 525 BCE a sequence of five unmarried, childless princesses of Libyan and Nubian descent were elevated to the existing position 'God's Wife of Amun'. At a time when the importance of traditionally male offices such as high priest and vizier were on the wane, this role accrued not just supreme religious, but also economic and political weight.[10]

In official representations, these women were given new 'throne names' framed by cartouches, and appeared leading royal festivals and making offerings directly to the gods – all of which were usually the prerogative of Egyptian kings. The God's Wives of Amun also owned some of the richest estates in Egypt, including the 'domain of the divine adoratrice', which contained extensive lands and a large staff of priests and scribes. The appointment of Nubian princesses to key political and economic roles in the Egyptian state permitted the Kushite royal household to govern at a distance. The princesses' celibacy, and that of high-ranking priestesses in their retinue, also precluded the emergence of rival sub-dynasties to challenge the authority of Kushite kings.

To have a situation in which women not only command power on such a scale, but in which this power is linked to an office reserved explicitly for single women, is historically unusual. Yet this political innovation is little discussed, partly because it is placed within a chronological framework that signals its transitory or even decadent nature (the 'Third Intermediate' and 'Late' periods of ancient Egyptian history). It is worth noting here that the overarching division of Egypt's ancient past into Old, Middle and New Kingdoms is not itself rooted in ancient sources: it began to be used by Egyptologists only in the nineteenth century, using terms (initially 'reich' or 'empire', and later 'kingdom') modelled on the modern history of nation states in Europe.[11] This scheme is now canonical for the historiography of ancient Egypt, with the result that the political history of ancient Nubia is often fitted uncomfortably into it, introducing subtle but significant biases.[12]

For the last five thousand years of history, our conventional vision not just of Africa's past, but of world history in general, resembles a checkerboard of kingdoms and empires. For most of this history, however, these states were exceptional islands of political hierarchy, surrounded by much larger territories whose inhabitants, if discernable at all to historians, are variously described as 'tribal confederacies', 'amphictyonies' or 'segmentary societies' – that is, as people who systematically avoided fixed, overarching systems of authority. Much is known about how such societies worked in Africa south of the Sahara, North America, Central and Southeast Asia, and other regions where loose and flexible political associations existed into recent times. Yet frustratingly little is known of how they operated in periods when they were, by far, the world's most common forms of government.

Considered in this way, the Nubian past takes on a particular significance. Arguably, the real puzzle of Nubia's ancient history and archaeology – at least since the Bronze Age (roughly 3000–1000 BCE) – is not whether it developed states or empires like those of neighbouring pharaonic Egypt. Rather, it is how its population managed to prevent the emergence of similar forms of domination in their own midst, despite the existence of Egyptian models of governance on their doorstep and the effects of recurring Egyptian predation on their people and resources. To answer *that* question, we also need to understand something about how kingship took root in Egypt in the first place. Let us continue with an overview of the emergence of kingdoms in the Nile Valley, extending back into pre-literate times. This deeper perspective brings into focus the shared conceptual roots of Egyptian and Nubian forms of kingship, as well as some contingent factors leading to their historical divergence and interplay.

EARLY NILOTIC LANDSCAPES
AND POLITICAL FORMATIONS

The waters of the Nile descend from sources in the Ethiopian highlands and the Great Lakes of Central Africa. Today, the river's main branches are the Blue Nile and White Nile, which converge near Khartoum; it is also fed by the Atbara River, a tributary that flows through the Butana grasslands in eastern Sudan. Further west lies the channel of the Wadi Howar, through which the so-called Yellow River once passed on its descent from the mountains of Chad, joining the main course of the Nile at Old Dongola in central Sudan. Along its 1,243-mile (2,000 km) extent, the flow of the Sudanese Nile is disrupted by six cataracts formed by outcrops of rock, which split the river into braided channels dotted with islands. The First Cataract is located near Aswan, marking the ancient border between Egypt and Nubia, north of which the Nile flows uninterrupted to the Mediterranean Sea, following a diversion into the Fayyum depression near Bani Suwaif and fanning out beyond Cairo to form one of the world's great deltas.

Each year during the autumn floods, the Nile deposited a wide blanket of mineral-rich sediment along the length of its Egyptian course, with roughly two-thirds of this deposit accumulating in the Delta. South of Aswan, the floodplain narrowed drastically; human populations became correspondingly smaller and more dispersed, with arable floodplain soils confined mainly to the regions of Shendi and Dongola, including the Kerma Basin. Agriculture in Egypt and northern Nubia was based largely on winter-growing crops of Asian origin such as wheat and barley, sown on the banks of the river after the retreat of the floodwaters; further south, native African crops such as sorghum and millet were adapted to a summer rainfall regime. Both winter and summer crops were grown in northeastern Africa by the fourth millennium BCE; emmer wheat and barley as far south as the Dongola Reach, and sorghum in savanna regions, such as the Butana.[13] Centres of trade and population frequently arose on the frontier between these two cropping cycles. The cultural roots of both Egyptian and Nubian kingship must, however, be sought in an earlier phase of prehistory from roughly 6000 to 4000 BCE.

At that time, cereal farming was still a marginal pursuit in the Nile Basin, although archaeologists refer to these societies as

'Neolithic' to signal their adoption – both in Egypt and Sudan – of domestic animals (cattle, sheep and goats) as sources of meat and milk. Cattle-keeping was pursued alongside mixed strategies of hunting, fishing and foraging on the Nile floodplain and in the oases and seasonal streams (wadis) of what are now its neighbouring deserts, but were then still watered by annual rains.[14] Neolithic populations moved freely in and out of this 'Green Sahara', both westwards through a network of seasonal lakes (now dry so-called playas) and eastwards to the Red Sea coast, where their presence can be traced in the archaeological remains of seasonal camps, cemeteries, a suite of mobile material culture (much of which could be worn or suspended on the bodies of people and their livestock) and in vivid rock paintings and engravings.[15]

In the course of the fifth millennium BCE, the mobility of Neolithic groups in the Nile Valley and adjacent regions led to a convergence of cultural features, which can be documented with striking consistency from the vicinity of Khartoum all the way to the el-Badari district of Middle Egypt. It is inconceivable that communities throughout this broad region (stretching for some 1,200 miles or 1,900 km) shared anything approaching a single form of ethnic identity. Instead, we are dealing here with what archaeologists refer to as a 'culture area', 'horizon' or 'interaction sphere' of the kind formed by Neolithic populations in many parts of the world; that is, to the existence of a common cultural milieu, out of which more local contrasts and group identities were constructed, but within which people moved widely and freely, often over large distances. What guaranteed this freedom was the existence of shared norms of hospitality and ritual practice, which cut across local affiliations.

In the Neolithic Nile Valley, this expansive cultural zone is known as the 'primary pastoral community' to signal the economic and symbolic importance of cattle, as well as the role of livestock-keeping in sustaining human mobility.[16] The prefix 'primary' also serves as a reminder that, while milking and dairying were widespread by the fifth millennium BCE, other 'secondary' animal products, such as traction power, were not yet widely exploited. The cultural uniformity of the primary pastoral community is demonstrated by comparing Neolithic settlements and cemeteries in southern Egypt and Sudan. Across this broad region, evidence for permanent village settlements remains hard to find; traces of herding and fishing camps, in contrast, are ubiquitous, especially along the margins of the floodplain. Such ephemeral sites – comprising loose configurations of postholes, concentrations of cultural material (primarily stone tools and pottery), dung deposits, ash middens and occasional fixed huts and storage pits – constitute the main evidence for human habitation, reflecting high levels of residential mobility and flexible social arrangements as communities alternated between seasonal herding camps and more dispersed hunting and foraging groups.

Cemeteries become a widely visible feature in the archaeological record of the Nile Valley for the first time, occupying what would have been prominent topographic locations on natural or anthropogenic mounds or at the mouths of wadis. In this way, a new type of cultural landscape took shape along the low desert bordering the valley, studded with ancestral burial grounds. These formed stable points of reference in an otherwise shifting social landscape, each marking a community's attachment to specific fishing and grazing lands as well as pathways of movement extending east and west of the valley. The contents of these burials show striking correspondences from central Sudan to Middle Egypt, with a common emphasis on new forms of personal grooming and adornment identified by traces of cosmetic pigments and minerals prospected from adjacent deserts, and by a dazzling array of beadwork, combs, bangles and other ornaments made of ivory and bone; also present are tools and weapons, such as stone maceheads, hafted flint knives and arrowheads.

Such objects were widely available to women, men and children, and indicate that populations throughout the Nile Valley shared ideas about how to care for the human body and person, as well as about the freedom of individuals to defend themselves, by violence if called for. In accounting for people's ability to move, spread, disperse and reintegrate, this common fund of social values matters just as much as the logistics and ecology of cattle-keeping. The ritual killing and consumption of livestock formed an important part of this social milieu, as indicated by the inclusion of cattle horns and other animal parts within human burials, carefully placed to rest alongside the deceased. A geographical point of origin for this primary pastoral community cannot be specified with any confidence, but on current evidence its earliest traces are to be found on the Dongola Reach in the vicinity of Kerma, where the excavation of a Neolithic cemetery at el-Barga reveals burials – replete with cattle skulls, cosmetic grinding palettes, stone maceheads, ivory bangles and other ornamentation – dating back to the first half of the sixth millennium BCE.[17]

The extended period that saw the formation of the primary pastoral community also witnessed the onset of significant changes in the environment of the Nile Basin, which eventually imposed new constraints on human mobility, especially in the more northerly regions of Egypt and Lower Nubia. The most important change over the long term was the beginning of a southward shift in the distribution of summer (monsoon) rains over northeastern Africa, leading to a contraction of grasslands and watercourses across the Sahara and eventually to the aridification of lands either side of the Nile, a process that appears to have been largely completed in Egypt by the fourth millennium BCE. In Sudan, the southward movement of this summer rainfall frontier was a more gradual process, reflected in the surviving distribution of rock engravings that depict herds of giraffes and elephant, alongside thousands of cattle carvings, as far downstream as the Second Cataract in Lower Nubia.

It is worth considering some wider characteristics of this shifting frontier, best illustrated by the later example of Meroë, with which this chapter began. Meroitic (Kushite) kingdoms of the first millennium BCE and early centuries CE were 'ecotone kingdoms', sitting astride the Nile Valley and the northernmost fringes of the African savanna: a nodal position that was pivotal to their trade wealth and political influence. By enhancing both the carrying capacity and religious significance of such locations, their rulers were able to build durable relationships with mobile groups, whose seasonal migrations brought Red Sea (and conceivably Indian Ocean) products to the Nile.[18] Meroitic rulers invested greatly in the construction of artificial catchment basins or *hafirs* – filled by overflow from rain-fed wadis – which extended beyond the Nile Valley deep into the Butana grasslands, where they offered a dependable source of water for people and livestock.[19] Temples were built adjacent to *hafirs*, becoming focal points for trade fairs and micro-cities that sprang up periodically in the Meroitic hinterland, only to disperse again out of season.

It is worth noting the absence of any evidence for fortifications or other means of controlling the movement of people. Kings of the savanna frontier did not rule over a large population of sedentary grain farmers, whose activities could easily be monitored or directed. By and large, their subjects were free from the constraints of agrarian production. More often, they were ambivalent or perhaps even seasonal subjects, whose freedom to move was underwritten by the summer rains, which opened vistas of grassland for them to cross with their herds of cattle. Indeed, for such populations, cattle remained – much as they were in Neolithic times – outstanding symbols of personal autonomy: living proof of a social existence based on the capacity to move away from arbitrary power and to define one's own path. In their homelands, the power of Meroitic rulers was thus based on attraction more than it was on coercion: like Apedemak, their lion-headed god of hunting and war, these kings of the Nile–savanna ecotone were a bridge between worlds, obliged to look in all directions at once.

To what extent did the organization of earlier Kushite and Nubian kingdoms foreshadow such arrangements? For much of the third and second millennia BCE, wadi systems fed by reliable summer rains and seasonal grazing lands extended as far north as the Dongola Reach; the savanna margin was located well downstream of its location in Meroitic times.[20] Many centuries before the rise of Napata and Meroë, the pre-eminent centre of Kushite religious and political power lay in the Kerma Basin near the Third Cataract, where evidence of large fauna, such as elephant, hippopotamus, lion and giraffe, is present – alongside copious remains of livestock – into the early part of the second millennium BCE. The environmental context of the Bronze Age polity that arose at Kerma is still poorly understood, but it seems at least plausible that this – arguably the earliest kingdom in sub-Saharan Africa – was also an 'ecotone kingdom', albeit differently structured from later Kushite examples and with access to a lucrative caravan trade passing through the oases of Egypt's Western Desert. Indeed, the prototype for a trade-oriented polity – where social power emerged less through direct control over people or territory than from rulers' abilities to concentrate (and consecrate) diverse influences from all around – may extend back further still, to the so-called A-Group of Lower Nubia in the fourth millennium BCE.[21]

If ancient Sudanic and Nubian polities were ruled by 'kings of rain', whose effective sovereignty was limited in scope and whose subjects moved freely between riverine, savanna and coastal environments, then those of Egypt might contrastingly be dubbed 'kings of flood'. Royal annals inscribed on the Palermo Stone of the 5th Dynasty mark regnal years by ritual appearances of the Egyptian king, linked both to taxation and to a measurement of the annual height of the Nile inundation.[22] It was the ascendence of these kings of flood on the alluvial plains of the Egyptian Nile that brought into being the world's first peasantries: settled populations of grain producers, whose mode of existence was tightly constrained in space and whose lives ticked by to the strict metronome of a floodplain farming regime. Unlike their Sudanic counterparts, Egyptian monarchs (both living and dead) extended a considerable measure of practical sovereignty over people and territory, enacted through a hierarchy of local officials, governors, scribes and soul priests.

THE MAKING OF ANCIENT EGYPT

Some basic contrasts have been identified between the early king-doms of Egypt and Nubia and in their environmental contexts, which made rigid patterns of authority more difficult to sustain the further south one went. The result was the emergence of different patterns of pharaonic and Sudanic kingship. Looking back more deeply into the past, we have also seen how these contrasting forms of kingship drew from the same reservoir of Neolithic cultural values in the Nile Basin: the 'primary pastoral community' of the sixth and fifth millennia BCE, with its shared notions of ritual and hospitality, its common aesthetics of social display and its relatively free and mobile existence associated with the keeping of cattle. Let us now examine how 'kings of the flood' ruling over dense populations of settled cultivators arose out of those fluid social arrangements of the Neolithic period.

We can begin by considering a phase of exceptional political violence, which accompanied the establishment of the first royal dynasties claiming sovereignty over the whole of Upper and Lower Egypt. It has been known for over a century that some of Egypt's earliest rulers, those of the 1st Dynasty around 3000 BCE, went to the afterlife amid the corpses of some hundreds or even thousands of retainers who appear to have been ritually killed on the king or queen's death.[23] Egypt is not alone in this respect. Burials of kings and queens surrounded by large numbers of human victims, killed especially for the occasion, can be found in almost every part of the ancient world where monarchies became established, from the early dynastic city-state of Ur in Mesopotamia to Shang China, the Moche and Wari societies of South America, the Mississippian city of Cahokia and – as we will see – the Kerma polity in Nubia. In the case of Egypt, the victims of ritual killing buried around the tombs of early dynastic kings (and at least one queen) seem to have been drawn almost exclusively from their own inner circles. The evidence derives from a series of five-thousand-year-old burial chambers, looted in antiquity but still visible near the site of the ancient city of Abydos in the low desert of southern Egypt. These were the tombs of Egypt's 1st Dynasty. Around each royal tomb lie long rows of subsidiary burials, numbering in the hundreds and forming a kind of perimeter. Such 'retainer burials' – including royal attendants and courtiers killed in the prime of life – were placed in smaller brick compartments of their own, each marked with a gravestone inscribed with the individual's titles. On the death of a king or queen, then, the successor appears to have presided over the death of his or her predecessor's courtly entourage, or at least a sizeable portion of it.

So, why all this ritual killing at the birth of the Egyptian state? What was the purpose of retainer burials? Given the belief that the living and the dead continued to exert an influence on each other's realms, was it to protect the departed king from the living, or the living from the departed king? Why did those sacrificed include so many who had evidently spent their lives caring for the king: most likely including wives, guards, officials, cooks, grooms, entertainers, palace dwarves and other servants, all grouped by rank around the royal tomb according to their roles or occupation? There would seem to be a terrible paradox here. On the one hand, we have a ritual that is the ultimate expression of love and devotion, as those who on a day-to-day basis made the king into something king-like – fed him, clothed him, trimmed his hair, cared for him in sickness – went willingly to their deaths to ensure he would continue to be king in the afterlife. At the same time, these burials are the ultimate demonstration that for a ruler, even his most intimate subjects could be treated as personal possessions, casually disposed of like so many baubles, blankets or flagons of wine.

Written records from the time do not indicate the official motives, but one thing that is quite striking in the evidence we do have – largely, a list of names and titles of the dead – is the mixed composition of these royal cemeteries. They seem to include both blood relatives of the early kings and queens, notably female members of the royal family, and individuals taken in as members of the royal household owing to their skills or striking personal qualities and who thus came to be seen as members of the king's extended family. The violence that attended these mass funerary rituals must have gone some way to effacing those differences, melding the victims into a single unit by turning servants into relatives and relatives into servants. In later times, the king's close kin represented themselves in exactly this way, by placing in their tombs some humble replicas of themselves engaged in acts of menial labour, such as grinding grain or cooking meals.[24]

Again, similar patterns of development can be seen in many parts of the world, including regions of Africa where 'great kings' emerged. When sovereignty first expands to become the general organizing principle of a society, it is by turning violence into kinship. The early, spectacular phases of mass killing in Egypt, China and elsewhere – whatever else they accomplished – appear to have lain the foundations of a political system in which all the kings' subjects are imagined as members of the royal household, at least to the degree that they are all working to care for the king. Turning erstwhile strangers into part of the royal household or denying them their own ancestors were ultimately two sides of the same coin. Or to put things another way, a ritual designed to produce kinship became a method of producing kingship. Internal violence accompanying the political unification of Egypt's 'Two Lands' (the Valley and the Delta) was mirrored by violence on its outer borders, notably the dismantling of a rival polity in Lower Nubia, commemorated in a rock carving near the Second Cataract.

Known to archaeologists simply as the 'A-Group' (from a pottery style), this Lower Nubian polity of the late fourth millennium BCE remains poorly understood, not least since most of its remains now lie submerged beneath the waters of Lake Nasser. As noted earlier, these local Nubian elites seem to have followed a divergent path to power from their contemporaries in Egypt, less grounded in control over territory or sedentary populations of grain farmers than in their mastery of trade routes linking the Nile corridor to the Red Sea and to lands beyond the Batn el-Hajar ('Belly of Stones'): a barren expanse of granite outcrops south of the Second Cataract. Goods accumulated in grand A-Group burials near the site of Qustul are testimony to this cosmopolitan outlook; they include many imported Egyptian (and even some Levantine) vessels, but also such distinctive local items as soft-stone incense burners. One such burner is carved with images of a seated ruler wearing a tall crown, as well as boats, one of which is depicted with a sail and contains the figure of a bound captive.[25]

An incense burner from the A-Group Cemetery L
at Qustul, Lower Nubia, c. 3100 BCE. Height 3½ in. (8.9 cm).

To what extent can the disappearance of the A-Group polity be attributed to punitive raids from Egypt? Alternatively, was this the result of more gradual processes, such as the movement of the Nubian rainfall boundary southwards and with it those mobile populations whose seasonal migrations to the Nile Valley were critical for the accumulation of trade wealth and foreign contacts in centres of royal power? No definitive answer is yet available, but what is clear is that by 3000 BCE, the regular movement of people, ideas and goods between Egypt and Nubia had been replaced by a frontier zone – possibly even a kind of 'no man's land' – from which Egyptian rulers could enjoy largely unmediated access to the gold and mineral deposits of the Nubian deserts. Egypt's southern border at Elephantine Island, on the First Cataract at Aswan, was fortified during the 1st Dynasty and, by no later than the beginning of the Old Kingdom (*c.* 2650 BCE), a permanent garrison was established overlooking the Nile at Buhen, deep within Lower Nubia.[26]

In Egypt itself, the practice of killing and burying retainers around royal burials ended during the 2nd Dynasty (2800–2650 BCE). The patrimonial polity continued to expand, not so much in terms of Egypt's external borders, which by now were established in Nubia and also west of the Nile Valley in what Egyptian sources call Tjehenu or Tjemhu (modern-day Libya), but more in terms of reordering the lives of Egypt's internal population. Within a few generations, large tracts of the Nile Valley and Delta were divided into royal estates dedicated to provisioning mortuary cults for former rulers; not long after that, workers' towns sprang up to house royal subjects engaged in the construction of pyramid-tombs and temples on the Giza Plateau, drawing seasonal labour (*corvée*) from up and down the country.[27] By this point, the sovereign's death had become the basis for the reorganization of much of human life along the length of the Nile.

To understand how this happened, we need to look at what Egypt was like before the 1st Dynasty. Burials of petty monarchs already appear in the Nile Valley and Lower Nubia by 3500 BCE, some five centuries earlier.[28] We don't know the names of these earliest rulers, since writing had barely developed yet. Most of their kingdoms appear to have been extremely small. Some of the largest were centred on Naqada and Abydos, near the great bend of the Nile; on Hierakonpolis further to the south; and on the site of Qustul in Lower Nubia. What preceded the 1st Dynasty, then, was not so much a lack of sovereign power as a great deal of it on a small scale: a surfeit of tiny kingdoms and miniature courts, always with a core of blood relatives and a collection of wives, servants and assorted followers. Some of these courts appear to have been quite magnificent in their own way, leaving behind large tombs and the bodies of sacrificed retainers. The most spectacular, at Hierakonpolis (Cemetery HK6), includes the remains of a male dwarf (dwarves seem to have become a fixture of courtly society very early on), a number of teen-aged girls and even a menagerie of exotic animals, including baboons, hippopotami, a leopard, a crocodile and an elephant.[29] This mortuary culture suggests that the first kings made grandiose and absolute cosmological claims, despite few signs that they maintained administrative or military control over their respective territories.

Alongside these local developments in elite culture, important changes were taking place in Egypt's economy. Archaeology allows us to discern their broad outlines. We might imagine these changes unfolding as a kind of extended debate, not just about the production of food, but also the responsibilities of the living to the dead. Do dead kings, like living ones, still need us to take care of them? Is this care different from the care accorded ordinary ancestors? Do ancestors get hungry? And, if so, what exactly do they eat? For whatever reasons, the answer that gained traction in Egypt around 3500 BCE was that ancestors do indeed get hungry, and what they required was something that, at that time, can only have been considered a rather exotic and luxurious form of food: leavened bread and fermented wheat beer, the pot-containers for which now start to become standard fixtures of well-appointed grave assemblages in Egypt (but not in Nubia, where bread moulds and beer jars remain absent from burials of the A-Group, just as the regime of agrarian labour that lay behind them failed to penetrate south of the First Cataract until much later times).[30]

Low-level wheat farming had been practised in Egypt since Neolithic times, but agriculture was only refined and intensified in the middle of the fourth millennium BCE, partly in response to the new demands of funerary rituals. The two processes – agronomic and ceremonial – reinforced each other and the social effects were epochal, especially after ploughs and oxen were introduced to Egypt (but again, not Nubia) around 3300 BCE. Families who found themselves unable to command such resources had to obtain beer and loaves elsewhere, creating networks of obligation and debt. New class divisions and dependencies began to emerge, as a sizeable sector of Egypt's population found itself deprived of the means to care independently for ancestors. For the first time, peasant societies took form, whose lives were tightly circumscribed and whose connections to a world beyond were increasingly confined to interactions with landlords, priests, merchants, tax collectors and other officers of the court. How and when exactly was the division of Egypt's arable lands into a grid of administrative domains (or *nomes*) achieved? Egyptologists have long debated this question, and increasingly they recognize a gulf between the ideal of a centralized bureaucracy – as projected on official monuments like the Palermo Stone – and messier realities on the ground.[31]

It is also around 3500 BCE that we begin to find remains of baking and beer-making facilities in cemeteries and, shortly after, attached to palaces and grand tombs, including a recently discovered brewery adjacent to the site of King Narmer's grave at Abydos. A later depiction, from the mastaba tomb of an Old Kingdom official called Ty, shows how these facilities could have operated, with pot-baked bread and beer produced in a single process.[32] The gradual extension of royal authority and administrative reach throughout Egypt began around the time of the 1st Dynasty or a little before, with the creation of estates dedicated to the provision, not so much of living kings, but of dead ones, and eventually deceased royal officials like Ty too.

By the time of the Great Pyramids (*c.* 2500 BCE), bread and beer were being manufactured on an industrial scale to supply armies of workers during their *corvée* on royal construction projects, when they too got to be relatives or at least caregivers for the king, and as such were themselves well provisioned and cared for.

Archaeological investigations of the workers' town associated with the Great Pyramids at Giza have produced thousands of ceramic moulds used to make communal loaves, known as *bedja*, eaten in large groups with meat supplied by royal livestock pens and washed down with spiced beer. Drinking was of special importance for the solidarity of seasonal work crews in Old Kingdom Egypt. The facts emerge with disarming simplicity, from graffiti on the reverse sides of blocks used in the construction of pyramids. 'Friends of [the king] Menkaure', reads one; 'Drunkards of Menkaure' another. These seasonal work units (or *phyles*, as Egyptologists call them) seem to have been made up only of men who passed through special age-grade rituals.[33] They also appear to have modelled themselves on the organization of a boat crew, although it's unclear if such ritual brotherhoods ever took to the water together. Pyramids were thus built by rendering male subjects into great social machines, afterwards celebrated by mass conviviality.

BEGINNING AND ENDING AT KERMA

Around the middle of the third millennium BCE, as the rulers of Egypt's Old Kingdom reached an apogee of pyramid-building on the Giza Plateau, an independent polity arose far to the south astride the Third Cataract of the Nile. Its epicentre was at Kerma, on the Dongola Reach, among the most densely inhabited sectors of Upper Nubia. Called Yam in Egyptian inscriptions of the Old Kingdom and Kush in later sources, the kingdom of Kerma existed for a thousand years, from 2500 to 1500 BCE. In that time, Egypt expanded its southern border as far as the Batn el-Hajar, where garrisons were established between Aswan and Semna as launching pads for gold-mining and stone-quarrying expeditions in Lower Nubia, and to control the movement of local populations beyond Egypt's southern frontier. Pharaonic propaganda portrayed the region's inhabitants as barbarians and their lands as eternally 'wretched', but the descendants of Egyptian colonists who settled in Nubia would eventually defect, switching their loyalties to the polity of Kerma.[34]

Egyptian sources refer to 'rulers' of Kush, but if Kerma was the centre of a large kingdom then it remained faceless, with no local or imported tradition of royal iconography, at least not in any form that has come down to us. The exception that proves the rule is a modest (10-in. or 26-cm high) sandstone stela at the border garrison of Buhen, which bears a schematic carving in sunk relief of a faceless figure who wears the White Crown of Upper Egypt and carries a mace and double-bent bow. Even here, however, there was no attempt to include an inscription, so we have little idea who or what status this enigmatic figure represents, if it was created by a Nubian or an Egyptian artist, or whether the intended audience for this image was Egyptian, Nubian or both.[35] Writing, as well as visual representation, appears to have been rejected for purposes of display in favour of oral recitations, perhaps reflected in Kerma's earliest documented traditions of monumental architecture, which include grand audience halls built of mud applied around a circular timber frame.[36] Indeed, the Ancient Egyptian word applied generally to Nubian populations, *nḥsj(w)*, may invoke a facility for powerful speech or incantations.[37] Nor does the kingdom of Kerma seem to have developed a military infrastructure for controlling its population, which grew through the incorporation of groups originating within and beyond Upper Nubia and from outside the Nile Valley altogether. Their gravitation to Kerma must have been largely voluntary, making the scale of the city and its religious precincts, including the northern conurbation at Dukki Gel, all the more notable.

At the city's heart stood its great temple, known today as the western *deffufa*, one of the largest ancient structures in Africa (see pl. II).

As reconstructed by archaeologists, the temple comprised a pylon (that is, a monumental gateway) and massive mud-brick walls, which still rise in parts to a height of 65 ft (20 m).[38] They were built above a long sequence of earlier shrines and date to around 1800 BCE. In the absence of written sources, the functions of the *deffufa* may be partly elucidated by comparison and contrast with Egyptian temples. In Egypt, temples were restricted stages for the divine cult, growing darker and more confined the further one descended to the inner sanctum; a movement through a cosmogonic landscape of origin, into the primordial waters of the inundation. Kerma's religious architecture was contrastingly oriented towards the sky: the most sacred area of the *deffufa* was its open roof terrace, accessed by ascending a great staircase and overlooking a plaza where large congregations could gather.[39]

Kerma was a religious centre for the inhabitants of the Nile Valley between the Second and Fifth Cataracts. Its eastern cemetery contained tens of thousands of graves and tumuli accumulated over almost a millennium.[40] Perhaps the very origins of Kerma – as with some more recent Nilotic kingdoms – lay in the power of prophets, magicians, oracles and religious revelation. Over time, it became the centre of a composite society or a sort of confederation, whose members were no doubt polyglot and as diverse in their ethnic affiliations as their architectural traditions, which run the gamut from Egyptian-inspired mortuary chapels to the curvilinear shrines of Dukki Gel, which may look to prototypes from the region to the south.[41] Other important spiritual centres existed in Kerma's sphere of influence, for example at Sai Island to the north, with little evidence of direct control from the capital.

Ancient Kerma is famous today for its ceramic sets of highly burnished drinking bowls and beakers used to serve unfiltered beers drunk communally through straws, including at funerary meals held by the graveside. In a setting where populations were still mobile and dispersed for much of the year, commensality at periodic gatherings played a vital role in the formation of larger social units, including

'Classic Kerma' (c. 1750–1500 BCE) funerary and feasting vessels.

the acceptance of strangers and non-kin.[42] Such aggregations also had a less pacific side, evident in the ritual killing and burial of dependents alongside a primary interment.[43] Often glossed as 'human sacrifice', this custom was by no means exclusive to kings or elites. It began on a small scale, perhaps as early as the Neolithic period (for example at el-Kadada),[44] when it seems best accounted for in terms of the detachment of certain individuals from their kin as a result of conflict, illness, bereavement, debt or other misfortune, followed by their social reattachment, possibly in servile relationships, to adoptive carers and protectors, whose death rendered their ongoing existence untenable.

The importance of personal protection is evident in assemblages of weapons and grooming equipment, which accompanied an important sub-class of Kerma burials. Copper-alloy daggers with ivory pommels replaced the chipped-stone blades of earlier periods; fighting sticks were also sometimes placed in the grave, as were longbows and double-bent bows (Egyptian sources refer to Nubia as Ta-Seti, 'the land of the bow'). Alongside personal weaponry, drinking vessels and leather clothing appear mirrors, razors, tweezers and other items associated with the care and training of the body.[45] The additional presence of cattle remains in these burials, especially horns trained into unique shapes, may extend such concerns. If so, then it would logically follow that the offering of cattle horns (bucrania) around focal tombs was a mark of personal loyalty, deference and perhaps military service to a lord. In the main cemetery at Kerma, this practice reached staggering proportions during the Middle Kerma period (2000–1750 BCE), when one high-ranking burial was flanked by some five thousand bucrania (including many with horns trained into elaborate and individual styles), assembled from far and wide and placed in carefully regimented rows around the southern flank of the main tumulus.[46] Some archaeologists take this recurrent combination of grave goods to signal the emergence in Kerman society of a warrior aristocracy, sharing a common ethos of individual achievement linked to combat and celebrated in spectacular funerary rituals.[47]

Bucrania (cattle skulls) arranged around a Middle Kerma tumulus burial.

In considering these various features of Kerma society, it is important to recall that throughout the third and second millennia BCE, the lands of Nubia were subject to almost continuous invasion from Egypt, in which large numbers of people and livestock were taken captive and deported.[48] Egyptian inscriptions of the Old Kingdom record raids resulting in the abduction and enslavement of thousands of men, women and children who were put to work in Egypt as agricultural labourers, soldiers or servants in elite households. Under the rulers of the Middle Kingdom, such as Senusret I (r. 1956–1911 BCE), Egypt established forced labour camps within Lower Nubia itself, where many Nubians were incarcerated, sometimes including prominent community leaders who were made to pan gold or work on imperial quarrying and construction projects.[49]

Less often considered is the impact of state-sponsored campaigns of raiding and abduction on those surviving kin left behind. In more recent times in Africa and elsewhere, it is often such 'detached' persons who form the core personnel of royal courts, congregating for refuge and asylum in the residence of a chief. Typically, these individuals become members of the chief's retinue, taking on the role of police-like enforcers, but also subordinate to his whims and commands. It is against such a background that we might interpret a series of striking developments associated with the last centuries of the Kerma kingdom's existence before its destruction at the hands of Egypt's 18th Dynasty.

By that time – the 'Classic Kerma' period (c. 1750–1500 BCE) – the kingdom was defended by an elaborate system of fortifications. In its eastern cemetery, tombs of increasingly impressive size and complexity had long been constructed, each linked to the staging of elaborate mortuary feasts, in which large numbers of cattle might be slaughtered, and to mortuary chapels that perpetuated the cult of the deceased among the living.[50] The emergence of powerful military and commercial elites at Kerma indicated by these remains is usually connected to the decline of Egypt's Middle Kingdom and the withdrawal of the Egyptian military presence from Lower Nubia, which opened new possibilities for expansion northwards. Kerma now set foot on a wider stage, making war on the Theban royal household of Upper Egypt and forging alliances with the Hyksos kings – rivals to Thebes, whose capital city Avaris was on the eastern side of the Delta and who conducted trade and diplomacy with Kerma via the oases of Egypt's Western Desert.[51]

At Kerma itself, this period sees the appearance of Egyptian-inspired palatial buildings incorporating a throne room, Egyptian forms of administration, and the introduction of exotic foods based on Egyptian examples into the established pattern of high-status funerary rituals. These ritual foods now included leavened bread produced in bakeries attached to Kerma's main religious and mortuary facilities, and perhaps also decanted beer and imported wine. Increasingly, Kerma's elites incorporated Egyptian elements into their own systems of courtly behaviour, as reflected in the modification of local types of prestige furniture (such as beds, used both for reclining and also for presenting the dead, which now gained Egyptian-inspired inlays and finials in the shape of bull's feet); in cosmetic kits (now including kohl pots and sticks for applying eye make-up); and in the deposition of imported Egyptian sculpture – likely taken as war booty – in high-status Kerman tombs, albeit without deference to Egyptian modes of decorum.[52]

To some extent, Kerma's ruling classes were styling themselves in the manner of Egyptian kings and queens through selective cultural borrowings (see pl. v). Yet these were adapted to fit in with Upper Nubian social norms, including the political autonomy of women, who continued to occupy high-status roles.[53] This ruling elite may also have begun to harbour similar expectations of obedience from their subjects, who now included a large number of sedentary cultivators engaged in producing grain surpluses for the city's temples as well as regiments of bodyguards, administrators, servants and others attached to the royal household. How far these interrelated processes had escalated by the middle of the second millennium BCE is indicated by another dramatic innovation in Kerma's eastern necropolis: the incorporation of courtly retainers into royal burial rites on an unprecedented scale. The killing and burial of victims extended into the hundreds, their bodies placed within and around the largest tombs according to rank. The central burials of these royal tombs – mostly looted in antiquity – were housed in chambers at the heart of massive tumuli (as large as 295 ft or 90 m in diameter) dressed with layers of white pebbles and a perimeter of black stones. A corridor adjacent to the central tomb contained the bodies of ritually killed individuals, up to four hundred in some cases, who appear to have been drawn from the local population and were buried alive.[54]

The kingdom of Kerma met its end around 1500 BCE as a result of invasions by the rulers of Egypt's 18th Dynasty, the first of the New Kingdom (1550–1069 BCE), which went on to assert its hegemony as far south as Kurgus, upstream of the Nile bend at Abu Hamed, for a period of roughly four hundred years.[55] Arguably, the independence of Upper Nubia was lost as much through internal as external factors: the emergence among its own populations of formally ranked societies, warrior elites and hereditary aristocracies resulted in the erosion of basic freedoms and forms of solidarity that had crystallized millennia earlier in that very same part of the Nile Valley. Once the shadow of Egyptian imperial domination lifted, many of those freedoms were quickly reasserted in Nubia and on the Middle Nile. Then, when kingship once again became a political force in those regions during the early centuries of the first millennium BCE, the pendulum again swung. This time it was Kush's 'kings of rain' in the ascendant over Egypt's 'kings of flood'.

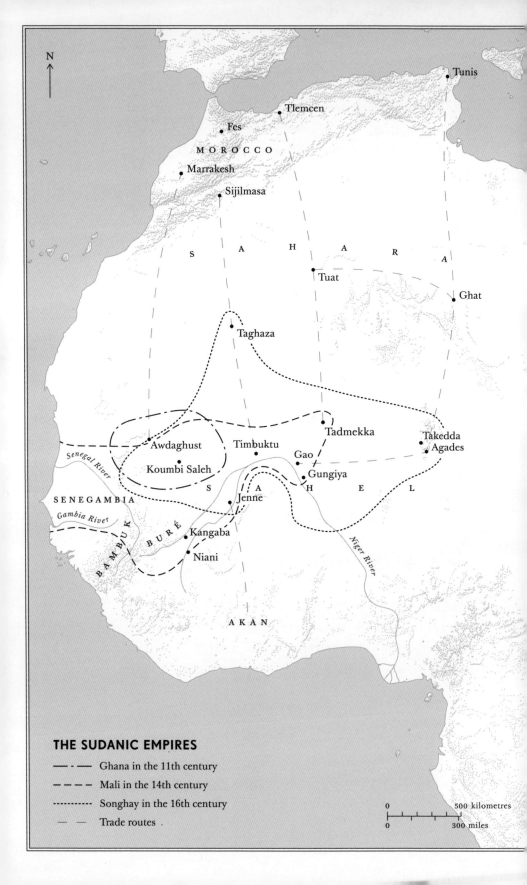

N

Tunis

Tlemcen

Fes

MOROCCO

Marrakesh

Sijilmasa

S A H A R A

Tuat

Ghat

Taghaza

Tadmekka

Takedda
Agades

Awdaghust

Timbuktu

Gao

Senegal River

Koumbi Saleh

Gungiya

S A H E L

SENEGAMBIA

Jenne

Gambia River

BAMBUK

BURÉ

Kangaba

Niani

Niger River

A K A N

THE SUDANIC EMPIRES

—·— Ghana in the 11th century

—— — Mali in the 14th century

·········· Songhay in the 16th century

— — Trade routes .

0   500 kilometres

0   300 miles

CHAPTER 2

THE SUDANIC EMPIRES
THE GOLD, THE ARTS, THE RIVER

Rahmane Idrissa

The Sudanic empires of Ghana, Mali and Songhay existed one after the other in a sequence spanning some thousand years of West African history. Each state emerged, in a sense, from that which came before it and the period of their domination coincided with the era that in European chronology is called the Middle Ages. The evidence suggests that Ghana began to take shape when the Western Roman Empire was on its last legs, around the fifth century CE; a millennium later, in 1591, at a time when modern Europe was emerging, Songhay was dealt a death blow by invading Moroccan forces. In the popular imagination – although medievalists vigorously disagree – the Middle Ages are the 'dark ages'. They were certainly a time of instability in Europe, one when the political map was in constant flux and when leaders struggled to consolidate sovereignties, let alone build empires. The rise of more stable centralized monarchies in the Atlantic-facing countries of northwestern Europe in the sixteenth century gives the false impression that France, England, Spain and Portugal were eternal entities. Yet the two Iberian nations did not exist for much of the Middle Ages, and all were younger than Ghana, emerging as the lucky winners in the muddled transition to the modern era. The situation in Europe presents something of a contrast with that in the medieval *bilad al-Sudan*, 'the land of the Blacks', as Arab geographers called Africa south of the Sahara Desert. In a stretch of territory that ran from the Atlantic coastline of present-day Mauritania and Senegal to the Aïr mountains in present-day Niger – a vast expanse considerably larger than western Europe, albeit less densely populated – it appears that political fragmentation was not allowed to set in. The transitions between the three empires were relatively short and smooth, even if the rise of some potential successor states, such as Soso, which appeared to have been on the cusp of succeeding Ghana, was thwarted. Each subsequent empire, moreover, was more expansive than the one before. Indeed, historians have recently been inclined to extend and complicate the imperial sequence by adding the early kingdom of Gao – from which Songhay would later emerge – as 'West Africa's starting point'.[1] Then there is the largely forgotten Jolof Empire, which dominated the region of Senegambia until the mid-sixteenth century.

West Africa's age of empire, however, gave out at the end of the sixteenth century. With the fall of Songhay, the western Sudan entered what might be described as its own 'dark ages', as the region fragmented and was overrun by predatory regimes: aggressively militarized states in the south; raiding nomad leagues in the north; and, in time, Islamic caliphates forged by jihadists whose state-building was based in part on the oppression of non-Muslim peoples. The consequences, although they remain largely unstudied as such, are still felt today in the modern Sahel. Yet things could have been different: if one considers the efforts of the Mande state-builder Samori Touré between the 1870s and 1890s – redolent of what Sonni Ali Ber, the founder of Songhay, achieved four centuries earlier – then this period of violence and disorder might instead have been brought to an end by a reconstructed imperial system. Samori's expansive state-building project was thwarted by the advent of a rival and better-armed imperial project, that of French colonial conquest. Yet given his early successes it is not implausible to imagine that much of the region might otherwise, by the early twentieth century, have been living within a new, Samorian empire.

The western Sudan, that is to argue, does seem to have an imperial vocation, embodied by the great states in the brighter age of its history as well as by a Samorian coda in the more recent era of fragmentation and decline.[2] This chapter is a study of that vocation: of its meanings, of its strengths and weaknesses, and of how it was organized in the successive regimes that epitomized it. It is about the ways in which these imperial states formed an integral part of the global world of their time, while at the same time representing the creative outcome of the strong and enduring West African cultures and civilizations from which they emerged. It is also about the modern consequences of the western Sudan's deep history of imperial state-building.

ORIGINS

There is not much debate about the origins of the Sudanic empires, and that is a problem. The nineteenth-century 'discovery' of a history of large-scale state-building south of the Sahara, as recorded in early Arab sources and in locally authored chronicles, came as a surprise to European scholars, who had assumed that the continent was a vast realm of naked savages – the kinds who the philosopher Georg F. W. Hegel had infamously banished from history. Soon, with the onset of a new era of European colonial conquest and the rise of pseudo-scientific evolutionary racism, the conviction took hold that such states must have been founded by representatives of a conquering 'White race' – Berbers or Arabs from North Africa, perhaps – and later bequeathed to lucky Black dynasts. The tales told by local Muslim elites, who sought exalted ancestors in the Middle Eastern heartland of Islam and claimed that their states were established by a wandering Arab (often from Yemen), tended to confirm this notion. But just like those tales, the so-called Hamitic Hypothesis was fantasy rather than science, and by the mid-twentieth century it had faded along with the era of European colonial domination of which it was part.

By the 1960s, a new origin theory gained credence. Robert Cornevin best expressed it in his classic *Histoire de l'Afrique* (1966), which explained that the fact that there were three successive 'organized states' in the western Sudan against only one in the eastern (in fact, central) Sudan – the kingdom of Kanem-Borno – was due to the 'nature of the commodities on offer for Mediterranean traders'.[3] Kanem-Borno, Cornevin argued, sold mainly enslaved people, whereas the western Sudan sold gold, which attracted more business and thus served as a stronger economic base for empire. In *Les siècles obscurs de l'Afrique noire* (1971), another early classic of French sub-Saharan historiography, Raymond Mauny argued that the rise of empires in 'Black Africa' was a consequence of the Arab conquest of North Africa. The subsequent expansion of trans-Saharan commerce, Mauny believed, drew the Sudanic zone into the sphere of Islamic civilization and provided the requisite statecraft and wealth for imperial state-building.[4] The location of the three empires in the Sahel and their orientation north towards the desert is crucial to this argument. Ghana emerged on the edge of the desert in an arid region that forms the frontier between the present-day republics of Mauritania and Mali (the latter taking its name from – but not to be confused with – the medieval empire). Gao, the future capital of the Songhay Empire, was a trading centre on the Niger River, which since the ninth century was also in contact with North Africa and had a significant Berber and Muslim commercial community. Emerging in the savanna region to the south, further away from trans-Saharan trade, Mali does not quite fit the pattern. Yet as there would not have been a Ghana or a Songhay without the caravan routes that ended (or started) in their capitals, the argument ran, there would therefore not have been a Mali. For most students of the western Sudan, the fact that trans-Saharan trade and Islam were catalysts for state-building is obvious. Hence the lack of debate on why the Sudanic empires were built: we think we already know.

More recent research has begun to question this established narrative of an external 'Arab stimulus' to Sudanic state-building. Archaeological evidence, most famously from the site of Jenne-jeno ('Old Jenne', near to the medieval city) in the inland delta of the

Niger River in present-day Mali, has demonstrated that social complexity, urban development and flourishing networks of regional commerce long preceded the arrival of North African traders.[5] In the region of Gao further to the east, epigraphic sources (i.e. inscriptions written on stone) have provided evidence not only for local rulers – including queens – stretching back before the arrival of Islam, but also for how the faith, once it did arrive, was actively appropriated by local societies rather than being an invasive cultural force.[6] Trade with Islamic North Africa and the Middle East beyond, it is starting to be revealed, did not necessarily trigger state formation and then empire-building south of the Sahara. Typically, it supported existing mercantile city-states of the kind that François-Xavier Fauvelle calls *royaumes courtiers* or 'broker kingdoms': localized regimes established in strategically located towns that offered protection to traders and were richly rewarded for their services.[7] Such entities appeared wherever Muslim trade extended its reach to the frontiers of the *dar al-Islam*, the 'abode of Islam', and beyond, including in the eastern Sudan (that is, the present-day Republic of the Sudan), on the Swahili coast of East Africa, in Hausaland (in northern Nigeria and the southern parts of Niger) and, indeed, in the western Sudan itself. One might add the Italian trading cities that also enriched themselves through trade with the Islamic world: Venice, Genoa, Pisa and Florence. When Jenne, the great entrepôt of the Middle Niger, was described to him during his stay in the Saharan oasis of Tuat in 1447, the Genoese commercial agent Antonio Malfante thought at once of those cities.[8] Gao was exactly such a broker kingdom for over seven centuries – before it emerged at the centre of a vast empire in the late fifteenth century.

From the traditions reported in Arab sources, Ghana had been an established regional power, if not an empire, long before it began trading with Islamic North Africa from the ninth century CE. Neither were Ghana, Mali and Songhay the only 'organized states' in the region; they are only the ones best known to historians, because their involvement in trans-Saharan trade brought them to the attention

of the outside world and generated written records. Before its imperial phase, the kingdom of Gao was of a similar size and nature as
the Mossi kingdoms to the southwest, in present-day Burkina Faso.
The implication is that the Ghana, Mali and Songhay empires were
the product of a political culture that they shared with other kingdoms in the western Sudan, which in turn suggests that the problem
of their origin is ultimately one of the emergence and nature of
kingship in the Sudan rather than of external influence.

Kingdoms, moreover, were by no means the 'normal' or 'natural'
form of political organization in the region. If there was such a form,
it was just as likely to have been what colonial-era European anthropologists called acephalous (literally, 'headless') societies: small-scale,
non-centralized communities governed by local assemblies of elders
paired with bodies of titled office-holders. In the Mande languages
such a self-governing community was called a *dugu*, and in the
Songhay languages, a *koyre*; their governance was overseen by a
ranking office-holder (the *dugutigi* and *laabu koy*, respectively). These
figures were not 'kings' and their fellow office-holders responsible
for various communal affairs neither answered to nor derived authority from them. Rather, authority came from intricate customary pre-
scriptions and lineage-bestowed rights that formed the ritual
constitution of the community. These self-governing village republics
– reminiscent of the *poleis* and *civitates* described by Aristotle or
Cicero – were essentially associations of patriarchal households which
managed local affairs without recourse to coercive power. They were
grounded in indigenous law and in religious practice – which together
constituted the 'customs' observed and recorded by colonial-era
ethnographers.

In this landscape of localized authority based on deeply rooted
rights and obligations, kingship tended to erupt as something outra-
geous and foreign – often, quite literally, in the shape of conquest
or imposition from beyond the frontiers of the community. It was
in any case a manifestation of force, as clearly indicated by the idioms
of political language throughout the region. In Mande, the king,

fama, means 'the forceful' or 'the powerful', the title derived from the word *fanga*, 'force' or 'predatory power'. The Mooré language of the Mossi peoples has a similar term, possibly derived from the Mande: *panga*. The political theorist Amy Niang describes *panga* as the origin of state power, which encroached on the ritual power of customary office-holders. '*Panga*, the predatory force conferred onto the *Naaba* [king], points to the emergence of the Mossi state as a centralized power structure with access to different forms of coercion', Niang explains. '*Panga* gives the state carte blanche: it frees it from the constraints of tradition, precedence and morality'.[9] Royalty and royal quarters in the Mossi kingdoms are *pangin*, 'where the force resides'; quite literally, 'the fortress'.

Yet kingship, created by the disruptions of force and perhaps reinforced by charisma and good fortune, could perpetuate itself only by inserting itself into the ritual constitutions of the village republics that it had subsumed. Force, that is, must be turned into lawful and sanctified power, constituted through the ruler's ordained connections with the ancestors and other spiritual forces. Only thus could a king become not just an oppressor, but a legitimate legislator, someone whose commands were accepted as lawful according to the fundamental ideas of established custom. In this process, the king was dependent upon the assistance of local office-holders, who often became members of his court and part of the college that after his death would elect his successor from among his eligible offspring or relatives. Yet there always was an element of 'carte blanche', as Niang puts it, about royal power: the fact that force was essential to it, however well concealed and apparently tamed. That could be revealed when a king chose to ignore or to contravene the negotiated terms of legitimacy and constraint. Repeated or grave transgressions could result in him being branded as a tyrant and therefore illegitimate, the fate that, according to tradition, befell Sumaworo Kanté, king of Soso in the thirteenth century. Should such violations result in the forging of a new empire, however, they would be remembered as superlative examples of the same force. As we will see, this was so for Sumaworo's foe and West Africa's most famous empire-builder, Sunjata Keita of Mali.

The historical processes that resulted in the rise and decline of Ghana, Mali and Songhay followed this broad logic. We now turn to the question of how these processes manifested in each of the three empires. Limitations in the body of evidence mean that it is impossible to answer this question with precision, although the tasks of reconstruction and interpretation grow somewhat less daunting as we move across time from the earliest to the most recent of the three states.

GHANA

Information on the kingdom of Ghana comes mostly from medieval Arab scholars who set about to document those parts of the world drawn into contact with the expanding *dar al-Islam*.[10] Following the conquest of North Africa by the forces of the Umayyad Caliphate in the decades after the death of the Prophet Muhammad in the year 632 CE, these realms included the so-called *bilad al-Sudan* beyond the Sahara. By the end of the seventh century, the Islamic empire had extended its reach along the Mediterranean to the Maghrib or 'far west' of its domains (present-day Morocco, Algeria and Tunisia) and in 711 CE its forces crossed the Straits of Gibraltar to conquer most of the Iberian Peninsula, or al-Andalus. Over the following century, Berber and Arab trading expeditions began tentatively to travel deeper into the desert, where they gathered information on and, ultimately, came into direct contact with peoples on the southern 'shore' or, in Arabic, *sahel* of the Sahara. Two centralized kingdoms in the western reaches of the *sahel* emerge most prominently from the early Arabic sources. One was Gao or, as it is written in the Arabic sources, 'Kawkaw', located on the eastern bend of the Niger River (which for centuries geographers mistakenly thought might be part of the Nile). The other, over 600 miles (1,000 km) to the west, beyond the Niger, was a larger state directly across the desert from the southern marches of Morocco. First mentioned in an Arabic source of 788–93 CE, it appears in the written corpus under a variety of names, among which 'Ghana' has prevailed. In his *Book of the Itineraries and Kingdoms* (1067–68), the Andalusi geographer al-Bakri calls the kingdom Awkar and notes that *Ghana* was the title of the king. The word in the local Soninké language for king is *maghan*, which may have yielded Ghana, although the traditional name for the realm appears to have been Wagadu. Again, the medieval kingdom should not be confused with the present-day nation of Ghana – although the fact that postcolonial African leaders chose to name their new countries after these great empires underlines how central they were to perceptions of the continent's history.

North African visitors to Ghana were informed that it had had some twenty rulers before the advent of the Prophet Muhammad, which suggests that it may have been founded as early as the third century CE. At that stage, it was likely to have been one of many emergent micro-states in the region, part of an age of increasing social complexity based on the development of agriculture, local trade networks and iron-smelting. The clearest evidence of these processes comes from the archaeological site of Jenne-jeno to the south. Excavations reveal that the settlement was founded in the third century BCE, making it the oldest known urban centre in Africa south of the Sahara. By the ninth century CE, it had grown into a substantial walled town, albeit one without evidence of monumental architecture, defined social differentiation or trans-Saharan contacts. Jenne-jeno's early development, like that of Ghana, was therefore the result of internal rather than external processes. In contrast with Ghana, however, there is every indication that the town continued to be governed without recourse to powerful kingship, along the lines of the autonomous non-centralized communities described above. As such, it provides an important counterweight to the established dominance of the 'imperial tradition' in the western Sudan.[11]

Today, the land occupied by Ghana is part of the barren fringe between the Sahel and the Sahara in the region of southern Mauritania still known as Aoukar. Yet sources suggest that its early medieval landscape was less forbidding, supporting a mixed agropastoral economy and characterized by groves of trees in which the Soninké – the Mande-speaking people who founded the state – located the shrines that sheltered their religious mysteries. It was also favourable to the use of horses, an important vehicle of empire-building in the Sudanic zone, both for war and for communication. The kingdom was thus in the first instance a political consequence of agricultural surplus. Its founding legends record this fact, along with the under-standing that the environment, although generous, was also fragile. In the stylized mythologies of these Soninké legends, the generosity of the land was represented by a great serpent, Bida, who required, not unlike the Minotaur of ancient Greek myth, the yearly sacrifice of the country's most beautiful young woman, in this case to ward off devastating drought. The Arabic sources indicate that the king was involved in a priestly role in these ceremonies of propitiation. By the time these sources began to report on Ghana in the late eighth century, the empire had extended its domination to neighbouring Mande states in the savanna country to the south. We do not know exactly how this imperial control transpired, but descriptions of the militaristic trappings of the royal court by al-Bakri together with the fact that Wagadu means 'the land of the Wago', the term for the Soninké military elite, point to at least the threat if not the reality of armed force.

The kingdom at its height was therefore a territorial system made up of a core Soninké state in the north and a periphery of Mande vassal kingdoms to the south. The king, or *tunka*, resided in a capital tentatively identified by archaeologists to be at the site of Koumbi Saleh, the ruins of which can be seen today in southeast Mauritania. The legitimacy of his rule appears to have been grounded in the Soninké religion, which surrounded his persona with sacred and priestly charisma. Yet despite its agricultural origins, the state also came to depend on trade with the Islamic world. In the late tenth century, Ghana conquered the rich Islamic emporium of Awdaghust, an oasis town in the desert to the northwest of Koumbi Saleh. Awdaghust was the main point of entry for trans-Saharan trade into the western Sudan, from where a caravan route headed north to Sijilmasa, the Berber trade centre in southeastern Morocco. In the kingdom's capital itself, a cosmopolitan mix of Berbers, Arabs and Sudanic converts to Islam resided in their own settlement separated from the royal court. A different protocol applied to them at court: while local peoples prostrated themselves in front of the king and covered their shoulders in dust to signify submission, Muslims were permitted only to clap their hands when approaching him. Given their literacy in Arabic, they also filled important positions in the *tunka*'s administration. This divided configuration ended up producing rival Islamic and traditionalist factions at court. But the details of their antagonism are lost to history, probably because it was mannerly and non-violent – until, that is, it turned into a burning issue in the final crisis of the empire.

If Ghana was not born from Saharan trade, its subsequent rise to prominence was based upon it. The kingdom became the principal transit point for West African gold bound for the Islamic commercial civilization built across three continents; indeed, it was that lucrative trade that drew Muslim merchants to its capital. Mined in the Bambuk goldfields beyond its domains to the south, gold was imported to Ghana and then exported north across the desert, while salt, copper and, in time, luxury goods from North Africa moved in the other direction. The system operated under a state-regulated fiscal regime: the Soninké traders who brought in the gold ceded a portion of their stock to the king, who came to be known as Kaya Maghan, the 'Master of Gold'. He and the kingdom's ruling elite became wealthy, as luxury goods from North Africa complemented the lavish consumption of locally crafted objects of gold and other materials. Visiting traders observed that the *tunka* lived in a palace with glass windows and flanked by a menagerie of animals. The king in session appeared as a bejewelled idol enthroned under a domed pavilion and attended by richly attired young nobles, the sons of his vassals. His court was so splendidly gilded that even the king's pet dogs reportedly wore golden collars studded with silver bells and his horses were covered in gold-embroidered caparisons.

Despite the growing presence of Islam, including among royal advisors, the king retained his role as the fulcrum of established religious belief and practice. The display in the royal palace of a large ingot of sanctified gold – a custom later reprised by the kings of Mali – symbolized the entanglement of the commercial and ritual realms. All of this was an irritant to resident Muslims, as became evident with the rise of the Almoravid movement in the desert to the north in the eleventh century. The Almoravids, *al mirabitun* in Arabic, took their name from the *ribat*, a fortified outpost manned by ascetic warriors of the faith. The movement emerged in the 1040s, when the militant reformer Abdallah ibn Yasin enlisted the nomadic Sanhaja Berbers in a campaign of religious purification. The principal target of ibn Yasin's Almoravids lay to the north in the Maghrib. In 1054–55, however, they sacked the Muslim town of Awdaghust – its pious men killed and its women raped – on the grounds that it paid tribute to an infidel king. Ghana was then ruled by Tunka Basi, a friend of the Muslim faction, but, in the face of Almoravid violence, his successor Tunka Manin (r. 1063–1076) favoured the traditionalists and created a front against the desert warriors. Yet in 1076 the latter appear to have prevailed. The evidence is unclear – and disputed – but the Almoravids reportedly overran the capital and killed Tunka Manin in battle.[12] This blow proved fatal to Ghana's regional dominance. Muslim kings in the Takrur region along the Senegal River had sided with the Almoravids, while the non-Muslim Mande confederates broke away and secured their independence. A rump Ghana state remained, although it had lost the ideological sway that Sudanic religion gave its king. It also lost control of the gold trade. A decline in agricultural production was perhaps caused by the advancing desertification but was remembered in Soninké oral traditions as being punishment from the serpent Bida. The remnants of the royal family moved southeast to Mema, where they would play a role in the rise of Mali in the thirteenth century.

As with all empires, Ghana's story is not simply one of territorial enlargement; it is also about influence in space and time. The kingdom's glory profoundly marked the political culture of the western Sudan, especially in places where kings ruled. Key aspects of its courtly culture and ritual performance, which sustained the legitimacy of the king by suffusing him with a sacred aura, were duplicated across the region. Sacred kingship was not 'invented' in Ghana, but Ghana gave it a unique form and éclat, which subsequent states appropriated and elaborated. The Mossi kingdoms of present-day Burkina Faso, for example, were located far from Ghana, yet they named their capitals in deference to its power: Tenkodogo (Tunka Dugu, 'royal town'); Wagodogo (Wago Dugu, 'noble town'). The mechanism of this diffusion was the practice of retaining at the *tunka*'s court the sons of vassals, who were tutored in the ways of the centre and imitated them once they assumed power at home. In that way, Ghana's Soninké political culture was reproduced by its Malinké vassals who would go on to forge the empire of Mali, appearing again in Songhay. In that sense, Ghana did not totally disappear: its spirit lived on as the starting point of Sudanic imperial kingship.

MALI

The foundation of Mali is told in a beautiful, complex epic popularly known by the name of its hero, Sunjata. A vessel for Mande and for broader Sudanic moral and ritual ideas, it is one of Africa's greatest oral traditions, rich with universal meaning. Love, sex, magic, justice and fortitude are central themes, interwoven in a tapestry of terrific action. Yet violence too is pervasive: the destructive violence of the king of Soso, Sumaworo Kanté, and the generative violence of his rival for power, the Malinké prince Sunjata Keita. This opposition is a good illustration of the dictum that history is written – or, in this case, recounted and sung – by the victors. The epic has been the object of two grand literary adaptations, the Guinean historian Djibril Tasmir Niane's *Sundiata: An Epic of Old Mali* (first published in French in 1960) and the Guinean novelist Camara Laye's *Le maître de la parole* (1978; translated as *The Guardian of the Word*); an excellent annotated prose translation has also recently been produced by the American historian David Conrad.[13] Yet it is through the performances of the Mande *jeliw* (sing. *jeli*), bards or praise singers better known as 'griots', that the triumph of Sunjata is best known. Performed as an epic cycle of songs and narrative interludes, the story has been kept alive down the centuries – and reinterpreted for new generations of listeners – by the famous *jeliw* families of the Manden, the Mande heartland, such as the Diabaté and the Condé.[14]

A photograph of a griot holding a kora, *c.* 1900, by Edmond Fortier, French West Africa's leading photographer and postcard producer in the early colonial period.

The content of the *jeliw*'s epic performances in combination with other historical evidence suggests that Soso, one of Ghana's former vassals, was, by the early thirteenth century, the rising power in the western Sudan. Under Sumaworo, Soso embarked on a campaign of military expansion that subjugated *jamanaw*, or chieftaincies, of the Manden, the historical heartland of Mande culture that today straddles the frontier between Mali and Guinea. Remembered as a powerful magician, Sumaworo nevertheless committed enough political mistakes for some powerful clans to rally behind Sunjata – then, according to tradition, a persecuted prince who had sought refuge in the exiled court of the ancient ruling family of Ghana. Eventually, Sumaworo was defeated around the year 1235 at Kirina. A convention was then sworn between Sunjata's confederates on the plain of Kurukan Fuga (near Kangaba in present-day Mali), which founded a new empire: Mali.

In its initial phase, this was an empire of the willing, based on an alliance between the so-called Manding clans (i.e. those of the Manden). The founding charter made Sunjata king (*mansa* or *maghan*), stipulated that future kings must come from his family and made them the father of the realm – subjects were to address them with a phrase that means 'King, my father'. With this mandate, the tradition records, Sunjata 'divided up the world' by establishing the rights and obligations of each of the confederate clans: the sixteen clans of 'quiver-bearing' nobles; the five maraboutic clans, cultivators of Islam; and the specialized caste groups or *nyamakalaw*, which included blacksmiths and *jeliw*. As Niane has suggested, it was this founding charter that underlay the striking lack of social mobility that characterized Manding social organization.[15] The expansion of Mali's power and the resulting far-flung influence of Mande culture meant that its hierarchical model of social order was also adopted by a range of neighbouring societies. The kingdom had become an empire, the influence of which extended beyond its frontiers.

The centrality of Sunjata's heroic role in the rise of Mali brings us back to the creative function of coercive force in the establishment of kingship. Sunjata had superior *nyama* (vital force) and *dalilu* (magical power or, more generally, 'means to achieve a goal'), which he inherited from both his paternal and maternal lines, but especially from his mother Sogolon Wulen Condé. Sogolon was daughter of the *mansa* of Dò ni Kiri and – like her sister Dò Kamissa, a shape-changing sorceress known as the Buffalo Woman – had a reputation as a formidable practitioner of *dalilu*.[16] Indeed, the name Sunjata is a contraction of Sogolon Jata, 'the Lion of Sogolon', although like all great men in the Sudan he was also known by a great many other names, including that used by the fourteenth-century Arab historian Ibn Khaldun: Mari Jata, 'the Lion King' (*mari* being a Mande form of the Arabic *amir*). Beyond the core confederates of Kurukan Fuga, the Manding expansion was a violent affair. Campaigns of conquest were directed to the west, north and east, first under Sunjata (r. *c*. 1235– *c*. 1250) and then under his son and successor Mansa Yerelenku, better known by the name reported in Arab histories, Mansa Ule (r. *c*. 1250– *c*. 1270). In the west, the Jolof kingdom was overrun, which carried Mande imperialism through present-day Gambia, the Senegalese region of Casamance and Guinea-Bissau to the Atlantic coastline. To the north, Ghana and Takrur were absorbed, and in the east, the trading cities on the Niger River were either conquered (Timbuktu) or submitted to vassal status (Gao) – although Jenne managed to preserve its independence.

Mali replicated and magnified the political structure of Ghana, although the new empire established a divide – which did not seem to have existed in Ghana – between its original Manding heartland and its conquered periphery. The domains of the former retained a considerable degree of autonomy, although according to the fourteenth-century Arab scholar al-Umari, only the ruler of Ghana continued to be styled a king. The conquered territories, in contrast, received Mande governors (*farin*) who closely supervised local rulers. In some districts, Manding troops were garrisoned, in most cases to protect trade. Under Sunjata, or perhaps later, the empire was split into two military regions: the north under the *Sura Farin* ('northern governor') and the south under the *Sankara Soma* ('head of the Sankaran', the basin of the upper Niger River). Although the location of the capital remains a matter of debate, it was possibly Niani, in the Sankaran.[17] There, the *mansa* reprised the Ghana custom of bringing up sons of vassals in his court. He oversaw two principal branches of central government: a powerful consultative council, the *gbara*, which institutionalized aspects of the original Kurukan Fuga convention; and the military body of the *donson ton*, originally the hunter's guild.

As in Ghana, the king was a sacred father figure who offered protection and dispensed justice – the latter usually while dressed in sensational trappings and during the course of awe-inspiring ceremonies. The intrepid Arab traveller Ibn Battuta observed such an occasion under Mansa Sulayman (r. 1336–1358), reporting it in much the same terms as al-Bakri's account of the court of the *tunka* of Ghana. In contrast with Ghana, however, the emperors of Mali were Muslim – a conversion that may have dated back to Sunjata himself, but certainly to his son Yerelenku, who made the pilgrimage to Mecca. Yet court ritual embodied the old political beliefs of the Sudan: people still approached the sovereign throwing dust onto their backs, and his sacred word was not uttered openly but to a spokesperson, the *wanadu*, and then projected in ornate, chant-like phrases by the *jeli ba*, the royal griot. Indeed, the mixture of Islam and indigenous culture perplexed the pious and somewhat sanctimonious Ibn Battuta during his visit in 1352–53. He admired the assiduous performance of daily prayers and the celebration of the great feasts of Islam, but, as John Iliffe notes, was less impressed by 'masked dancing, public recitation of pagan traditions, self-abasement before the king, eating of unclean foods, and scanty female clothing'.[18]

Even more than Ghana, Mali was the land of gold. Its domains now encompassed the new Buré goldfield on the headwaters of the Niger and it also had access to rich new sources further south in the Akan forest region of the present-day country of Ghana. The fiscal regime by which wealth was accumulated in imperial Ghana's royal treasury was also in use in Mali but applied to much larger quantities of gold. The result was that Mansa Musa I (r. 1312–1337), whose reign can be seen as the apogee of the empire, is reputed as having been among the wealthiest men in all history. Famously, that was demonstrated when he undertook the pilgrimage to Mecca in 1325: on passing through Cairo, his profligacy was such that he reportedly depressed the gold market for many years across the Middle East. Echoes of that power and wealth also reached Europe, where a map of the world produced in Majorca in 1375 depicts Mansa Musa as 'Rex Melli', seated in majesty holding a golden orb (see pl. IV).

Yet gold appears to have been less of a strategic asset for the emperor of Mali than it was for that of Ghana. During his stay in Cairo, Mansa Musa explained that he in fact drew more revenue from the export of copper to the forest region to the south. Mali, that is, was not just the 'broker kingdom' that Ghana was: it encompassed production zones for a wide variety of agricultural commodities, as well as drawing salt from the Saharan mines at Taghaza and copper from those at Takedda. It organized the entire western Sudan into a vast integrated economic zone in which trade was protected by military garrisons and by the rule of law. Ibn Battuta was amazed at the level of security for persons and for property, while the seventeenth-century author of the Timbuktu Chronicle *Tarikh al-fattash* believed that the resulting prosperity made Mali only second to Syria 'among the beautiful countries of the world'.[19] The occupation of the Atlantic coastline even led to dreams of expansion beyond the sea: according to one Arabic source, Mansa Muhammad (r. c. 1310–1312) reportedly launched several dugout flotillas on the ocean and when none returned, he embarked on one himself – and was never seen again.

In the Sudanic theory of kingship, however, sacred authority was ultimately anchored in force. The *mansa* depended on military capability for the maintenance of authority, and great army leaders of the *donson ton* were the pillars of the throne. Some of these commanders acquired legendary status, such as Sunjata's and Yerelenku's general Turama'an Traoré (or Tirmakan) and Saran Mandian, who under Mansa Musa I led the campaigns to subdue the predatory Saharan nomads. The most illustrious, however, was Sakura, who translated military force into usurpation and *mansaya* (kingship). The Kurukan Fuga charter had sought to stabilize *mansaya* by making it a mandate of Sunjata's family, but it neglected to establish firm rules of succession within it. This dangerous flaw led to political turmoil as early as the 1280s, when the *gbara* and the *donson ton* engaged in furious intrigues against each other and state disintegration became a real possibility. In response, Sakura staged a coup, restored stability and crowned himself king. The *jonni* or 'little slave', as his enemies called him, then set about securing his dubious legitimacy by military means, expanding and fortifying the frontiers of the empire. By the late 1290s, Sakura's grip on power was sufficiently secure for him to undertake the lengthy pilgrimage to Mecca – on the

A terracotta figure of a mounted warrior from Mali, 13th to 15th century. The cylindrical form of the torso and limbs of both horse and rider together with the detailed rendering of the helmet, quiver and bridle are characteristic of the so-called Jenne style of terracotta art. Height 27¾ in. (70.5 cm).

return from which he was killed by brigands in Libya. That event brought Sunjata's family back to power, but the Sakura episode demonstrates that if sacred authority was essential to *mansaya*, then so too was coercive force.

After the reign of Mansa Musa I, Mali entered a period of gradual decline, as a sequence of less impressive emperors put the established structure of power under increasing strain. The Manding heartland, with its strong cultural and constitutional bonds to the emperor, largely remained loyal. The conquered periphery to the north and east, however, gradually broke away – including, fatefully, the kingdom of Gao. No forceful general emerged to stem the crumbling of central power, and by the early fifteenth century there was a Mali kingdom in the Manden but there was no longer a Mali empire encompassing the western Sudan.

SONGHAY

In contrast to Mali, we know more about the history of Songhay through written sources than through oral traditions. The most famous of these sources are the so-called Timbuktu Chronicles, particularly al-Sa'di's *Tarikh al-Sudan* (1653–56) and Ibn al-Mukhtar's *Tarikh al-fattash* (1664). Composed in the great urban centre of commerce and Islamic scholarship in the aftermath of the collapse of Songhay power, these literary works are important in part because they were written by local scholars rather than by foreign visitors. They therefore provide an indigenous perspective all too rare in medieval African history. Indeed, it was their discovery by the outside world in the nineteenth century that gave rise to the notion of a distinctively Sudanic statecraft: their aim, Paulo de Moraes Farias has written, was to portray the region 'as a vast geopolitical entity defined by the notion of imperial kingship'.[20] Recent scholarship has therefore sought to re-examine the *tarikh* tradition in the context of its production. Far from simply celebrating the social and political hierarchy that had existed under Songhay imperial rule, Farias argues, it also sought to come to terms with the reality of the end of that rule by urging a reconciliation with the Arma, the local Moroccan regime left behind after the invasion of Songhay in 1591. Written sources, that is, need to be approached with the same critical awareness as oral traditions.

Songhay's origins lie in the ancient kingdom of Gao, which became known to North African traders at the same time as Ghana to the west and Kanem (which would later evolve into Kanem-Borno) to the east. Crucial to an understanding of early Gao and to Songhay was its location on the Niger River. The nucleus of Songhay society was the Sorko fishing community. The Sorko occupied a similar riverine niche as the Bozo and Somono peoples of the upper reaches of the Niger but developed a more complex society, with a class of riverbank farmers, the *gabi*, and a military elite, the *san* (pl. *sanyey* or *sonyey*), the origin of the word Songhay. Songhay religion and governance was closely bound up with the Niger and early settlements always emerged on islands in the river, ruled by communal chiefs constrained in their authority by rules inscribed in the ritual constitution. Such riverine communities do not seem to have possessed a natural imperial vocation: throughout their history, the Bozo and Somono remained mere helpers for the successive state-building projects of the Malinké of Mali, the Bamana of Segu and the Fulbe of Masina. But by moving to Gao to control trade revenue in perhaps the early eleventh century, the Songhay chiefship of Gungiya broke that mould: stepping out of the river and onto dry land, it waxed into a kingship.

Yet that kingship remained rooted in the old riverine culture. Its tradition of origin recorded that the ancestors of the king created the country by lighting its first fire, and on his accession the king received the *din tuuri*, the snuffed-out firebrand said to be the one used in that momentous event. That and other royal regalia were handed to the new king by the *hikoy*, the Sorko 'chief of boats', who was the only man at court not bound by rites of submission: the throwing of dust on one's back and addressing the king indirectly through his spokesman. As the guardian of the rules of kingship, including those of succession, the *hikoy* spoke freely to the monarch as a peer – a reminder of the 'amphibious' nature of Songhay kingship based on the partnership of boat and spear. Sonni Ali Ber, the fifteenth-century founder of the empire of Songhay, made extensive use of the river fleet in his wars and on one occasion even attempted to dig a canal through the desert to reach one of his targets. Until the successor Askia dynasty, the Gao kings always kept a residence at Gungiya (or Kukiya) – an alternating island–dryland pattern of residence that still exists at Ayorou in present-day Niger, a refuge for the exiled Sonni family. Governance and law were closely shaped by Songhay religion, the chief priests of which were Sorko and who worked their rituals on riverine islands.

Uniquely among the great Sudanic states, royal succession at Gao was by male primogeniture or, in the absence of the eldest son, the eldest brother. The rationale was clear: there should be no vacuum at the top of the state at any time. The result was a high degree of dynastic stability, although when Askia Dawud died in 1582, his son Elhaj exploited the fact that his elder brother Muhammad Benkan was not in Gao and seized power. His other brothers accepted the fait accompli, but told him that 'had Muhammad Benkan been here, you would not have been king'. Ten years later, when Askia Ishaq II took his son with him in his escape from the invading Moroccans, the *hikoy* Laha Sorkiya protested, telling him that he could go, but alone, for he must not deprive the state of its rightful successor.

When they moved onto dry land, perhaps in the tenth or eleventh century, the Gungiya kings of the Za Der Banda dynasty also converted to Islam – one of the first recorded ruling families in Africa south of the Sahara to do so. From around the tenth to the thirteenth century, the kingdom of Gao was a modest equivalent of Ghana, operating a transit economy based on the trade in salt and gold. Its Islamized elite, too, lived in considerable luxury, a fact reported by al-Bakri and al-Idrisi and which archaeological excavations had

just begun to confirm when the region was overrun by jihadist political violence in the 2010s. In common with Mali, Gao's religious
culture was also characterized by a complex interaction between
Islam and indigenous belief. Songhay religion had unmistakable
elements in common with the peoples to the south: Dongo, the
thunder god, for example, can be associated with the great Yoruba
deity, Shango. The Gao kings were pious Muslims who considered
their domains to be an outpost of the *dar al-Islam* and were recognized as thus: their regalia included a copy of the Quran allegedly
sent by the Abbasid caliph in Baghdad. Yet they were revered by
their overwhelmingly non-Muslim subjects as near-divine lords and
protectors of the kingdom. 'Court ceremonial', John Hunwick writes,
on the basis of al-Bakri's account, 'was clearly pagan'. 'When the
ruler ate, a drum was beaten and women danced, shaking their heads.
All work ceased during the sovereign's meal time, and when he had
finished, the remains of the food were thrown into the Niger with
loud cries and work was allowed to start again.'[21]

The riverine kingdom of Gao was incorporated into the empire
of Mali in the late thirteenth century and was liberated a century
later by Za Der Banda princes who took the title Sonni. During this
period of vassalage, Gao sent royal sons to the imperial capital and
took in Mande political culture in large draughts. The decline of
Mali may have freed Gao, but it also ended the imperial security
system that had ensured commercial prosperity across the Middle
Niger region. With the Mande shield down, predatory groups began
to have a field day. Timbuktu was harried by Tuareg raiders from
the desert and by the Mossi from the south, while the inland delta
of the Niger became the playground of Fulbe warlords. While there
is no direct evidence that Songhay expansion began as a conscious
effort to reimpose order, a search for security in an increasingly
disordered world may well have motivated the founding of a new
imperial system by Sonni Ali Ber in the 1460s.

A Sonni prince with parentage in the ancestral southern reaches
of Songhay, Ali Ber consolidated control over his home territory

before waging a merciless war on the predatory raiders to the north. The Tuareg were subdued, and turned from being the pillagers of desert caravans into their protectors; the Mossi kingdom of Yatenga was subjected to a punitive campaign aimed at teaching its rulers to keep out of the Middle Niger; while the Fulbe, who had occupied the productive heart of the region, saw their warrior class decimated in a series of brutal campaigns. Meanwhile, the great commercial and scholarly centres of Timbuktu and Jenne were occupied. Indeed, Sonni Ali's entire reign, from 1464 until his death in 1492, was spent on the warpath. His son Sonni Baru, however, ruled for only a few months before being toppled in a coup by the military commander Muhammad Sylla (whose name is often given, mistakenly, as Touré). Sylla, who kept the military title 'Askia' as his regnal title – which became that of his dynasty – continued Sonni Ali's policy of imperial expansion, rounding off Songhay's acquisitions with the desert-side trading city of Agades and the salt mines of Taghaza, deep in the Sahara.

Yet Askia Muhammad was keener on governance than on war. Songhay freely borrowed from Mali's administrative system but, as was already evident under Sonni Ali, it was more tightly centralized. Askia Muhammad's grand project in the first decade of his rule was to Islamize the state. He was a Soninké from a line of Muslim clerics on his father's side, and his coup against Sonni Baru had the support of the empire's Islamic faction. This opened the gates for a constitutional crisis over the ritual groundings of the state. Sonni Ali, condemned by posterity – like Sumaworo – as a 'magician king' or a 'witch', was seen to have favoured indigenous religion over Islam. He was said to have relished provoking pious orthodox Muslims and actively cultivated the sacred nature of Songhay kingship. Sonni Ali's disappearance, reportedly in a swimming accident – swallowed by the river that flowed through the heart of local belief – presented a golden opportunity for the aggravated Islamic party and the multi-ethnic military elite that was less bound in loyalty to the king. After his victory over the perceived forces of pagan tradition, therefore,

Askia Muhammad made the pilgrimage to Mecca. Unlike that other military usurper, Sakura, he returned safely, proceeding to seek clerical advice on Islamic governance. The most radical counsel came from the stern Berber theologian al-Maghili, from Tlemcen in present-day Algeria. Al-Maghili told Askia Muhammad that God had elevated him so he could reform the faith and the wayward conduct of his subjects rather than be their lord and master: 'You are through the whole extent of your kingdom a shepherd, not a proprietor'.[22] These words, which alluded to the bad behaviour of Sonni Ali, were a clear attack on Songhay's traditional kingship.

That kingship in many ways persisted, but Askia Muhammad presided over the rise of a powerful 'religious estate', a Muslim clergy that became an indispensable ingredient of his government.[23] An Islamic style of governance became increasingly pronounced during the Askia period. In 1528–29, Askia Muhammad was in turn deposed by his son Musa, who, according to al-Sa'di's *Tarikh al-Sudan*, confronted his aged father in the great mosque of Gao during the prayer for the festival of Eid al-Adha.[24] Yet to the end, court ceremonial remained rooted in established Sudanic manners: Askia Dawud (r. 1549–1582) was once blushingly forced to apologize to Arab visitors for such 'barbarous' conduct as the throwing of dust on the back by supplicants or the rushing to present one's sleeve when the king was about to spit.

There is every indication that Songhay replicated the prosperity of the earlier Sudanic empires. As with Ghana, the goldfields lay beyond its territorial control, but the precious metal continued to flow in from the south – increasingly from the Akan region – to the entrepôts of the Middle Niger. Gao may have been the most populous metropole in West Africa in the sixteenth century, its status heightened by the concentration of wealth in the imperial court. Agricultural production – more important for the common people than gold or other luxury commodities – was the mainstay of the economy, overseen by the *fari monzo* or 'regent of the fields', the post occupied by Askia Musa before his coup. The ruler was the empire's biggest land-owner, possessing vast farmlands cultivated by large numbers of bonded workers. In accordance with the ideology of the king as provider of his subjects, the output of these estates was mostly slated for clientelist redistribution. Yet the imperial regime and the broader land-owning class, which included the clerical elite, was highly exploitative of the rural population, both freeborn and enslaved.[25] Communities of servile craftspeople also supplied a range of goods to the king's household, which was managed by a powerful official, the *hugukuraykoy*, 'chief of the interior of the house'.

The 1550s witnessed the start of recurring episodes of political tension between Songhay and Morocco, at the heart of which lay the control over the lucrative Saharan salt mines at Taghaza. These were compounded in the 1580s by the rise to power of the ambitious Moulay Ahmad al-Mansur, whose victory over a Portuguese army supplied him with the resources to recruit mercenaries and purchase European firearms. The resulting imbalance in military technology between the Sudan and Morocco – one of spears and arrows versus guns – convinced al-Mansur that the Songhay Empire, which he imagined to be swimming in gold, was an easy prey. Pressuring his own Islamic 'religious estate' to declare that the Askia did not deserve to rule the Sudan, he proceeded to mount an expedition of conquest. Many of the soldiers he launched across the Sahara in November 1590 were Spanish mercenaries or the descendants of Muslim refugees from al-Andalus: the same kind of tough fighting men who had assailed the Aztec and Inca empires of the Americas earlier in the century. In early 1591, the invaders routed the Askia's army at Tondibi ('the Black Stone') close to Gao, stunning their enemy with muskets and cannons. Askia Ishaq (r. 1588–1591) sued for peace and offered to become a vassal of Morocco, but al-Mansur rejected the proposal and ordered his forces to move on to occupy Timbuktu. The sun had set over Songhay.

Historians of Songhay tend to read its entire history in the light of its destruction at Tondibi. For many, it is a tale of steady decline culminating in political infighting in the 1580s, which left the regime ill-equipped to confront the threat from Morocco. This view has been shaped by the Timbuktu Chronicles, which begin by affirming that Songhay was doomed to catastrophe from the beginning – an opinion pleasing to the Arma of Timbuktu and consonant with the fatalistic conceptions that found easy purchase among a clerical readership. Yet what is striking about Songhay, despite the dynastic shift from the Sonnis to the Askias, is its political stability. It is not at all clear that Songhay would have collapsed without the Moroccan attack, and its defeat – which prefigured the dilemmas of many African kingdoms faced with European firepower three centuries later – was largely the consequence of the technological disparity on which al-Mansur had shrewdly counted. More importantly, what the defeat of 1591 marked was not just the end of Songhay, but of the entire imperial tradition of the western Sudan. Morocco was unable to establish its own stable imperial domination over the region, and the Arma degenerated into one of the many predatory elements competing for power. What it did was to open the way for a resumption of the disorder and violence against which Songhay had been built in the first place.[26]

CONCLUSION

At a time when historians are increasingly suspicious of grand narratives, the 'imperial tradition' in Sudanic West Africa has in recent years been critiqued and qualified. The history of the region, it has begun to be argued, goes beyond that of the three great states of Ghana, Mali and Songhay and more attention should be directed to the enduring cultural and political forms that underlay their dynastic rise and decline. Yet the imperial era remains a topic of fascination. Michael Gomez revisits it in his recent *African Dominion*, which seeks to insert the region into the broader global history from which it has for so long been excluded. It ended a long time ago, at Tondibi in 1591, but lasted much longer than the intervening period since. Under the aegis of the three successive empires, the Sudan built much of its civilization as we know it today. The distinctive mud-brick architecture exemplified by the great mosque in Jenne (see pl. III); the griot tradition that continues to flourish in the music of Mali, Guinea, The Gambia and beyond; the dynamic mix of Sudanic and Islamic religious cultures: all were produced or reconfigured in the context of the imperial system.[27] There can be little doubt, too, that the post-imperial phase of the last four centuries has been one of relative disorder and decline, when the contradictions inherent in some of these constructs have threatened the fabric of society. The high degree of inequality and of predation directed towards the enslavement of the vulnerable and the 'pagan' grew increasingly unregulated in the time of petty wars and chronic violence that set in after Tondibi. Although much African history is made to revolve around the advent of European colonial conquest, the multiple legacies of this prolonged *ancien régime* remain profound for the peoples of the region of the Sahel. There is much good that needs to be preserved, and much bad that must be overcome.

CHAPTER 3

THE SOLOMONIC CHRISTIAN KINGDOM OF ETHIOPIA

Habtamu Tegegne and Wendy Laura Belcher

The northeast African kingdom of Ethiopia has been the dominant power in the Horn of Africa and the western Red Sea for most of the last three millennia. Indeed, Ethiopia has maintained one of the longest national traditions in the world, with a charismatic monarchy that has existed without interruption over the last two millennia.[1] Moreover, Ethiopia's prehistory extends far deeper in time than that. Archaeological evidence points to it being the very cradle of humanity: it is the site of the oldest human fossils (those of the genus *Homo*) yet found, dated to 2.8 million years ago; of the oldest fossils of anatomically modern people, dated to 195,000 years ago; and of the oldest tools and therefore the earliest evidence of advanced human behaviour. Ethiopia is also one of the seven earliest sites in the world where agriculture developed. Its people domesticated several important and distinctive crops, including teff – a small grain traditionally used to produce the region's famous soured flat bread, *injera* – and another that would eventually spread around the world, coffee. The Afroasiatic family of languages, which includes Hebrew, Arabic, Berber and the languages of Ethiopia, probably emerged in the region some ten to eight thousand years ago. Two of the languages that would subsequently evolve from that early Ethiopian language were Sabean, spoken across the Red Sea from Ethiopia in what is now Yemen, and classical Ethiopic, also called Ge'ez.[2]

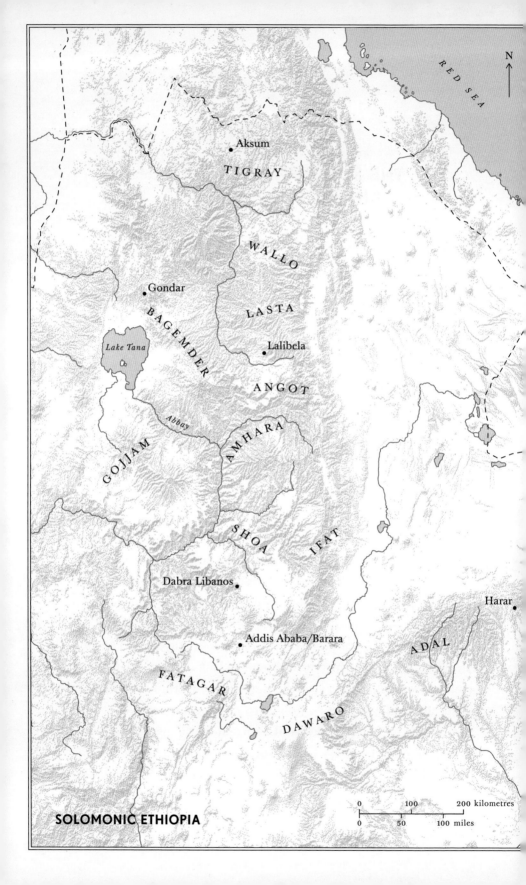

N

RED SEA

Aksum

TIGRAY

WALLO

Gondar

LASTA

BAGEMDER

Lake Tana

Lalibela

ANGOT

Abbay

AMHARA

GOJJAM

SHOA

IFAT

Dabra Libanos

Harar

Addis Ababa/Barara

ADAL

FATAGAR

DAWARO

0   100   200 kilometres

0   50   100 miles

SOLOMONIC ETHIOPIA

Early on, Ethiopia created an ancient literate culture. Ethiopians invented a script for Ge'ez, based in part on the Sabean script but instead written from left to right and with marked vowels.[3] They then used it to develop Ge'ez into the scholarly and liturgical language of Ethiopia, starting in the fourth century CE. It maintained this status into the twentieth century, despite being replaced as the language of the court and daily life around 1000 CE by regional languages such as Amharic and Tigrinya. Bound books written in Ge'ez also began to be produced as early as the sixth century. Ethiopians spent much of the first millennium translating the Bible and other religious materials into Ge'ez, but in the medieval period they also composed thousands of original books of biography, theology, poetry and short stories, as well as richly detailed historical chronicles. As a result, locally written sources have enabled modern historians to reconstruct many aspects of the region's deeper past.

Ethiopians built these innovations on earlier ones. As early as 2500 BCE, they may have created the wealthy Red Sea kingdom of Punt, with which Egypt traded precious goods. Certainly, in the first millennium BCE, Ethiopia participated in forming an ancient zone of connectivity stretching from the Mediterranean down both sides of the Red Sea and the Nile River Basin. This zone was a cosmopolitan and multicultural space through which Ethiopia was linked not only to neighbouring South Arabia, Nubia and Egypt, but also to the more distant lands of the Levant and the Hellenic world, as well as to South Asia and the Indian Ocean. By the fifth century BCE, Ethiopians had created trade networks that spanned these diverse cultural and economic regions, and Ethiopia emerged as a major trade hub. As Classical Greek civilization was emerging in the eastern Mediterranean, Ethiopia was already an important place. Its role in the larger world waxed and waned over the centuries, but the mention of 'Ethiopia' in the Bible – where the term was used to refer to the entire continent – repeatedly revived interest in it. In the twentieth century, diasporic African Americans claimed the ancient Christian kingdom of Ethiopia as symbolic of a proud African heritage, pointing to Ethiopia's defeat of

European imperial invaders during the Scramble for Africa and its independence throughout the era of colonial rule. The kingdom became a powerful symbol of Black freedom and of Africa's glorious past.[4]

This chapter is a history of the so-called Solomonic Christian kingdom of Ethiopia, with a focus on its origins in the powerful empire of Aksum, its rise in the medieval period (1270–1550) and its later developments (1636–1974). Over a millennium, at the crossroads of global networks, this kingdom had a genius for adaptability and innovation. From its conversion to Christianity in the fourth century CE to its invention of complex administrative systems, its dynamic intellectual tradition, and on to its recovery from devastating foreign incursions, Ethiopia has invented new futures and forged its own path.

THE AKSUMITE EMPIRE

In the first millennium BCE, several important developments happened in northern Ethiopia. First, the civilization that had arisen on the northern reaches of the mountainous plateau took on a distinctively urban character, with Ethiopians creating large towns and constructing massive stone temples, monuments and other structures. The ruins of Yeha, one of these ancient towns that flourished in the eighth century BCE, include a large temple with exquisite masonry and the remains of dams and irrigation canals, indicating that Ethiopians also developed sophisticated water management technology. The people were united by a common religion, worshipping a god represented by a disc and crescent. Yeha established a small kingdom called D'mt, about which little is known, although the region appears largely to have remained a diffused assortment of independent towns. Meanwhile, a town called Aksum was settled in the seventh century BCE. It was from these developments that the Aksumite Empire arose in the early first millennium CE.[5]

The Aksumites built their mighty empire in the same region of northern Ethiopia as Yeha and D'mt.[6] During the first century CE, the city of Aksum brought all the other towns under its sway and united them into a powerful kingdom. By the third century, the Aksumite Empire reached the peak of its power, which continued until the advent of Islam in the seventh century. This was no minor power. The Persian prophet Mani (216–276 CE) ranked Aksum as the third greatest empire of the ancient world: 'There are four great kingdoms on earth. The first is the kingdom of Babylon and Persia; the second is the kingdom of Rome; the third is the kingdom of the Aksumites; the fourth is the kingdom of the Chinese.'[7] Indeed, this Ethiopian empire can be ranked among the great kingdoms of the world for its military might, monumental buildings and prosperous economy. Aksumite rule extended from its heartland in present-day Eritrea and northern Ethiopia to the Red Sea coast, to the lowlands south of the highlands and to the west in present-day Sudan. In some periods, it even extended across the Red Sea into South Arabia, in the region of present-day Yemen.[8] In terms of building technology, Ethiopian engineers erected the tallest known monolithic stelae in world history (see pl. VII). Their many stone monuments were inscribed in local and international languages: Ge'ez, Sabean and Greek.

Ethiopian innovations in agriculture, trade and currency under-pinned Aksum's emergence as the wealthiest power in the Red Sea region. Farmers owned the land they cultivated, paying taxes in agri-cultural produce to their rulers. The empire's shipbuilding technologies and specialized mariners played a crucial role in maritime trade routes. Revenue from trade – in which enslaved people, ivory, gold, tortoise shell and other products were exchanged for imported luxury goods – was the fiscal bedrock supporting Aksumite power. As a result, the empire's port city of Adulis on the Red Sea coast was a vibrant centre for international commerce during the glory days of Aksum. Its rulers minted their own currency: gold, silver and bronze coins.

The greatest rulers of the Aksumite Empire were the fourth-century emperor Ezana and the sixth-century emperor Kaleb (whose throne name was Ella-Asbeha). Ezana is remembered not only for conquering the kingdom of Meroë in present-day Sudan, where he left many monumental stelae and inscriptions in three languages (including Greek), but also for converting to Christianity around 340 CE. Christianity reached Aksum from Egypt and the Ethiopian Church would remain intimately connected to that in Egypt into the twentieth century, headed by a bishop appointed by the Coptic patriarch in Alexandria. Between the fifth and the seventh centuries, the Bible was translated into Ge'ez and the faith began to spread throughout the Ethiopian highlands.[9]

Kaleb was the last of the great kings of Aksum, known for his naval expeditions to South Arabia and presiding over the vigorous missionary activity that resulted in widespread popular conversion to Christianity by the end of the sixth century. By then, however, Aksum was showing signs of decline. The rise and expansion of Islam in the seventh century would lead to its final eclipse: not only did the empire lose its territories in South Arabia and on the western Red Sea coast, but also the great port of Adulis was destroyed. By the tenth century, the city of Aksum itself was largely abandoned. Yet Ethiopian kingship and Christianity survived. Various Ethiopian dynasties have risen and fallen over time, but the Ethiopian Orthodox Church founded under the auspices of the great Aksumite rulers has remained a strong and constant presence in the region to the present day. The language, script, architecture, art and Christian faith of the Aksumite civilization would continue to shape Ethiopia for many centuries to come.

THE RISE OF THE SOLOMONIC DYNASTY

After a fallow period of several centuries, a new dynasty arose, popularly known as the Zagwe. Little is known about the Zagwe dynasty, although it appears to have emerged in the early twelfth century under a ruler from the region to the east of the previous centre, Aksum. One of its most lasting achievements was the construction of a dozen churches of splendid workmanship chiselled several storeys down from ground level into the solid rock. These churches are located in what later came to be known as the city of Lalibela, the Zagwe capital named after King Lalibela (r. *c.* 1185–*c.* 1225), who sponsored the construction of some of them, and they are now a famous UNESCO World Heritage Site.[10] Meanwhile, Islam was also spreading from the Red Sea coast along the trade routes into the southeastern highlands and adjacent lowlands, where several sultanates, most prominently that of Ifat, emerged in proximity to the frontiers of Christianity.

In 1270, the so-called Solomonic dynasty came to power when its first king, Yekuno Amlak, defeated the last of the Zagwe kings on the battlefield.[11] The Solomonic kings ruled Ethiopia for seven centuries until the overthrow of Emperor Haile Selassie in 1974, making the dynasty one of the longest in human history. Its rulers claimed direct descent from the Aksumite kings and to be the rightful heirs of their ancient civilization. Whereas the Aksumite Empire and the Zagwe dynasty had been located in the northern region of Tigray, however, the new Solomonic dynasty shifted the political and ecclesiastical centre of Ethiopia south to the provinces of Amhara and Shoa, in the watershed between the Abbay (Blue Nile) and Awash

The excavated rock-cut church of
Bete Giyorgis (St George) at Lalibela, 13th century CE.

rivers. The kingdom profited from its ability to tax the trade goods that came from the lands around it as they flowed to the ports of the Red Sea and beyond. At its greatest territorial extent, the medieval kingdom incorporated most of what are now modern Ethiopia and Eritrea, which it succeeded in transforming from a collection of loosely tied regions into a centralized kingdom of many ethnicities.

The ruling ideology of the Solomonic dynasty can be described as one of 'African Zionism'. Grounded in a founding myth of biblical descent, it claimed that Ethiopia and its kings had replaced the Israelites as the chosen people of God. That is, they asserted that their kings were descended from the biblical King Solomon and the legendary Queen of Sheba, who from ancient times had been associated with Ethiopia.[12] According to the myth, the two monarchs had a son, Bayna Lekhem, popularly known as Menelik I, who was responsible for the transfer of God's providence from the Levant to Africa. He did so by bringing the first-born sons of the Israelites to advise his rule and the Ark of the Covenant from the temple in Jerusalem, which he deposited at Aksum. The textual underpinnings of this ideology lie in a book of uncertain origin titled the *Kebra Nagast* (The Glory of Kings), which was translated from Arabic into Ge'ez around 1320.[13] Appearing soon after the founding of the Solomonic dynasty, the *Kebra Nagast* played a critical discursive role in highland Ethiopia's various ethnic groups coming to see themselves as a unified people with a joint destiny. It served to justify Ethiopia's existence as a singular nation, the special focus of God's blessings, and contributed to its kings' ability to wield authority over a vast swathe of territory containing many different peoples and polities.

GOVERNANCE UNDER AMDA SEYON

The two most famous Solomonic rulers – who most decisively shaped the politics and culture of Ethiopia – were Amda Seyon (r. 1314–1344) and Zara Yaqob (r. 1434–1468). The reign of Amda Seyon was a defining moment in the emergence of medieval governance. The grandson of Yekuno Amlak, he is remembered as a great warrior king, consolidating Ethiopia's vast territories, including north to the Dahlak Islands in the Red Sea, west to Gojjam (the region of the Beta Israel or Ethiopian Jews) and south to the Damot and Hadya kingdoms. Amda Seyon's strongest foes were the Islamic sultanates in the east, led by Ifat, the oldest and historically most significant, and his successful campaigns against them are the best documented in the Ge'ez chronicle of his reign. This larger Ethiopian kingdom offered still greater opportunities for extracting revenues, while presenting considerable challenges in terms of imposing centralized rule. Amda Seyon addressed these challenges by creating an administrative hierarchy containing both directly appointed officials and hereditary local rulers. He laid out this new system in a handbook of governance that subsequent Ethiopian kings would elaborate and revise. This was the *Ser'ata Mangest* (The Law of the Government), which also defined the rules for the organization of the royal court, the coronation of the king, the investiture of officials, the manner of legal jurisdiction and the relationship between the church and the monarchy.[14] Its main thrust, however, was to emphasize the authority of centralized power over that of local and provincial hereditary rulers. The kingdom was accordingly organized into an elaborate bureaucratic hierarchy, the *Ser'ata Mangest* providing detailed lists of monasteries, districts and provinces together with their corresponding administrators, as well as lists of other civil, religious, judicial and military titles and officeholders with their various privileges, entitlements and administrative duties. All these officials were installed with much pageantry and were responsible for the day-to-day implementation of royal policy.

Amda Seyon is also remembered for his solution to the problem of royal succession. As in many regions of Africa, the principle of primogeniture in Ethiopia never existed; rather, the only requirement for succession was descent from the previous king's male line. Sons of the king's concubines, his nephews and even cousins could be legitimate kings, so potential claimants to the throne were many. For instance, six brothers and sons of Yekuno Amlak had vied for power in a fourteen-year succession struggle from 1285 to 1299. Amda Seyon therefore devised the institution of the royal prison: the brothers and sons of the reigning king were held in an impregnable natural fortress called Amba Geshan. Although succession struggles did continue to arise from time to time, the royal prison significantly reduced their capacity for disruption, with the result that the kingdom was consistently well governed during the medieval period.[15]

Over time, the Solomonic kings expanded on a long-established local method of extracting economic resources. Called *gwelt*, it gave fief-holding rights to officials and religious institutions as a reward for service and loyalty.[16] This system of administration was therefore an efficient way of securing the authority of the centralized state in the regions and of collecting wealth from peasant farmers and merchants. In turn, *gwelt*-holders had obligations to the government: if secular office-holders, they were required to raise soldiers and lead them into battle; if Church officials, they were required to carry out a variety of religious services such as missionary work, the founding of new churches or monasteries and scribal duties. In the fourteenth and fifteenth centuries, the Solomonic kings also established military colonies, known as *chawa*, throughout the kingdom, especially on the vulnerable frontier to the east. The intent was to police and defend the domains of the kingdom from enemy encroachments and to ensure the flow of trade essential to its prosperity.

ADMINISTRATION UNDER ZARA YAQOB

The reign of Zara Yaqob from 1434 to 1468 marked the peak of the Solomonic period. A vigorous, highly educated man with a gift for systematizing mechanisms of governance, Zara Yaqob instituted organizational changes that transformed the Ethiopian kingdom. He invented a new model for Church–state relations, in which the secular state was the dominant force, creating an indigenous absolutism based upon the concept of Solomonic legitimacy. He reformed the Church in ways that unified the country, thereby further consolidating royal power. While the permanent capital at Barara (in the region of Shoa, located in and around Ethiopia's modern capital of Addis Ababa) might have predated Zara Yaqob's reign, he developed it into an important centre.[17]

Zara Yaqob inherited from his predecessors the policy of active military campaigning. Under his rule, the kingdom reached its territorial apex, approximating the modern boundaries of Ethiopia, which meant that he governed a much larger domain than previous kings. This gave rise to further problems of governance. The kingdom's cultural diversity, mountainous terrain and sheer expanse meant that regional hereditary rulers and local authorities continued to play a key role in controlling territory and people. Indeed, in many regions the centralized kingdom had only a minimal impact on the older social and political order. In Muslim-majority regions where the Ethiopian kings had no doubts as to the loyalty of traditional chiefs or their capacity for self-government, for example, they permitted local ruling houses to continue to govern. Zara Yaqob, however, set out to govern the provinces less as a collection of disparate polities and more as a contiguous territory to be administered and defended as a whole. He also believed that religious ritual could play a central role in uniting his Christian subjects and his project of further centralizing the governance of the kingdom.[18] He instituted uniformity by decreeing a feast day in honour of the Virgin Mary each month, the reading of her miracles in every church service, and that every Christian should wear a cross and be tattooed on the forehead with a mark of the Holy Trinity.[19]

Zara Yaqob achieved this consolidation of centralized kingship in several ways. First, he directly appointed royal officials, including his own daughters, to administer several provinces. Second, he used a series of internal and external threats, in particular the presence of the sultanate of Adal to the east, to justify the need for a greater degree of royal authority. Indeed, when the Ethiopian king was strong, Adal paid tribute, but when the king was weak the Adali rulers refused to do so and raided the eastern frontier provinces. Third, he placed an unprecedented emphasis on legislative and religious uniformity, imposing a range of religious-juridical reforms that sought to shape the behaviour of his Christian subjects. Fourth, and perhaps most importantly, Zara Yaqob shifted the balance of religious power by establishing royal churches as a counterweight to the powerful and largely autonomous monasteries. This succeeded in generating enthusiastic support in the churches for the king, their patron. In turn, the agency of the royal churches stymied opposition to central power, particularly among dissident monks, the leading intellectuals of the day. In other words, the powerful elites that controlled these royal churches worked closely with the monarchy to maintain political stability. In this way, Zara Yaqob established the precedent of Solomonic absolutism that Ethiopian rulers in later centuries followed.[20]

The emergence of Barara as a permanent capital is an important development that has been consistently overlooked by scholars. It was long argued that medieval Ethiopia had only moving capitals, with the kings living in tents while constantly moving about their domains to assert their power. Scholars misread the annual royal processions to sub-capitals and mistakenly assumed that kings lacked the resources to support a fixed royal court. Yet as early as 1450, the Venetian cartographer Fra Mauro's world map depicted Barara as the principal residence of the king; the capital of Aksum lasted for over eight centuries, moreover, while the later capital of Gondar was maintained for over two centuries. In short, the governance of medieval Ethiopia did not depend on personal royal contact. Rather, it was in fact heavily bureaucratized, with an almost bewildering array of administrative, military, religious and legal institutions. Barara was the kingdom's cosmopolitan centre, with many artisans and merchants from Italy, Syria and Egypt living there, and was a critical site in the Afro-Eurasian world until the destructive assault by its Muslim neighbour in 1531.[21]

I A pyramid field at Jebel Barkal in present-day Sudan, near the ancient city of Napata.

II An aerial view of the western *defuffa* in the ancient Nubian city of Kerma, after restoration.

III The Great Mosque of Jenne, in present-day Mali. First established in the 13th century CE, the mosque was extensively rebuilt in 1907 and continues to undergo periodic reconstruction.

IV Mansa Musa of Mali, as depicted in the Catalan Atlas of 1375. Holding aloft a golden orb, the ruler of 'Guinea' ('Ginyia') sits in majesty surrounded by the great cities of his domain: Gao ('geugeu'), Timbuktu ('tenbuch') and the 'City of Mali' ('ciutat de melli'); to the left of the orb lies the Saharan oasis town of Taghaza.

V Statues of Nubian pharaohs in the museum at Kerma.

VI A page from an 18th-century Ethiopian *Ta'ammera Maryam* (Miracles of the Virgin Mary) manuscript, painted in the second Gondarine style.

VII A stelae field at Aksum, in present-day northern Ethiopia, *c.* 350 CE. The tallest remaining standing stela (second from left), created from a single block of granite, is 69 ft (21 m) in height and carved to represent a ten-storey building with a false door at the base.

VIII A brass wall plaque from the royal palace of Benin, 16th to 17th century. Depicting an *oba* wearing the distinctive beaded crown and collar, swinging two leopards by their tails and with his lower limbs mysteriously transformed into mudfish, this image highlights the ability of the king to dominate and harness the potent forces of the animal world. The plaque's catalogue number in the British Museum, Af1898,0115.30, tells a different story about domination: it forms part of the so-called Benin Bronzes, looted by invading colonial forces

IX A terracotta head from Ife, 13th to 15th century. Unearthed in 1958 at the Ita Yemoo site in the Yoruba city of Ile-Ife, the woman portrayed wears an intricate five-tiered beaded crown, giving every indication that she was a queen or other high-ranking royal. Height 8¾ in. (25 cm).

X An *ade* or fringed beaded crown from the Ekiti region of Yorubaland, *c.* 1920. The birds depicted on the upper part of the crown are said to symbolize the ritual forces possessed by powerful women, which the king seeks to harness in order to rule effectively. Height 30 in. (76 cm).

MONASTERIES AND DISSENT

Any understanding of early Solomonic Ethiopia must consider the religious impulses of the era.[22] The kingdom and the church worked together to create a new Zion in Ethiopia. A tradition of monasticism that had developed during the Aksumite period played a key role in these efforts, as pioneering holy men established monasteries on the frontiers of the kingdom. Great monastic centres, such as Dabra Libanos, founded by the abbot St Takla Haymanot (d. 1313) in Shoa around 1284, were outposts of evangelization and vibrant sites of church education and intellectual activity, including writing, book-making and public debates about doctrine. They drew the best minds in the kingdom and produced the most important artists and writers of the era. In turn, their thinking and networks had a powerful impact on Ethiopian society and culture. Monks and priests were the cultural avant-garde, key bearers of Ethiopian culture whose scholarly production included the writing of chronicles and hagiographies.[23] They also played a fundamental role in community life, as the standard bearers for tradition, morality and education.

Yet monks had a complex and ambivalent relationship with monarchs. On the one hand, the Christian king was the highest patron and protector of the church, encouraging it to advance the project of evangelism; monks, in turn, provided ideological support to the king and served as key local agents of the monarchy. On the other hand, monks played a critical role in defining the parameters of royal control and the relationship between the monarchy and society. The proliferation of monasteries contributed to a growing number of monks, whose ideas of personal religious freedom and spirituality altered their relationship with secular authority. The more ambitious and energetic monks were religious and social reformers who argued for a role in regulating morality – including, in some cases, that of kings. One area in which monks challenged royal power was in denouncing as unchristian the customary practice of royal polygyny.

Others distanced themselves from secular patronage, which brought them closer to the laity. The monks saw themselves as engaging in an ascetic life, denying the things of this world, a lifestyle that became synonymous with the quest for liberty and freedom. Some even refused to acquiesce to monarchial demands, rejecting royal patronage and seeking to establish institutional independence.[24]

A tradition of radicalism and dissent was therefore an important feature of medieval Ethiopian history. Ethiopians wrestled with a wide range of profound dilemmas about Christian religious doctrine and practice, political authority, competing definitions of loyalty and the relationship between the Church and the monarchy. Many worried that doctrinal errors might lead the community of faith astray. One of the most notable dissidents was a monk named Ewostatewos (c. 1273–1352). Ewostatewos and his followers argued that the Sabbath should be celebrated on both Saturday and Sunday, in order to honour the practice of the Old Testament, but central Church authorities denounced this as heretical. As a result, so-called Ewostateans turned to dissidence, establishing their own monasteries in which they preached that contact between the Church and the monarchy should be circumscribed and pledged allegiance to no one except themselves. Church authorities could not stop the dramatic growth of the 'Sabbath movement' emerging on the margins of the kingdom. While monastic nonconformists composed only a small minority of the Church establishment, they nonetheless succeeded in shifting popular understandings of the Sabbath. By the mid-fifteenth century, the pro-Sabbath party was firmly rooted in countless monasteries. Then, in 1450, Zara Yaqob presided over a religious council on the issue, which favoured the Ewostateans. Evolving attitudes towards such demonstrations of faith and religious practice highlight the process of negotiation as well as the impact of local issues on national identity and discourse.[25]

Two of the leading dissident monks in the fifteenth century were Estifanos (whose followers were called Estifanites) and Zamika'el (whose followers were called Zamika'elites).[26] Both derided as heretical and unbiblical the veneration of the cross and the Virgin Mary. In a direct affront to the monarchy, the Estifanites also argued for the equality of all Christians before God and the law, judging the idea of divine kingship to be political nonsense. The anti-Marian and anti-royal streak of these monks shocked Zara Yaqob, who was actively promoting the cult of Mary. In the ensuing royal backlash, the two monks' teachings were banned. They and their followers were suppressed and eventually forced to relinquish their radical position on these matters. Zara Yaqob established new laws, which aimed to control dissident monastic-centred spirituality and ritual, demanding mandatory religious instruction and regular attendance in church on Sundays and embedding the Marian cult by disseminating texts about the Virgin to churches.[27] He also denounced the lingering influence of pre-Christian beliefs and ritual practices on Ethiopian Christians. Thus, the king's greatest legacy was a narrowing of religious pluralism by imposing a greater degree of uniformity in religious practice than had been the case in the earlier medieval period and setting the Ethiopian Church apart from other churches, including the Egyptian Church.

ART AND FOREIGN RELATIONS DURING THE SOLOMONIC PERIOD

The early Solomonic kings became so wealthy that they could spend fortunes on the construction of churches, the creation of art and the writing of literature. Much of this cultural production arose in connection with the eastern Mediterranean world in the period of late antiquity.[28] Ethiopians appropriated book-making culture from Egypt, architectural motifs from Classical Rome, icon motifs from Byzantium and diverse styles from Islamic, Coptic and Italianate art. They then refined these with local aesthetic themes and techniques, such as the bold use of primary colours, the rejection of three-dimensionality and the introduction of indigenous architectural elements. The result was a unique and distinctive body of art in various media, again demonstrating the Ethiopian kingdom's genius for adaptability and innovation.

This art-making began early. The oldest extant illuminated gospels in the world are the Ethiopian Abba Garima Gospel manuscripts, dated to between 330 and 650 CE.[29] Their highly stylized and richly embellished page frames, including architectural elements and various species of birds, flowers and geometrical motifs together with the use of bold red, yellow, blue and green colours, were typical of the Ethiopian process of creating magnificent manuscripts that were sacred objects in and of themselves.

A thousand years later, manuscripts describing and depicting the *Ta'ammera Maryam* (Miracles of the Virgin Mary) reveal some of the continuities that dominated Ethiopian art.[30] In the earliest extant *Ta'ammera Maryam* manuscript, created between 1398 and 1409, the elongated almond-shaped eyes of the human figures are inspired by Islamic art and the framing arches by early Renaissance art.[31] Framing the Ge'ez text in black and red is a special feature of Ethiopian illuminated manuscripts: an ornate band called a *harag*. This Ge'ez word means literally 'the tendril of a climbing plant', apt for the interlaced floral designs that frame liturgical texts in Ethiopic codices.[32] They became common in the late fourteenth century, the golden age of *harag* design. The adoption of foreign elements, however, did not signify a submission to foreign culture. The bold colours, frontality of the figures and two-dimensionality represent an active rejection of emerging European ideas of art as a window onto the real world. Rather, Ethiopians sought to use the 'spiritual efficiency of the images' to draw the believer into the world beyond the real.[33] Meanwhile, that the manuscript is about the miracles of Mary reflects the devotion of King Dawit (r. 1382–1413) to the Virgin, whose cult, as we have seen, was further elevated by his son Zara Yaqob.

The connection to Europe, that is to suggest, is often over-emphasized in Ethiopian art history. In a later *Ta'ammera Maryam* manuscript, in the so-called second Gondarine style (which flourished in the seventeenth-century capital of Gondar), we see something less remarked on: the influence of Indian art (see pl. vi). Images from this period often depict the increasing opulence and pageantry of court life, sometimes through detailed reproductions of luxurious textiles imported from India to be worn by Ethiopia's aristocratic class. In this image, Mary wears a long Indian-style caftan robe that covers her hair and body. Also often neglected is the influence of Egypt, such as the penchant for colouring the entire image and leaving no empty space, as seen here.[34] Egypt may also be the ancient origin of the 'continuous narrative' of this painting, with three different moments in the story depicted in the same image. Mary's faithful follower first crowns her with roses, then prays before her, and then prostrates himself before her. Yet distinctively indigenous cultural elements are also present, such as the Ethiopian cross depicted on the robe where it covers Mary's forehead. The Virgin's neck folds signal an Ethiopian aesthetic of beautiful plumpness, while a cross typical of Ethiopian churches tops her icon. Her follower has a natural Ethiopian hairstyle and his crossed arms and folded-down cloak represent the appropriate behaviour of a worshipper in an Ethiopian church. Ethiopian art drew on a wide variety of foreign influences, but evolved its own traits, sensibilities and tastes.

As these interactions show, foreign diplomatic connections were of great interest to early Solomonic Ethiopia, which saw itself as an integral part of the international Christian community. In the period between 1270 and 1527, Ethiopian rulers dispatched no fewer than eleven diplomatic missions to Mamluk- and then Ottoman-ruled Egypt alone, often to fetch a new *abuna* (patriarch) for the Ethiopian Church.[35] In the other direction, connections to the Indian Ocean were also regarded as crucial to the kingdom's economic well-being. As these long-established cultural and mercantile links were maintained, new connections with Christian Europe were also forged. Neither did Ethiopia's rulers wait for Europe to come to them; rather, they actively and shrewdly sought to engage with Europeans, sending delegations to Venice, Rome, Naples, Valencia and Lisbon in the fifteenth and sixteenth centuries. Long active in the transregional commercial networks that linked the Red Sea, the Middle East and the Indian Ocean, medieval Ethiopia was in dialogue with Christian Europe as well.[36]

Scholars have examined the diplomatic, military and commercial motivations for Ethiopia's desire to secure good relations with fellow Christian kingdoms. The acquisition of European technology and art, however, has had less attention. Throughout the medieval period, there was an imperative to access European crafts, artisans and technology.[37] The kings who reigned from the early 1400s to the mid-1500s were particularly notable in their efforts to achieve technological transfer, sending ambassadors to Europe specifically for this purpose. The arrival of skilled artisans from Europe in the early fifteenth century spurred later kings to strengthen foreign connections as well. Another motivation was religious. Ethiopia formed many of its links with the Eurasian world through the movement of Ethiopian pilgrims and church missions. Indeed, it was monks and pilgrims rather than diplomats who propelled the initial Ethiopian encounters in the Middle East and Europe. For Ethiopian Christians, membership in a global faith community offered the opportunity for solidarity and direct contact with fellow Christians in the Mediterranean and the Middle East. The same can be said for the position of Ethiopian Muslims in the world of Islam. Such burgeoning networks enabled pilgrims and other travellers to create new forms of spiritual kinship and intellectual exchange.[38]

As Ethiopians looked outwards to establish diplomatic relations with others, they also dealt with outsiders who came to them for the same purpose. There had long been a belief in medieval Europe that a mighty Christian domain ruled by a priest-king named Prester John existed somewhere in 'the East', from where he might assist in the struggle against perceived Islamic enemies. By the fourteenth century, as an awareness of the Solomonic kingdom began to reach Europe, this mythical land was increasingly identified with Ethiopia. Several enterprising European traders found their way to the

Ethiopian court in Barara during the fifteenth century. The myth of Prester John would also play a role in the gradual fifteenth-century exploration by Portuguese mariners of the Atlantic coast of Africa, which was spurred on not only by a desire to break into the trans-Saharan gold trade and other lucrative commodity flows from Asia, but also by the fantasy of securing for Christendom a powerful ally against Islam. By the opening decade of the sixteenth century, the Portuguese had reached India, pioneering the maritime route via the Atlantic to the Indian Ocean and forcing their way into the region's commodity trade. Direct Portuguese contact with Ethiopia would intensify in the following century.

At the same time, Ethiopian rulers also looked to Europe for support in the fight against regional rivals. Queen Eleni (*c.* 1431–1522), considered Ethiopia's most powerful female ruler during the medieval period, sent an Ethiopian delegation to Portugal to propose a military alliance against their shared Muslim enemy. The Portuguese responded by sending a diplomatic mission in 1520 to the court of Lebna Dengel (r. 1508–1540), who suggested that they should build forts at Zayla on the Gulf of Aden and on the Red Sea coast. Lebna Dengel's dual strategy was to protect his coast with the assistance of his new military allies and to secure access to European goods and technology. Portugal would provide much-needed military support during the assault on the Christian kingdom by the sultanate of Adal in the 1530s–40s.[39]

THE CONSEQUENCES OF IMAM AHMAD'S CONQUEST

Following the death of the assertive Zara Yaqob in 1468 and that of his son and successor Ba'eda Maryam in 1478, Christian Ethiopia entered a period of political turmoil. The efforts to centralize power began to unravel. Over the next forty years, the kingdom was often ruled by boy kings, which made it vulnerable to military incursions.[40] The warrior king Amda Seyon had brought most of the sultanates in the east under his control in the early fourteenth century, including the most politically significant, Ifat. Following his reign, however, a militant branch of the rulers of Ifat regrouped further to the east, creating a new sultanate called Adal, which from 1525 would be based in the city of Harar.[41] Recurring conflict between Adal and the Solomonic kingdom had occurred for two centuries, but the situation was transformed by the rise to power, in Adal, of a charismatic *imam*, Ahmad ibn Ibrahim al-Gazi, known in Ethiopia as Ahmad Gran, 'the left-handed', in the 1520s. Ahmad preached a message of *jihad* against the Christian kingdom and received military support from the rulers of southwest Arabia. In 1529, his forces secured a major victory over the Christian army at the Battle of Shembra Kure and he would go on to dominate the entire Horn of Africa region until his death in battle in 1543.

The fourteen-year conflict was Ethiopia's longest and most destructive. Ahmad's forces mounted a devastating assault on the Solomonic kingdom: centres of Christian culture, such as Aksum, the great monastery of Dabra Libanos and the churches of Lalibela and Amhara, were plundered and desecrated. Entire communities were destroyed and many were forced to convert to Islam; others refused to do so and fought on, despite the strength of their adversaries. Clerics and laypeople, soldiers and civilians, women and men, elites and commoners: all were equally affected, and many forced to weigh their options between Islam and Christianity. In recently conquered frontier provinces only partially integrated into the Christian kingdom, some found common cause with the Muslim invaders as a strategy to regain their independence.

The Ethiopian–Adal War was also connected to developments beyond Ethiopia, notably Ottoman and Portuguese imperial designs to dominate the Red Sea. The arrival of a small but well-armed contingent of Portuguese musketeers helped Christian Ethiopia finally to prevail. In 1543, a joint Ethiopian–Portuguese force led by King Galawdewos (r. 1540–1559) defeated the Islamic army and killed Ahmad. Galawdewos succeeded in re-establishing royal administration in most provinces of the kingdom.[42] The impact of the conflict, however, was profound and long-lasting. Highland society was destabilized and centuries of steady progress in urbanization and commerce was stalled or reversed; with the destruction of churches and monasteries together with their libraries, moreover, countless precious books and works of art were lost. In the end, Ahmad's surviving forces withdrew back to the city of Harar. The war had cost so much that Adal went into decline and had disappeared by the end of the sixteenth century.

While the defeat of Adal represented an opportunity for the Christian kingdom to reassert its authority, what followed was an era of political fragmentation. Due to their losses during the war, regional nobles lost respect for the monarchy and centralized rule was weakened by a succession of power struggles. King Sarsa Dengel (r. 1563–1597) spent the first fourteen years of his reign fighting rebellious nobles and their Ottoman allies. His death in 1597 then triggered a ten-year succession crisis. One of these aspirants, King Za Dengel (r. 1603–1604), sought to replace Ethiopia's traditional military class system – which depended heavily on professional soldiers and the exploitation of servile peasants – with a new system.[43] As Za Dengel's decree decreased the power of professional soldiers, he was soon killed. His reform died with him, and peasant servitude would continue for centuries. After this, the nobility openly debated abolishing the monarchy altogether. Then the throne was seized by Susenyos (r. 1607–1632), who sought in turn to break the power of the nobles, in part through a radical experimentation with Catholicism.

Susenyos's experiment with Catholicism was another consequence of the Ethiopian–Adal War. Portuguese missionaries had arrived in Ethiopia in 1557 in the footsteps of the military expedition in support of the fight against Imam Ahmad. Members of the newly created Jesuit order, they pursued the peculiar quest of converting the Ethiopians from their own ancient form of Christianity to Catholicism. At first, Susenyos approached their evangelistic efforts with caution. Yet many members of his court converted and in 1622 so too did the

king himself: while refusing to submit to the Pope, he openly professed his new Catholic faith and then decreed that it was to be the
national religion. But the Jesuits' hatred of all things Orthodox and
their denouncements of local religious practices – for instance, telling women that their dead children were in hell because they had
not been baptized at birth – engendered such fury that the country
was plunged into civil war. Leading the charge against the new religion were many of the women of the royal court, including the king's
wife, mother, niece and daughters.[44] Local monasteries were also
hotbeds of resistance and many peasants took up arms. Susenyos
saw that his experiment was proving counterproductive, doing nothing to lessen the power of the Orthodox Church or the nobles.
In June 1632, after brutally crushing yet another rebellion and dis-
heartened by the unnecessary bloodshed, he abdicated in favour of
his son, Fasilidas.

Fasilidas (r. 1632–1667) set the kingdom on a new path, expelling
the Jesuits and eliminating Catholicism; by the 1640s, not a single
professing Catholic was left in the country. Its impact, however,
would continue to reverberate: Jesuit teachings spurred doctrinal
debates within the Ethiopian Church, leading to a bitter Christological
controversy (that is, about the nature of Christ) between rival groups
of monks. The result was the emergence of two sects, which remained
locked in conflict until 1878, when sectarianism was finally banned.
Meanwhile, Fasilidas, fearing what else might come from Europe,
sought to secure alliances with regional powers such as Yemen, India
and the Ottoman Empire. These diplomatic moves were shaped by
the perceived need to develop defences against Europe; by reaching
out to Muslim states, moreover, bitter memories of the conflict with
Imam Ahmad were swept under the rug. This wariness towards
Europeans would prove useful in the nineteenth century, when Italian
colonial efforts were confronted and defeated.

Perhaps the most significant consequence of the Ethiopian–Adal
War was to open the way for the Oromo ethnic group to conquer
and settle territories on the southern frontiers of the kingdom. Oromo

expansion represented a crisis for the beleaguered central government. Sarsa Dengel and his seventeenth-century successors were forced to devote much of their time and resources on war with the Oromo. As centralized royal governance became increasingly ineffective, Ethiopian rulers realized that constant campaigning to maintain a presence in the region south of the Abbay River was untenable. In the late 1570s, seeking to shore up the power of the monarchy, Sarsa Dengel temporarily moved the royal court north, from Shoa to a locality north of Lake Tana. This shift in the geopolitical centre of Ethiopia became permanent under Fasilidas, who inaugurated the so-called Gondarine kingdom by founding a fixed capital in the town of Gondar in 1636. By abandoning the southern reaches of the highlands, the government effectively rolled back the frontiers of the kingdom, leaving it in direct control of only a few key provinces in the north. Although sporadic efforts were made into the early eighteenth century to reconquer these lost territories, the Oromo peoples had permanently settled in many of them and they became the southern boundary of the kingdom until a renewed phase of expansion in the nineteenth century. Oromo expansion was also cultural, accompanied by the 'Oromoization' of indigenous populations. The Oromo name for this system of assimilating non-Oromo and renaming places was *mogasa*.[45] By the nineteenth century, when the Ethiopian kingdom reconquered these areas, their indigenous peoples had been entirely assimilated into Oromo culture. Ethnic identity in the heartland of the Ethiopian kingdom had been fundamentally altered.

THE GONDARINE KINGDOM

After their retreat northwestwards to Gondar, Ethiopian rulers struggled to establish peace and stability out of the scattered remnants of the medieval Ethiopian state. Gondar served as Ethiopia's capital between 1636 and 1769, with its influence as the royal residence continuing into the late 1800s. Following their illustrious medieval predecessors, the Gondarine kings sought to revive the monarchical tradition of Zara Yaqob, in which power rested on local structures of government, and became active military campaigners. The kingdom again flourished under Fasilidas, his son Yohannes I (r. 1667–1682) and grandson Iyasu I, 'The Great' (r. 1682–1706). Although Iyasu's reign ended with his assassination and the following fifteen years were turbulent, his son Bakaffa (r. 1721–1730) restored peace and order. He was effectively succeeded by his consort, Queen Mentewwab, arguably the most remarkable female leader in Ethiopian history. When her infant son was crowned, so too was Mentewwab – an elevation with no precedent. She ruled from 1730 to 1767 through her son Iyasu II (r. 1730–1755) and grandson Iyo'as (r. 1755–1769). Having stabilized things politically, Mentewwab presided over a period of tremendous cultural creativity. Her cosmopolitan court attracted musicians, artists and poets from Ethiopia and beyond, including such visitors as the Scottish adventurer James Bruce.

The castle at Gondar built by the emperor Fasilidas (r. 1632–1667).

Gondar grew into a vital urban centre, with tens of thousands of residents and extensive trade networks. It attracted the best minds in the Church, who debated doctrinal issues at lively councils. Gondar's monarchs built over forty churches and a magnificent royal compound. Major works of history and biography were written using information from medieval texts. The arts flourished, with the emergence of new styles of manuscript and mural painting drawing on a range of exotic influences and referred to by art historians, as we have seen, as the Gondarine style.

Yet the Gondarine monarchs had to solve the problem of land and income. Not only had they lost much territory and revenue, but also the influx of refugees into what was left of Ethiopia made land a much scarcer commodity. In an effort to maintain its authority, the ruling elite adopted a new policy of confiscating land from peasants. New methods of land surveying were developed, resulting in a reordering of property relations.[46] The possession of such detailed information about land enhanced the power of the kings. Meanwhile, the political assimilation of the Oromo into the Gondarine kingdom through intermarriage and military service laid the foundation for a greater degree of ethnic integration in the nineteenth and twentieth centuries.

THE ERA OF THE PRINCES

The Gondarine period ended abruptly. The kingdom's long unresolved structural problem of finding a balance between the power of kings and that of the great nobles came to a head, leading to the turbulence of the so-called Era of the Princes (1769–1855). Mikael Sehul, the governor of Tigray, assassinated Mentewwab's grandson in 1769 and became regent. Twenty-five years later, a coalition of nobles removed him, but other kingmakers arose. The Solomonic kings became financially impoverished and their authority did not extend beyond the shadow of their palaces. The country fragmented into autonomous regions: the central provinces were ruled by a Christianized dynasty of Oromo-Muslim background, while such areas as Tigray, Gojjam and Shoa became autonomous provinces. The old medieval lands, south of the Abbay River and in the eastern highlands, remained beyond Solomonic control. Meanwhile, the Ethiopian Church was bitterly divided into hostile sects, which marginalized and isolated its bishops.

The Era of the Princes is often gloomily presented by historians as a period of recurring violence and social decline. In fact, it was a period of some dynamism and a greater degree of continuity than hitherto thought. Regional rulers followed the same style of governance as the once-powerful Solomonic kings, using established legal and administrative models and keeping order through standing armies. As Church patronage was transferred to regional rulers, they built new churches to establish their own rapport with the priesthood. These churches drew worshippers, which in turn brought prosperity to the towns in which they were located. By the mid-1800s, the devolution of power to the regions had resulted in the development of towns, the expansion of regional trade and intensified land markets. The increasing political assimilation of the Oromo also aided interregional integration.[47]

In the second half of the nineteenth century, centralized royal power was revived. In part, this was due to the emergence of regional rulers so strong they could serve as national leaders. It was also due to consolidation in reaction to the looming threat of European colonialism. A new movement seeking national reunification was pioneered by Kassa, a powerful governor who secured Ethiopia's throne in 1855 through a series of dramatic battles. He became Tewodros II, who styled himself as *negus*, 'King of Kings', ending the era of a weak monarchy.[48] Tewodros had remarkable modernizing ambitions and crafted a framework for uniting the country that generations of Ethiopians would follow. His agenda included restoring the authority of both the Church and the monarchy, ending sectarianism and encouraging moral reformation. He believed royal support of the Church was essential to reviving royal power. He also adopted

Western military technology while shaping a more disciplined national army. Among his modernizing efforts was breaking with the Gondarine land policies, which had so benefited the religious and secular elites. Neither, however, took kindly to this innovation and by 1865 Tewodros II had lost control of the country and become politically isolated. Meanwhile, a diplomatic row with the British led to a military confrontation in the late 1860s. When he was defeated and died in April 1868, Tewodros II controlled little more than his own royal camp.[49]

However, Tewodros's political rivals, who emerged to dominate the rest of the century, followed his precedent and realized his radical objectives. In 1872, a regional leader from Tigray became king as Yohannes IV (r. 1872–1889). Yohannes stood out for his spectacular success in uniting the church and ending sectarian strife among its clergy. As sectarianism was almost entirely along regional lines, this was a huge step towards national unification. When Yohannes died fighting an incursion by Mahdist forces from the Sudan in 1889, he left behind a much more united country. The throne was quickly seized by his main rival, a regional ruler from Shoa, Menelik II, who reigned as the king of Shoa from 1865 to 1889 and then as emperor of Ethiopia from 1889 to 1913. He continued the unification policies of his predecessors, with such success that he is widely regarded as the founder of modern Ethiopia. During the 1880s and 1890s, Menelik put most of the old medieval kingdom of Ethiopia under his authority. By 1900, he had re-established the systems of the old Gondarine era, which were so strong that they endured until 1974.[50]

CONCLUSION

The final century of the Solomonic dynasty saw its greatest victories and worst defeats. Italy conquered and colonized the Red Sea province of Eritrea, but then Emperor Menelik's army defeated the Italian army at the Battle of Adwa in 1896 and secured Ethiopia's independence in the era of European colonial rule in Africa. In 1935–36, Italy attacked and brutally occupied Ethiopia, but, with British assistance, Ethiopia regained its independence and the territory of Eritrea in 1941. In other words, Ethiopian rulers in the nineteenth and twentieth centuries used what they had learned from previous Solomonic rulers to reunite the nation and defend its sovereignty against European colonialism. As a result, the ancient dynasty loomed large in the African diasporic imagination. Black peoples around the world

Emperor Haile Selassie I, photographed at his coronation in Addis Ababa in 1930.

celebrated the Black Christian emperors who had triumphed over European enslavers. In the religion of the Rastafari, Emperor Haile Selassie I (who reigned as Ras Tafari from 1916 to 1930 and as emperor from 1930 to 1974) became the Messiah who would save Black peoples everywhere. Fittingly, Haile Selassie pursued an aggressive pan-African diplomacy in the 1950s and 1960s as part of his anti-imperialist effort. He helped found the Organization of African Unity (now the African Union) in 1963, and it remains headquartered in Addis Ababa, a showcase of the triumph of Ethiopian diplomacy.

But then, having reached its greatest territorial extent, the Solomonic dynasty fell. Haile Selassie had attempted to make modernizing reforms, but by the late 1960s many Ethiopians had come to view the monarchy as an anachronistic obstacle to modernization. In 1974, the monarchy was swept aside by revolution and a new socialist government seized power, bringing the seven-hundred-year-old Solomonic dynasty to an end. Over a period of seven centuries, that dynasty had forged an expansive multi-ethnic kingdom, which it ruled with acumen and ingenuity. Convinced that they were destined to rule, its kings cultivated a legitimating ideology of African Zionism, making Christianity integral to national identity and fostering a unique Church. Through administrative innovations and a global outlook, the dynasty created such power and wealth that many Ethiopians continue to look back to it as a source of inspiration.

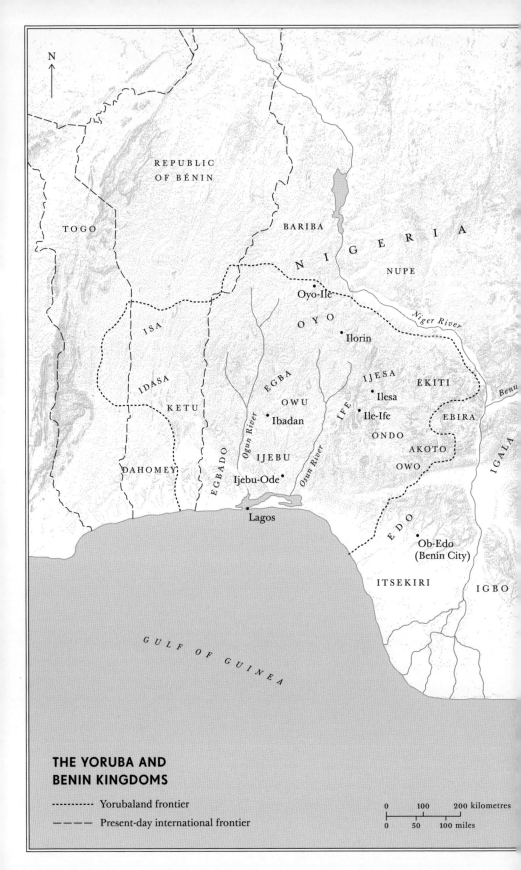

CHAPTER 4

THE YORUBA AND
BENIN KINGDOMS

```
---------- Yorubaland frontier
--- --- --- Present-day international frontier
```

THE YORUBA AND BENIN KINGDOMS

Olatunji Ojo

The region of present-day southwestern Nigeria is inhabited by diverse groups of people, including the Yoruba, Edo, Itsekiri, Ijo and Egun. This chapter is about kingship among the two largest of these groups, the Yoruba and Edo, renowned for their long history of state-building, urbanization and dazzling artistic production. The Edo, creators of the powerful kingdom of Benin, occupy the easternmost part of the region, with the Niger River to their east forming a frontier with the Igbo-speaking region of southeastern Nigeria. To the west of the Edo lies the more expansive territory of the Yoruba-speaking peoples, bounded by the Niger in the north and the Atlantic Ocean in the south and extending across the frontier of Nigeria into the neighbouring republics of Bénin (not to be confused with the historic kingdom) and Togo. There, on its western frontier, the Yoruba region merges into that of the linguistically and culturally related Aja-speaking peoples, most notably the Fon, creators in the seventeenth century of another powerful kingdom, Dahomey. Today, an estimated 40 million people speak Yoruba, making it one of Africa's largest language communities. The Yoruba have also had a profound impact on the creation of diasporic African identities in the Americas, especially in Brazil, Cuba, Haiti and Trinidad. Not only has Yoruba culture been the fulcrum of a cultural zone stretching from the historic West African kingdoms of Dahomey in the west to Benin in the east, its pantheon of gods, the *orisa*, has emerged as the focus of devotion in a 'circum-Atlantic', globalized religion.[1]

An understanding of the history of the Yoruba and Edo peoples must proceed from a consideration of their own oral traditions (in Yoruba, *itan*), which record diverse forms of state formation ranging from small-scale village governments to centralized kingdoms and on to powerful and expansive multi-ethnic 'empires', such as Benin and Oyo. The city-states of the Yoruba and the Edo kingdom of Benin were rooted in the coming together of families into villages and walled towns, in part to provide security against outside aggression. For the Yoruba, a crucial component of identity is that of *ile*, meaning family, lineage or 'house', which would remain as a fundamental building block of the larger town, or *ilu*. 'Houses' did not receive protection free of charge: they surrendered some degree of independence to the *ilu* and the sacred kings who came to rule over them. Over time, communities came to accept the hegemony of the most powerful settlements and their hereditary *oba* or king, who then spared no effort to bring yet more outlying communities under his authority by persuasion, alliance or, if need be, coercion. In this way, the earliest 'micro-states' came into existence in the ecological frontier between the forest and savanna zones to the south of the confluence of the Niger and Benue rivers. Archaeological evidence suggests that this process was unfolding in the second half of the first millennium CE; the most prominent early Yoruba kingdom, Ife, located just within the northern edge of the forest, was developing by the sixth century. It was Ile-Ife, the kingdom's principal urban centre, that emerged as the first *ilu alade* or 'crowned town', recognized as the 'cradle of the Yoruba' or the 'cosmic metropolis' from where the ideology of sacred kingship was perceived to have spread throughout the region and to Benin.[2]

Today, the historical consciousness of the Yoruba and Edo peoples remains focused on the existence of long-standing centralized kingdoms and the sophisticated forms of statecraft by which they were governed. Such an impression is sustained by authoritative traditions of origin and by a rich artistic heritage, both of which were, to a large extent, fashioned according to the requirements of ruling elites.

Yet neither the Yoruba or Edo in fact form a single ethnic group; rather, both consist of diverse elements with different origins, which came over time to be united by a common language and culture. The Yoruba language, first written down in the mid-nineteenth century, consists of some thirty-five mutually intelligible dialectic groups.[3] Traditions seek to conflate the advent of kingship with the origins of the people themselves. Yet this tendency often stemmed from a strategic attempt to give legitimacy to dynasties that claimed the right to rule in the line of their founding ancestors, who in turn derived authority from a divine source. Hence, the origins of the Yoruba and Edo peoples, of their kings and of the political systems they presided over are all tied up with the mythical figure of Oduduwa, reputed to be founder of Ife. A closer look, however, reveals that communities and kingdoms were formed by different groups of people, who in the early period of their history had varied roots and ways of governing themselves. This chapter will seek to move away from the established view of the Yoruba and Edo as homogeneous political communities to a more critical analysis of the history of state and society in the two regions.

ILE-IFE AND THE ORIGIN
OF THE YORUBA KINGDOMS

Before the nineteenth century, the various groups now called Yoruba did not have a common name for themselves. The term Yoruba appears to have been originally that given to these peoples by the Hausa from the Sudanic savanna region to the north. From around the seventeenth century, it came to be most closely associated with the powerful kingdom of Oyo, but began to gain wider currency only when it was applied to the whole region by nineteenth-century European travellers and Christian missionaries. Many of the latter were themselves Yoruba-speaking peoples, most famously the pioneering churchman Rev. Samuel Ajayi Crowther and the historian

Rev. Samuel Johnson, for whom an entangled Christian and Yoruba identity was forged in exile from their homelands in the British colony established in Sierra Leone for people liberated from enslavement.[4] What has been called the 'cultural work' of Crowther, Johnson and other local intellectuals in the nineteenth and early twentieth centuries not only forged a modernizing Yoruba identity, it also added an important body of written sources to the oral, archaeological, linguistic and artistic evidence available for the reconstruction and interpretation of the past. It in turn laid the foundations for a second wave of research in the opening decades of Nigeria's independence, when a new generation of scholars at the University of Ibaban and elsewhere put the region's past at the cutting edge of the emerging field of African history.[5]

Yoruba traditions of origin have various, often conflicting, versions, recounting stories both of localized creation and of migration from the northeast and elsewhere. Some migration traditions record ancestral origins as far away as Egypt or Arabia, although these are best seen to represent relatively recent efforts to assert a link to ancient civilizations or to the heartland of Christianity or Islam.[6] Migration traditions appear to be entirely absent from many groups in eastern and southern Yorubaland, such as the Ijebu, Ekiti, Owo and Ikale, whose ancestors are remembered as indigenous to their current regions.[7] Recent archaeological and linguistic evidence does, however, point to a more proximate northeastern point of dispersal from where the ancestral Yoruba-speaking community fanned out to settle the forest to the south: the area around the Niger-Benue Confluence.[8]

The coexistence of different traditions of origin suggests that what would emerge as the Yoruba peoples are a fusion of indigenous and subsequent migrant groups. In cases where the migrants did not assimilate into established communities, they appear to have imposed themselves on indigenous peoples, resulting in the prominence of migration traditions among ruling elites of chiefs and kings. As a pan-Yoruba identity took shape only from the nineteenth century, the chronology and content of traditions of origin are peculiar to the various communities, kingdoms and the individual *ile*, 'houses', from which they were built. In eastern Yorubaland, many families subscribe to an origin from Ife but others point to origins in Ijesa, Nupe, Ijumu, Igbomina, Igala, Ondo or Benin. Rather than necessarily indicating primordial migrations, such accounts can be seen as figurative expressions of the assimilation of foreign cultural traits or of conquest by others. In Ekiti, Owo and Ikale, for example, identification with Benin gained popularity from the fifteenth century with the emerging domination of eastern Yorubaland by the expansionist kingdom.

Whatever their traditions of origin, however, all communities came to identify Ife as the centre of diffusion from which the Yoruba-speaking peoples spread out to form different regional groups. Ile-Ife was held not only to be the cradle of the Yoruba people, but also the place where the world itself and all humanity began. It was here that Oduduwa was said to have descended from heaven and created the Yoruba social order. In 1830, people in Oyo told Richard and John Lander that 'Iffie' was where 'their first parents were created, and from whence all Africa has been peopled'.[9] In 1846, in Freetown, Sierra Leone, an elderly liberated man styled Ife as 'to the other [Yoruba] countries what England is to [Sierra Leone]', the mother nation.[10] Yet the kingdom was not associated with large-scale military conquest or imperial expansion; it had, moreover, been in decline since its peak in the fourteenth century. Ife's emergence as the foundational Yoruba home has therefore been a crucial issue for historians. At no point was early Yorubaland governed by a single state; rather, the kingdoms emerged as independent city-states under their own rulers. How did Ife therefore establish and maintain its mystical aura among the Yoruba?

One theory is that Ile-Ife was the site where the core principles of Yoruba cultural identity were first elaborated into a sophisticated political ideology and urbanized civilization. Archaeological evidence suggests that this was under way by the eleventh century and reached its peak in a 'classical' period from around 1250 to 1350. In a recent book on the deep-time cultural history of the Yoruba, archaeologist Akinwumi Ogundiran identifies three key components to what he calls Ile-Ife's 'knowledge capital': divine kingship, artistic production, and cosmological thought and ritual practice focused on the pantheon of *orisa*.[11] It was these forms of knowledge rather than merchant capital, Ogundiran argues, that spread from Ife to the rest of Yorubaland and beyond. The implication of his term 'knowledge capital' is that these things were a kind of commodity. By exporting them, the kingdom became a place of 'reverence and reference', the aura of which came to be mobilized by ruling elites throughout the region to legitimize their own claim to kingship.

There has been much debate among scholars over the decades about the relationship between political power and sacred authority in Africa and elsewhere. Was kingship originally a sacred office, and to what extent did it remain so once dynastic rulers accumulated additional, 'secular' forms of power? Were kings regarded as divine beings, or did they merely have certain sacred attributes? Either way, to what extent did a ruler's sacred identity enhance his capacity to exercise power or, alternatively, constrain that capacity? Yoruba political culture has been an important part of this debate because its core ideology of *oba-alade*, as it first emerged in Ile-Ife, has been interpreted as one of 'divine kingship'. This notion was rooted in the maxim *oba alaase ekeji orisa*, 'the *oba* has a power like that of the gods' or, in Aribidesi Usman and Toyin Falola's translation, is 'the commander and companion of deities'.[12] For Jacob Olúpònà, the *oba* was in principle a 'god-king': one of the praise names of the *ooni,* as the king of Ile-Ife was known, was Olofin Ajalaye, 'Divine Ruler of the World'.[13] For Usman and Falola, too, the king was 'semi-divine', 'set apart from his subjects by the spiritual powers he acquired at his installation'.[14] '*Oba*s do not die', John Pemberton and Funso Afolayan write; rather, they are seen to 'sink into the ground'. 'Death is a change in status. It is to become more powerful; it is to become an *òrìṣà*.'[15] Ogundiran goes somewhat further, arguing that in what

The *alaafin* of Oyo, Adeyemi I Alowolodu (r. 1876–1905), wearing the
ade or fringed beaded crown. Son of Atiba Atobatale (r. 1837–1859),
the first *alaafin* to rule after the abandonment of Old Oyo, and grandson
of the great king Abiodun, Adeyemi was the last ruler of an independent
Oyo and the first to be brought under British colonial rule in 1894–96.

represented a 'profound shift in Yoruba political ideology', the living
ooni of Ile-Ife came to be regarded as an *orisa* who was 'deified upon
assuming office and putting on the *ade*' – the fringed beaded crown,
which covered the face of the king in public, symbolizing his sacred
and secluded identity (see pl. x).[16]

Sacred kingship, then, was intimately connected to the central
role of the *orisa* (pronounced 'orisha') in Yoruba cosmological thought
and religious practice. The number of *orisa* was vast, said to total
201, or even 401. The final '1', Olúpònà notes, demonstrates 'the
inclusivity of the Yorùbá religious worldview, which is always willing
to add one more deity to the pantheon' – the extra deity perhaps

being the *ooni* of Ile-Ife himself.[17] Religious devotion, however, tended to be focused on a smaller number of great *orisa*, whose cults expanded and contracted over time in different parts of Yorubaland and beyond: notably the male deities Sango, Ogun, Esu, Obatala and Orunmila, and the female deities Osun and Yemoja. Of these deities, Orunmila (or Ifa), the animating power of the *ifa* divination system and arguably 'the intellectual anchor of the Yorùbá pantheon', may have been particularly important in the spread of what Ogundiran describes as Ile-Ife's soft power.[18] Others would later be harnessed to the more militarized state-building project of the Oyo kingdom: Sango, the thunder deity, and Ogun, who underwent a transformation from the god of iron and those skills associated with it to a potent symbol of a new era of warrior kings. The rise of Osun, meanwhile, can be seen as a 'counter-hegemonic' response to these hypermasculine deities – a female critique of male power that has also been preserved in the Yoruba-derived religions of the Americas.[19]

Ife's extraordinary artistic creativity was a further aspect of its foundational role in Yoruba civilization. Its most famous artworks are the naturalistic and life-size portrait heads sculpted in terracotta and in copper or copper alloy ('bronze'), some two hundred of which have been unearthed and dated from the eleventh to the fourteenth centuries (see pl. IX). The copper-alloy heads are identified with the classical period of Ife culture between 1250 and 1350, particularly with the reign of Ooni Obalufon II, who may have commissioned many of them as part of an effort to reassert his authority after a period of dynastic conflict. While some appear to be portraits of individual kings or to represent Ife's successive dynasties, most are in fact of non-royals and were probably components of mortuary assemblages or ancestral shrines. Designed to capture and project *ase*, the vital inner force or energy of those portrayed, they possess a profound dignity and serenity that resonate down the ages and would inspire a further burst of artistic creativity in the kingdom of Benin.[20]

Less striking but perhaps more important in the projection of Ile-Ife's cultural authority was another art form: glass beads. Used to fashion the fringed crown and other regalia displayed by an *oba*, they too served to validate the ideology of divine kingship. In contrast to the rarefied sculpted heads, however, the humble bead became a staple trade commodity: produced in large quantities under the patronage of the *ooni* at the Olokun Grove site within the walled city, they were not only the most widely recognized material signifier of *oba alade*, but also made a significant contribution to Ife's mercantile wealth. Their symbolic and monetary importance, moreover, continued after a disruption in the established order marked the end of Ile-Ife's classical period and of its creation of sculpted heads. The two art forms would subsequently come together in Benin, where red coral beads came to symbolize dynastic power and were often portrayed in a renewed tradition of royal portraiture.[21]

THE OYO EMPIRE AND
YORUBALAND'S ATLANTIC ERA

The reason for the decline of Ife by the late fourteenth century is unclear. One factor may have been its location in the forest, which posed problems for physical expansion, the deployment of military force and the development of an active role in trans-Saharan trade. Others may have been the emergence of factional conflict between indigenous and migrant groups, dynastic disputes and outbreaks of epidemic disease. What is clear is that Ife's role as the regional centre of gravity was replaced by that of the rising power of Oyo, located some 100 miles (160 km) to the north on the forest–savanna fringe. Oyo was founded around the thirteenth century, reputedly by Oranmiyan, said to have been a son or grandson of Oduduwa who was also credited with the transfer of divine kingship to Benin. Exploiting its favourable location in the open savanna, Oyo forged a role as a broker in trade between the forest kingdoms to the south and those of the Sudanic zone to the north. By around 1600, these commercial connections extended to the Atlantic coast, where the arrival of European traders ushered in a new phase in the history of Yoruba state-building: one characterized no longer by Ife knowledge capital but by Oyo merchant capital. If the material symbol of the former was the glass bead, then that of the latter was the cowrie shell, vast imports of which served to monetize expanding commerce. Other Yoruba kingdoms, such as Ijebu-Ode, Ijesa, Igbomina and Ondo, also rose to prominence in this period, but it would be Oyo that most effectively mobilized newfound mercantile wealth and military power to create an expansive imperial state.

In contrast to Ife, Oyo's power rested in large part on military force. Around the early sixteenth century, the kingdom was attacked by the horsemen of the non-Yoruba savanna state of Nupe to the north; the capital, Oyo-Ile, was evacuated and the royal family temporarily fled to neighbouring Borgu. Over the following decades, Oyo rebuilt its army around a cavalry force, with both horses and horsemen imported from the north. By time of the reign of the *alaafin* (the specific Oyo term for an *oba*) Obalokun (r. *c.* 1590s–*c.* 1620s), it had reasserted itself using this new military technology and was beginning to raid southwards into the forest. Over the course of the following century, Oyo extended its rule over much of Yorubaland and imposed its authority in non-Yoruba states to the north, such as Bariba and Nupe. As elsewhere in Atlantic Africa, militarized state-building generated war captives and Oyo became an important supplier of enslaved people to European slave traders of the coast. In the 1720s, it imposed tributary status on the kingdom of Dahomey and in the reign of Alaafin Onisile (r. 1746–1754) finally secured control over a commercial corridor to the Atlantic. It had become one of the most powerful imperial states in West Africa.[22]

Oyo was a force for regional stability, J. F. A. Ajayi wrote in an important survey of the rise and fall of the empire. This stability of governance, Ajayi argued, 'helps to explain the comparative infrequency of major intra-Yoruba wars until the 1820s'.[23] At the imperial capital of Oyo-Ile, political power was carefully shared between key interest groups and institutions: the *alaafin*; the *oyomesi*, a council of seven chiefs who represented the leading non-royal *ile*; and, if the system as observed by Samuel Johnson and others in the nineteenth century can be extrapolated back in time, the Ogboni, a ritual association or civic 'cult'.[24] The imperial cult of the thunder god Sango was also important. Believed to be (at least in part) an early *alaafin* who at his death was deified as an *orisa*, Sango was closely associated with royal authority and emerged at the centre of a cult that held sway in the core region of Oyo and in its Yoruba-speaking vassal kingdoms.[25] In these vassals and in the non-Yoruba tributary states beyond, imperial control tended to be maintained with a light touch. Even in neighbouring kingdoms, such as Egba and Egbado, Ajayi argues, local identities were acknowledged and their *obas* enjoyed considerable autonomy. They were overseen and advised by *ajele*, imperial residents who supervised the delivery of annual tribute, and were required too to contribute troops when necessary to the imperial army. Provided they recognized the *alaafin*'s suzerainty and paid the stipulated tribute, the constituent kingdoms were largely left to their own devices. If this recognition was withheld or repudiated, however, they were subjected to punitive military campaigns and brought into line.

By the mid-eighteenth century, Oyo's system of governance was coming under strain. This was due in part to the nature of the empire's formidable cavalry-based military power. As the *alaafin* had no monopoly over the import of horses and cavalry warfare was a highly skilled, professionalized undertaking, the armed forces were largely under the control of the non-royal lineages. A degree of royal oversight had been maintained by their organization under seventy captains called *eso*, who answered initially to the ranking member of the *oyomesi* council, the *basorun*, and then, from the mid-seventeenth century, to a new supreme commander of enslaved origin titled the *Are-ona-Kakanfo*. Yet military prowess resulted in these figures accumulating great prestige and authority. 'The Kakanfo became as powerful as, sometimes more powerful than, the Basorun', Ajayi writes, 'and the Alafin receded further into the background'.[26]

Indeed, according to oral traditions collected by Samuel Johnson, not one *alaafin* died a natural death in the eighteenth century. Every king was either forced to commit suicide or was poisoned. With just two exceptions – Ojigi, the conqueror of Dahomey, and Abiodun, who succeeded in reasserting royal power at the end of the century – the traditions record the *alaafins* as weak or minor figures, while the *basorun* and *kakanfo* emerge as the real powers behind the throne.[27] From around 1754 to 1774, the state was dominated by the ruthlessly ambitious *basorun* Gaha, who personally sent four kings to their death before he was overthrown by Alaafin Abiodun (r. *c.* 1770–1789). Johnson – himself a proud descendant of Abiodun – portrays his reign as a new golden age in terms of commercial prosperity, cultural sophistication and artistic production. Yet he was to be Oyo's last great king. Yorubaland's 'Atlantic age' had brought considerable prosperity and stability for those able to exploit the opportunities offered by the rise of merchant capital. The spread of new forms of mercantile wealth and power, however, had created deep contradictions and social tensions, which would explode into open conflict in the early nineteenth century. 'By 1810', Usman and Falola write, 'Oyo had been reduced to a city-state or kingdom, as it was before the sixteenth century'.[28] As we will see below, its final collapse in the 1830s triggered a period of widespread violence and dislocation for the remainder of the nineteenth century.

YORUBA POLITICAL ORGANIZATION

The two great centres of Ile-Ife and Oyo-Ile are evidently of crucial importance in any understanding of Yoruba state-building. Yet in recent years, historians have been concerned to move on from the established view of the region's past, dominated by what Ogundiran describes as a 'parade of kingdoms and city-states'.[29] Even for scholars of an earlier generation, there was a question of whether the primacy in statecraft of Ife and Oyo – and of Benin – was historical reality or subsequent ideological fabrication. As early as 1973, Robin Law described the mystical aura of ancient Ile-Ife as a work of propaganda by Yoruba monarchs seeking to validate their own dynastic power. For some kingdoms, identifying with the aura of Ife appears to have been a relatively recent strategy: a rejection of Oyo hegemony in the eighteenth and nineteenth centuries.[30] In this light, the myth of Oduduwa's sixteen sons spreading out from Ile-Ife to establish a penumbra of kingdoms is what can be described as a 'fictive kin allegiance'. Existing independent city-states, Suzanne Preston Blier argues, were more likely to have sworn allegiance to Ife 'in exchange for diplomatic ties, trade, protection, and ritual engagement'.[31]

Yoruba historical experience, that is to argue, tended to remain local in orientation, firmly rooted in the *ile*, the house, and the *ilu*, the town. Indeed, the latter was a distinctive feature of Yoruba civilization and governance, which was focused on the autonomy of the *ilu-alade*, the 'crowned town'.[32] Outlying villages were typically headed by an uncrowned ruler or *baale*, and their inhabitants, in another act of fictive kin allegiance, often traced their ancestry to the capital and referred to its *oba* also as '*baba*', the father of the kingdom. As we have seen in the case of Oyo, political authority was carefully apportioned between various interest groups. The *oba* was advised by a council – in some cases multiple councils – of chiefs. In theory, he possessed absolute authority, including power over life and death, but in practice was a constitutional monarch bound to consult his councils of chiefs at regular, often daily, meetings. The highest council was typically composed of the most senior lineage chiefs of the kingdom, whom the *oba* ignored at his peril. He was therefore under constitutional restraint from ruling tyrannically.

The long and complex process involved in the installation of an *oba* provided the opportunity to inculcate the new ruler in the arts of government. A period of three months typically elapsed between election and coronation. Once the ruling house (or, where kingship rotated between different lineages, that segment of the ruling house whose turn it was to provide an *oba*) had submitted nominations, the kingmakers would consult the practitioners of *ifa* divination, the *babalawo*, to determine the best candidate. Elaborate ceremonies would then be performed to consecrate the new king. In many kingdoms, the *oba*-elect's powers of restraint and endurance would be tested by him being flogged and made to wear rags. This ritual was designed also to make him experience the hardship of the poor so that in his exalted position he would always be mindful of the common people. He then spent three months in confinement, during which he was instructed in the history of the kingdom and the significance of his role as father of his people. Having received the sacred powers of all his predecessors, the *oba* was finally crowned and his face covered with the *ade*, the fringed beaded crown.

Despite this sacred status, should an *oba* fail in his duty or attempt to exercise unjust or excessive power, he risked serious sanctions. We have seen how the *oyomesi* council played a leading role in the governance of Oyo; in Johnson's words, it represented 'the voice of the nation'.[33] The *oyomesi* also had a degree of control over religious life: of its seven members, the *alapinin* was head of the Egungun masquerade; the *laguna* of the cult of Oko, the *orisa* of fertility; the *agbakin* of the cult of Oranmiyan; the *asipa* of the cult of Ogun; and the *basorun* of the cult of the king's *orun* or spiritual double, 'with the power of signifying to the Alafin that he had been rejected by the gods'.[34] Among the Ijebu and Egba, the Osugbo or Ogboni cults were so dominant that the *oba* in fact had little real power.

In those parts of Yorubaland where the Ogboni or Osugbo cults did not play an important political role or where, in contrast to Oyo, the council of chiefs had no constitutional power to remove an *oba*, a despotic ruler could be removed only by insurrection. The chiefs usually began such a process by refusing the traditional daily homage paid to the king at his palace. The community might also relocate the marketplace or women might protest by pronouncing curses, desecrating sacred places or, in a striking display of a gendered 'politics of undress', by resorting to public nudity in order to shame the king.[35] The sanctified and secluded body of the *oba* was highly vulnerable to such defilement. This seclusion was underlined by the fact the *oba* tended to remain in the background of day-to-day governance. Often, he did not even attend council meetings, which were usually held on the veranda of his palace and decisions from which were communicated to him for ratification.

Neither was government the concern of the *oba* and his leading councillors alone. Commoners (in the sense of freeborn adult men and, often, prominent women as well) were also involved. Yoruba towns were intricately organized into distinct quarters (*ogbon*) headed by titled chiefs: those comprising Oyo numbered thirty-six, Ijebu-Ode twenty-five, and Ilesa, the capital of the kingdom of Ijesa, seventy. Chiefs were required to inform their people of the deliberations of the *oba*'s council, while the people in turn expressed their views and wishes through their compound heads to the quarter chiefs and on to the *oba*. In those parts of Yorubaland such as Ijebu, Ekiti, Egba and Ondo where the chiefs belonged to civic associations like Ogboni, matters of governance were also discussed with their members. In Ekiti, the young men expressed their views in meetings of 'age-grades' (i.e. generational associations), which were transmitted to the *oba*. Effective administration also depended upon a hierarchy of palace officials. These were the personal servants of the *oba* and were referred to by a variety of terms: *ilari* in Oyo, *odi* in Ijebu and *emese* in Ife, Ekiti and Ilesa. They were mostly of enslaved origin although in some regions also included freeborn men.

The *oba* and chiefs derived revenue from various sources, first and foremost from the proceeds of their farms. They typically had large retinues of servants, many of whom were enslaved or so-called pawns (i.e. in debt bondage), who were typically put to work on their agricultural estates. Gifts, fines, tributes, tolls and, in times of military conflict, war booty were the other principal sources of royal and chiefly revenue. The *oba*, however, had no preferential right in trade: both chiefs and ordinary commoners were free to participate in local and long-distance trade. In most cases the wives, the enslaved and free servants of *obas* and chiefs traded on their behalf. The *oba* also inherited the property of his predecessor, as well as receiving death duties from the family of deceased chiefs of substance. As no clear distinction was made between the state treasury and the *oba*'s personal wealth, however, a substantial part of the latter was inevitably spent on providing services to his subjects. This was also the case for the great chiefs, who were regularly required to perform rituals to the *orisa* and to feast lineage members during festivals. In his position as the father of his people and the head priest of the kingdom, the *oba* spent a large part of his income on performing rituals to guarantee the physical and spiritual well-being of his subjects.

Central government was further articulated to the periphery by an elaborate system of chiefly patronage. These patrons were also known as *baba* ('father'), who communicated with their 'children' through agents in the vassal towns called *baba kekere* ('little father') or *baba isale* ('father in court').[36] Matters affecting the subordinate towns were taken to these patrons, who raised them in the chiefs' council. Tribute was paid through the patrons, who took their own share before delivering the rest to the *oba*. In Oyo, patrons were appointed from among the senior chiefs of the capital, but to guard against intrigues the *alaafin* usually delegated one of his *ilari* (royal servants) to the patron's entourage to act as the 'eyes of the *oba*' (*oju oba*). *Ilari* were sent from time to time to report on the activities of both the *ajele* and the *baale*, while the *alaafin*'s ritual authority was also bolstered by the posting of priests of the great *orisa* Sango on the peripheries of the empire. Thus, despite the secluded and ritualized status of the king, an elaborate network of influence allowed him to rule rather than simply to reign.

The pattern of government summarized here had many local variants. It was also modified over time as towns increased in size and complexity and the territorial reach of kingdoms was extended. The expansion of some kingdoms inevitably meant the decline of others; many subordinate towns claimed to have been in existence long before the arrival of centralized government and some maintained that their own rulers had unjustly lost the right to wear the beaded crown of an *oba*. What has often been overlooked in histories focused on a 'parade of kingdoms' is that some regions retained quite distinctive and stubbornly decentralized forms of governance. One was the Egba region on the southern frontier of imperial Oyo, which was characterized by a highly complex political structure. The Egba people were divided into three kingdoms: Egba Agbeyin, Egba Agura and Egba Oke-Ona. All three were federations of many towns – 144 is the number given for Egba Agura – which continued to have an unusually high degree of autonomy, each with its own ruler and intricate hierarchy of Ogboni chiefs and those of other local civic associations Olorogun and Parakoyi. Each town also supplied chiefs to fill offices at the federal level. The link between the three federated kingdoms remains unclear, although Ajayi Ajisafe argues that the *oba* of Egba Agbeyin, the *alake*, was recognized as the senior king.[37]

Eastern Yorubaland on the frontiers with Benin had an even more fragmented political structure. Ekiti, Ijebu, Ondo, Owo and Awori all remained beyond the reach of Oyo imperial power and were characterized by a striking absence of centralized authority. Ekiti oral traditions record the ensuing political struggles when the descendants of Oduduwa arrived from Ile-Ife, perhaps in the sixteenth century, seeking to impose their rule on the region's existing small kingdoms.[38] The situation was further complicated by the subsequent arrival of migrants from Ijebu-Ode, Oyo and Benin. Thus, the demographic composition of Ekiti came to be made up of a fusion of the original inhabitants, the Oduduwa group from Ile-Ife, Edo migrants and, finally, new waves of Oyo and Igbomina refugees displaced by the wars that plagued Yorubaland in the nineteenth century.

The Awori were probably the least centralized of all, each town governed by a council of male elders, the *igbimo*, which enforced its orders through a secret society. The office of *oba* did exist, but the incumbent remained more a priest than a secular ruler. In the Awori kingdom of Lagos, the monarchy seems to have been somewhat stronger than in neighbouring settlements. This is probably due to the influence of Benin, which had contacts with the port town as early as the sixteenth century; in the following century the local king or *olofin* was overthrown and Lagos became a Benin vassal. The authority of the *olofin* (or the *ologun* or *eleko*, as the *oba* of Lagos was variously called in the past) was probably also enhanced by the town's emerging role in the Atlantic slave trade.[39]

The view of the Yoruba past dominated by dynastic power, therefore, requires some qualification. Yoruba government, rather than being either 'centralized' or 'decentralized', tended to be characterized by an inventive and fluid combination of the two. Everywhere, subordinate towns sought to continue to appoint their own rulers and were often fiercely protective of local rights and identities, as enshrined in founding charters, in the *oriki* or praise poems dedicated to hallowed historical figures and in patterns of *orisa* devotion. Metropolitan paramount rulers such as the *ooni* of Ife and the *alaafin* of Oyo were all too aware of this. So long as reciprocal obligations continued to be met, they were reluctant to interfere in the internal business of the outlying towns over which they exercised suzerainty. Herein can be seen to lie the genius of Yoruba statecraft.

THE KINGDOM OF BENIN

The Edo founders of the kingdom of Benin traced their origins to an ancient domain called Igodomigodo ruled by the *ogiso*, the 'king of the sky' or 'king of heaven'. The remains of villages enclosed by extensive earthworks suggest that ancestors of the Edo began to settle the forest region to the east of Yorubaland late in the first millennium CE. Oral traditions record that although the *ogisos* were powerful and respected kings, their dynasty eventually foundered. There are different versions of how a new dynasty was then created, although all have one element in common: the central role of Ife in the forging of a new model of sacred kingship. In one, a dispute between the crown prince Ekaladerhan and a faction within the palace resulted in Ekaladerhan being defeated and fleeing from

Benin to Ife. When the *ogiso* died, the Benin kingmakers recalled the exiled prince and installed him on the throne. The other tradition was first written down in the nineteenth century and popularized in the 1930s by the pioneering local historian Chief Jacob Egharevba, whose work was inspired by the outpouring of historical research in neighbouring Yorubaland. In Egharevba's version, the Benin kingmakers appealed to the *ooni* of Ife to intervene in a dynastic crisis. The *ooni* sent his son Oranmiyan to take the throne. Although Oranmiyan failed to secure the support of the Edo chiefs, he married a local woman and it was their son, Eweka, who would emerge as king and founder of the new dynasty. Oranmiyan was said to have returned to Yorubaland, where he went on to found Oyo and became its *alaafin*.[40] When Eweka died, however, his remains were returned to Ife. Egharevba explained in the 1930s that this mortuary practice continued for every third *oba* 'until very recently': symbolic, Olúpònà writes, 'of the return of the "stranger-king" to his autochthonous place'.[41]

In contrast to these divergent traditions, the expansion of Benin in all accounts is associated with the dynamic reign of Oba Ewuare (r. c. 1440–c. 1473). Ewuare created a strong army and a council of advisors; he also rebuilt the capital city, which he named Ob-Edo, laying out broad streets and organizing craftspeople into guilds and the citizenry into age grades. Two classes of chiefs were created: town chiefs or *Eghaevbo n'Ore* and palace chiefs or *Eghaevbo n'Ogbe*, who were charged with assisting the king and the council of kingmakers (the *uzama*) in legislative and judicial duties. The so-called *uzama* chiefs, whose role dated back to early Edo and who hitherto had wielded great influence, gradually lost their powers to the *oba* and his appointees. With the kingdom's territorial expansion, the new chiefs played a key role in provincial administration and the collection of tribute. Ewuare is also remembered as introducing the system of royal primogeniture to end the bitter succession disputes, which had in the past been the cause of much conflict. He appointed his designated heir Edaiken to the *uzama*, ostensibly to familiarize him with workings of government policies but in fact further to check the power of old kingmakers.

Royal authority in early Benin therefore appears to have been put on a stronger constitutional footing than in Yorubaland to the east. The structure of rule forged by Ewuare certainly had staying power: in contrast to the rise and decline of Ife and Oyo, the kingdom of Benin maintained its position of regional prominence since the fourteenth century – and its second dynasty continues to reign in Benin City today. Kingship was not, however, to be absolute. The *Eghaevbo n'Ore* may well have served to nullify the authority of the kingmakers, but their ranking member, the *iyase*, would emerge as a dominant figure in Benin politics over the centuries. Indeed, the *iyase* came to be portrayed in both oral and written sources as the focus of opposition to the *oba*'s power, serving as the head of the Benin army before the creation of a new military commander, the *ezemo*, in the eighteenth century.[42]

Under Ewuare, Benin's territorial expansion extended into eastern Yorubaland. It was during the reign of his successor Ozolua (r. *c*. 1481–*c*. 1503) that Benin was first visited by Portuguese mariners, who reached the coast around 1485 and sought to open commercial relations with the powerful kingdom. One commodity the Portuguese purchased was enslaved captives, who were initially resold at regional ports from the Gold Coast east to the island of São Tomé. As in Oyo and elsewhere in West Africa, the process of militarized territorial expansion thus became entangled with that of enslavement and participation in the Atlantic slave trade. A further phase of expansion occurred under Oba Ehengbuda (r. *c*. 1578–*c*. 1606), who, like Ewuare, was 'recognized both as a powerful healer-magician and as a great warrior'.[43] In time, Benin power was carried west along the line of coastal lagoons to Lagos, north through the Yoruba regions of Ekiti and Owo towards the Niger-Benue Confluence, east to the frontiers of Igboland, and south into the Niger Delta. That section of the Atlantic coast between Lagos and the Delta began to appear named on European maps as the Bight of Benin.

European sources provide information on some of these wars, as well as on other aspects of Benin state and society.[44] As early as 1516, a force of Portuguese soldiers, accompanied by some Capuchin friars, joined the Benin army in a campaign against the Igala kingdom. A century later, by which time rival European powers had begun to challenge the Portuguese monopoly of maritime trade in West Africa, German and Dutch mercenaries were also lending their services to the kingdom. These soldiers are portrayed on some of the brass wall plaques that once adorned the great royal palace at the centre of Ob-Edo – a projection of the *oba*'s patronage of Europeans and his access to their goods and military technology. Europeans, in turn, portrayed their Benin allies, both in writing and in art. Perhaps the best known is the account of the kingdom written by Olfert Dapper, first published in 1668 but drawing on a range of earlier European sources. Dapper's description of the palace, which was accompanied by an engraving depicting the *oba* emerging from it in procession, indicates how impressed early visitors were with the royal city:

> The King's palace is on the right side of the town, as you leave by the gate of Gotton. It is a collection of buildings which occupy as much space as the town of Harlem, and which is enclosed with walls. There are numerous apartments for the Prince's ministers and fine galleries, most of which are as big as those of the Exchange at Amsterdam. They are supported by wooden pillars encased with copper, where their victories are depicted, and which are carefully kept very clean. The majority of these royal houses are covered with branches of palm-trees, arranged like square planks; each corner is adorned with a small pyramidal tower, on the point of which is perched a copper bird spreading its wings.[45]

Dapper's description points to Benin's impressive achievements in art and architecture and to their role in the projection of dynastic power. Traditions collected by Egharevba record that brass-casting too was introduced from Ife, during the reign of Benin's Oba Oguola in the late fourteenth century. As at Ile-Ife, terracotta figures appear to have preceded those produced in metal, but by the fifteenth century the most striking form of artistic creation were naturalistic copper alloy portraits, so-called *uhumwelo* or 'handsome heads'. These included stunning representations of queen mothers, distinguished by their lofty crowns and thought to date to the early sixteenth-century reign of Oba Esigie, who created the office of queen mother in recognition of the crucial role in government played by his own mother, Idia. The creation of the more than nine hundred known brass wall plaques adorning the palace complex is also believed to have begun under Esigie. 'The power of the king was based ideologically on his divinity', the leading art historian of Benin, Paula Girshick Ben-Amos, writes, 'but concretely in his control over a military machine'. The iconography of royal art was therefore dominated by

The *oba* of Benin emerges from his palace, accompanied by leashed leopards, musicians, armed retainers and court notables, from Olfert Dapper, *Naukeurige Beschrijvinge de Afrikaensche Gewesten* (Amsterdam, 1668). The sculptures of hornbills and other birds atop the turrets of the palace were a visible reminder of the cosmological connection between the animal world and royal power.

these aspects of dynastic power: 'the twin themes of warfare and courtly splendour'.[46] A further theme was more esoteric: the portrayal of birds, snakes, mudfish and other animals in order to underline the complex cosmological connections between the natural world and royal power (see pl. VIII).

The death in 1606 of Oba Ehengbuda in a canoe accident while fighting on the coastal lagoon led to a decree banning his successors from personally leading their armies into battle. This law had unintended consequences: limited to the capital and secluded in the royal palace, the *oba* began to lose authority. The vacuum was filled by the *Eghaevbo n'Ogbe*, the palace chiefs, who exploited this opening to their advantage by asserting their influence over the king and, despite the law of primogeniture, over the process of royal succession. A combination of palace intrigues and a sequence of youthful or weak kings further enabled the chiefs to exploit the situation to their own ends. Yet the chiefs lacked the means to usurp all power, which remained contested. Like the Yoruba kings, the *oba* of Benin embodied potent spiritual as well as secular authority. In contrast with the Yoruba, moreover, the Benin chiefs were mostly royal appointees rather than being established representatives of their lineages. Tactically using their position as the ultimate source of power and carefully balancing the various levers of government, the more skilful *obas* succeeded in playing one set of chiefs off against the other and in maintaining their role as the indispensable personification and sacred soul of the state.

Nonetheless, the ongoing contest between the king and his chiefs weakened Benin. By the 1650s, chiefly factions engineered the accession to the throne of princes from obscure branches of the dynasty remote from the capital, which undermined the mystical aura of royal authority. At the same time, economic change in the volatile arena of Atlantic commerce served to transfer power and influence from the palace to new commercial agents stationed in the Niger Delta and to ambitious military entrepreneurs. Unlike in the sixteenth century, when the Portuguese purchased pepper and enslaved captives only with the express permission of the king or his agents, new patterns of trade – increasingly based on the import of textiles – began to undermine the royal monopoly. The result was the outbreak of civil war, which lasted from 1689 until 1720.[47]

The palace emerged triumphant from this prolonged conflict. Oba Ewuakpe (r. 1690–1713) succeeded in reasserting the law of primogeniture, while his successors Akenzua I (r. 1715–1735) and Eresonyen (r. 1735–1750) further restored dynastic legitimacy. This process can be seen in the changing nature of artistic production. As Ben-Amos demonstrates, eighteenth-century iconography was distinguished from that which came before by an overriding concern with ancestral legitimacy and by looking back to the age of the kingdom's great warrior kings. The art of this period can be shown not simply to have been a representation of royal power, but also to have been strategically deployed to accumulate it. Explicitly Yoruba-based motifs also begin to appear, as Benin's kings strove to strengthen the origins of their power in the mythical founder Oranmiyan. New artistic media included elaborately carved elephant tusks; 'novelty itself', Ben-Amos writes, 'became a strategy'.[48]

THE TUMULTUOUS NINETEENTH CENTURY

As elsewhere in Africa, the nineteenth century was a tumultuous and challenging period for the Yoruba and Edo peoples. The most profound change occurred in Yorubaland, where the collapse of the Oyo Empire was the catalyst for what Ogundiran describes as a cataclysmic breakdown of social order.[49] The reasons for the decline and then implosion of Oyo have been much debated. Ogundiran points to the contradictions in Yoruba society created by the entanglement with Atlantic trade, but Oyo's dynastic crisis was the culmination of multiple factors, both internal and external. The political strains were already apparent in the struggle for power between the *alaafin* and the lineage chiefs headed by the *basorun*. This created an opening by the early nineteenth century for some tributary kingdoms – including Dahomey – to break away from imperial overrule. The proximate cause of collapse, however, was associated with the outbreak of Shehu 'Uthman Dan Fodio's revolt in the Hausa region and the creation of the Sokoto Caliphate (see chapter 7). Although Islam had made only limited inroads into the northern reaches of Oyo, in 1817 a dissident *kakanfo*, Afonja, incited a revolt among Muslims in the province of Ilorin. Ilorin, Ajayi writes, 'thus developed from a rebellious province of Oyo into a frontier post of the Fulani *jihad*'.[50] A combination of internal revolt and military pressure from jihadist forces resulted in Oyo-Ile being overrun. By the mid-1830s, the city had been abandoned, its inhabitants fleeing to the south. The imperial state had been destroyed.

The consequences reverberated throughout Yorubaland to the end of the nineteenth century and from there into the enslaved African diaspora in the Americas. The following decades saw the region plunged into waves of violent conflict, resulting in large-scale population movement, militarization, social dislocation and enslavement. Despite the British abolition of the Atlantic slave trade in 1807, from the 1790s to the 1860s an estimated 500,000 enslaved Yoruba people were transported across the Atlantic, the majority to Brazil and Cuba. Hundreds of thousands more lost their lives in war, millions of others were displaced, and a new generation of warlords sought to usurp the ancient authority of the *obas*.[51] Refugees from the fighting created new towns such as Ibadan, a former war camp, which emerged as the dominant power in the land. Social dislocation also resulted in religious change in the shape of increasing conversion to both Islam and Christianity. By 1871, Ibadan had its first Muslim ruler, the *Are-ona-Kakanfo* Momoh Latosisa, while New Oyo, created to the south of the abandoned capital, reportedly boasted twelve mosques. Another newly created city in the Egba region, Abeokuta, was an early headquarters of Christian missionary endeavour and of returning Saros (that is, 'Sierra Leonians'), who would play such a key role in the forging of a new Yoruba identity.[52]

The creation of the Sokoto Caliphate also impacted on Benin. By 1815, the jihad had spread to the northern districts of the kingdom and three years later, when Oba Osemwende dispatched forces to put down an uprising in Ekiti, they were defeated by local forces and those of Sokoto. The peaceful coexistence that had long been established between Oyo and Benin was shattered by the rise of Ibadan, which expanded aggressively into Benin's Yoruba-speaking frontier regions of Ekiti, Owo and Akoto. Benin also struggled to contain the repercussions of the abolition of the Atlantic slave trade. Although the kingdom was no longer a major supplier of enslaved captives, the lucrative new palm oil trade that gradually replaced it was concentrated in the Niger Delta, beyond its direct control. The campaign against the slave trade and the transition to so-called legitimate commerce also drew the British into the region: Lagos was occupied in 1850 and a protectorate declared in 1884 over the Niger Delta, the administration of which was granted to a private, militarized

A printed cloth commemorating the thirtieth anniversary of the coronation of Oba Erediauwa of Benin (r. 1979–2016) in 2009. The cloth is bordered by lines of circles containing two crossed swords, the *ada* and the *eben*, which symbolize the idea of the *oba* as both sacred and secular ruler. 42 in. (107 cm) × 75 in. (190 cm).

trading consortium, the Royal Niger Company. In 1897, in response to the defeat of an earlier attempt to infiltrate Benin, a British punitive expedition marched on the kingdom. After fierce fighting, Benin's defenders were defeated and the *oba* deposed and later exiled. Meanwhile, colonial forces set about looting the kingdom's artistic treasures. Large numbers of these stolen objects were acquired by museums and private collectors in Europe, where over a century later, most remain. An international campaign is now under way to restore them to Nigeria, to be displayed in a planned new Edo Museum of West African Art adjacent to the royal palace in Benin City.

Yorubaland too was incorporated into what became the British colony of Nigeria, albeit in different circumstances. With the exceptions of Ilorin and Ijebu, colonial conquest proceeded by way of treaty rather than military campaigns: in Ajayi's words, the 'wars and divisions among the Yoruba made large-scale conquest unnecessary'. Rather, the British insinuated themselves into the region by negotiating the end of hostilities between the warring factions, in 1893 cajoling Ibadan, Abeokuta and what remained of Oyo to sign 'treaties of friendship'. 'The British thus emerged as the power most able to fill the vacuum left by Old Oyo', Ajayi writes. Gradually, however, they were to reveal 'that they were no longer friends or allies but rulers far more effective and domineering than Old Oyo ever was'.[53]

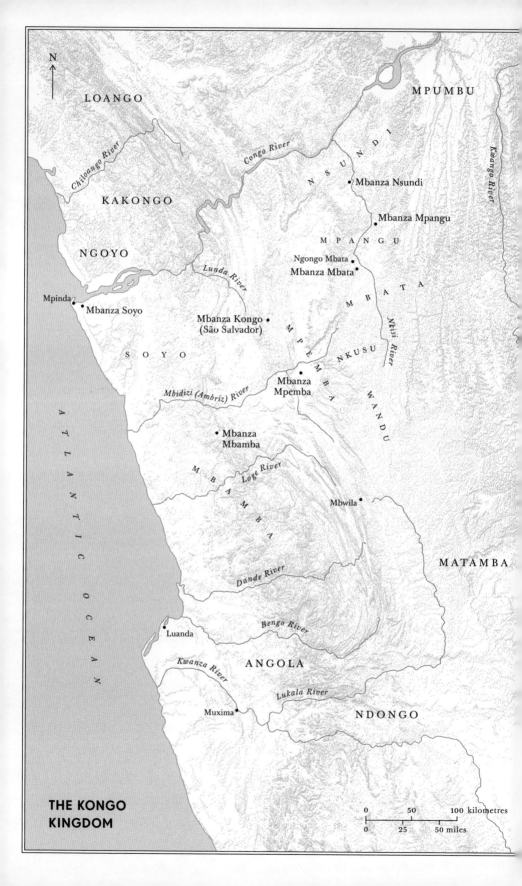

N

LOANGO   MPUMBU

Chiloango River

Congo River   *Kwango River*

KAKONGO   N S U N D I

                                    • Mbanza Nsundi

NGOYO   M P A N G U
                                    • Mbanza Mpangu

                          Lunda River   Ngongo Mbata •
                                    Mbanza Mbata •

Mpinda   M B A T A
   •
   Mbanza Soyo

                 Mbanza Kongo •   M P E M B A   N K U S U
                 (São Salvador)   *Nkisi River*

          S O Y O   W A N D U

              Mbidizi (Ambriz) River   Mbanza •
                                          Mpemba

                          • Mbanza
                            Mbamba

                 M   *Loge River*
                   B
                     A
                       M   • Mbwila
                         B
                           A   MATAMBA

                       Dande River

A T L A N T I C   *Bengo River*

   O C E A N   • Luanda

              Kwanza River   ANGOLA

                       Lukala River

              Muxima •   NDONGO

THE KONGO
KINGDOM

0   50   100 kilometres
0   25   50 miles

CHAPTER 5

THE KONGO KINGDOM

Cécile Fromont

In 1506, upon the death of his father João Nzinga a Nkuwu, Afonso Mvemba a Nzinga (r. 1506–1542) claimed the title of Mwene Kongo, ruler of the land of the Kongo. The title, we learn from the correspondence Afonso wrote in Portuguese to the vassal rulers under his authority and to his counterpart in Lisbon, Manuel I, meant king, and his dominion was a kingdom.[1] As was often the case in moments of political transition in the region, his claim faced opposition: another member of the royal dynasty also asserted a right to the kingship and stood ready to fight for it through a mix of palace intrigue and armed struggle. Afonso had strong arguments supporting his bid: his father had made him heir apparent by naming him as ruler of the wealthy Nsundi province of the kingdom, a privilege the Mwene Kongo generally reserved to his favoured successor. Yet Afonso also had reasons to expect a contest. His position at the royal court and reputation beyond had suffered as members of competing political factions spread rumours about his violent ruling style and efforts to seduce his own father's wives. He also knew that being the heir apparent gave only limited weight to his hopes of becoming the Mwene Kongo, as the kingship was not in his father's gift. Rather, after the death of a king, a council of electors bestowed the title on the candidate they considered the most suitable. Indeed, the figure behind the rumours against Afonso, his half-brother Mpanzu a Nzinga, also hoped to succeed to the throne. Upon the death of their father, Mpanzu a Nzinga manoeuvred to gain support from key electors and prepared to take up arms against Afonso. Such fraternal competition appears to have been an established part of Kongo succession – and would continue to threaten political stability in the centuries to come. Yet the dispute of 1506 hinged on a matter of more profound significance than institutionalized palace intrigue. It unfolded along an emerging political and spiritual rift that divided competing views about the very nature and future of the kingdom.

Kongo was the westernmost of the arc of Bantu-speaking states that emerged along the southern fringes of the Central African rainforest. It was the earliest and, in many ways, the best-known polity in this zone of state-building described by the pioneering historian Jan Vansina as 'the kingdoms of the savanna'.[2] Located largely to the south of the Congo River that drained the vast equatorial basin into the Atlantic Ocean, Kongo's core domains are today encompassed by the nations of Angola and the Democratic Republic of the Congo. In the three decades that led up to the disputed succession of 1506, the kingdom experienced a sequence of events that shook its established social order and religious identity. Portuguese mariners reached its shores in 1483 and in the years that followed, both African and European cultural mediators began to travel – some willingly, others by force – between Lisbon and Central Africa. Christianity started to gain ground as early as 1491, when key members of the ruling elite, including Nzinga a Nkuwu and the Mwene Soyo, ruler of the coastal province of Soyo, received baptism. The Mwene Soyo took the Christian name Manuel and the Mwene Kongo the name João, the latter borrowed from his Portuguese counterpart. The personal and political significance of this gesture remains unclear, as little is known about Nzinga a Nkuwu's engagement with the new faith. Whatever his intimate convictions, the king authorized the settlement of a Portuguese community, which included Catholic clerics. Supported by the Kongo crown and working alongside elite Africans returned from Portugal, these priests established an educational system that fostered literacy in private and public affairs and disseminated

Christian teachings. The result, unique in the early modern history of tropical Africa, was the emergence by the early sixteenth century of a Christian kingdom on the continent's Atlantic coast.

As a member of the Kongo ruling elite, Afonso Mvemba a Nzinga therefore grew up learning the history and mythology of the kingdom, but as an adult also studied that of the Christian Church. If little is known about his father João's relationship with Catholicism, there is a wealth of oral and written sources that point to Afonso's piety. Stories of his dedicated study of Church teachings and history, of his erudition in the scriptures and of his zealous proselytizing efforts became key elements in Kongo historical memory.[3] In the narrative Afonso crafted after having secured the throne, it was this embrace of Christianity that gave him the edge in the succession struggle with his brother and the Kongo traditionalists who opposed the advent of the new faith. Indeed, holders of the office of Mwene Kongo were always in need of legitimizing their rule in the face of rival political factions, and Christianity afforded Afonso an opportunity to present his rule as supported by historical precedent and by powerful new supernatural forces. The events surrounding his rise to power are known principally through his own written accounts, in which he began to advance this narrative. The fate of the kingdom, he declared, was sealed on the battlefield: Mpanzu a Nzinga's 'heathen' battalions had the upper hand when, moments before an assault that was certain to prove fatal to his cause, an army of knights on horseback appeared, swords in hand, under a resplendent celestial cross. The miraculous troops swept away all before them, giving Afonso a resounding victory over his brother and handing him the throne of the Kongo.

Accounts of battles turning on divine intervention on behalf of the victors are of course common throughout history in many parts of the world. Yet Afonso's victory had a profound impact on the history of Kongo. The new king wrote the story of his rise as a narrative that combined established Central African understandings of political power with Christian lore, and it would resonate for centuries to come. As a heroic tale it consciously echoed the foundation myths of Kongo and other Central African kingdoms, in which an enlightened ruler and astute warrior brings a new, sophisticated civilization to a benighted land mired in a disordered past. Afonso's narrative couched this as a holy war between a righteous Christian prince and a pagan opponent – a re-enactment of Emperor Constantine's efforts to win over Rome to Christianity. It therefore formed a space where Central African myth and Christian lore could merge into a single Kongo story, as the kingdom found a place in the expanding Christendom of the sixteenth century.

The tradition of origin of the Kongo kingdom that underlay Afonso's account is known from various versions written down by Africans and by European visitors between the sixteenth and twentieth centuries. Its central protagonist is Lukeni lua Nimi, who would also become known as Ntinu Wene, literally 'king of the kingdom'. A prototypical stranger king, Lukeni lua Nimi was said to have crossed the Congo River from Vungu to the north (or in some versions the Kwango River to the east) and to have seized control of territories inhabited by indigenous peoples ruled by an older local dynasty. By committing the grave transgression of murdering his own father's pregnant sister, Lukeni lua Nimi set himself apart from ordinary people; he became, that is, an extraordinary man unbound by established social norms. In the words of anthropologist Luc de Heusch, he became a 'sacred monster' – a king.[4] Like other founding 'culture heroes' of the savanna kingdoms, he also came armed with a transformative political philosophy and, according to some versions, insinuated himself into the established social order by marrying a woman of the local ruling elite. From the capital of Mbanza Kongo, Lukeni then extended his control over the surrounding principalities of Mpemba, Nsundi, Mbata and Soyo, which would become the core provinces of the new kingdom.

The narrative of Afonso's rise to power resonates with this ancient tradition of origin. Like Lukeni lua Nimi, Afonso was no longer an ordinary man but a sacred king, whose legitimacy was underpinned by potent spiritual forces. Some eighteenth-century versions of the story have him upholding the newly Christianized culture of his domain at the price of a monstrous transgression like that of Lukeni: taking the life of his own mother when she refused to destroy sacred objects he considered to be pagan idols.[5] Afonso's pivotal reign inaugurated a new era for Kongo – as well as for the writing of its history. The kingdom was not the only centralized state in the region, but its cosmopolitan Christian culture and engagement with the broader Atlantic world from the late fifteenth century have made it the best known. Kongo's use of writing in internal as well as international affairs, moreover, has enabled scholars to study its deeper past to an extent that is unusual in Africa south of the Sahara. As the editors of a recent book on its early history have written, Kongo has become 'a famous emblem of Africa's past' and 'an important cultural landmark for Africans'.[6] Yet Kongo's wealth of written and oral sources have raised complex problems of interpretation, for example as its historians have sought to understand and to reach beyond Afonso's efforts to recast the past and to shape the future. How and what can we know, then, of the kingdom over which Afonso and his brother fought in 1506?

KONGO BEFORE 1500

The origins and early history of Kongo have been the subject of much debate. One point of contention has been the narrative of Lukeni lua Nimi's founding of the kingdom, a process that historians tend to date to some point in the late thirteenth or early fourteenth century. This is a debate that extends beyond the region and even beyond Africa, as at its core is the issue of the relationship between 'myth' and 'history'. Kongo was one of many Bantu-speaking kingdoms in Central Africa of which the traditions of origin turned on the arrival of a noble stranger from across a river, who seizes power from an older, often despotic, dynasty and inaugurates a new civilized social order based on sacred kingship. Vansina's pioneering efforts to mobilize these accounts tended to take them quite literally, assuming that culture heroes like Lukeni lua Nimi, Kalala Ilunga of the Luba and Cibinda Ilunga of the Lunda were historic state-builders whose conquests could be dated by counting the generations of remembered kings back from verifiable successors.[7] Subsequent interpretations, however, rejected the idea that these were historical figures. The anthropologist Luc de Heusch, most prominently, argued that traditions of origin were mythical charters, albeit ones with profound and deeply rooted meanings for local societies.[8] Historians also came to adopt a more critical approach to the processes by which oral traditions were generated and transmitted. Different and, at times, conflicting versions of the story of Kongo origins recorded over the centuries, for example, can be seen to have resulted in part from the 'political work' that the tradition was called upon to perform. Oral traditions, that is to say, were far from immutable: they often tell us as much about the circumstances of their telling as about the histories they record.

These debates are far from over. In a recent intervention, the historical anthropologist Marshall Sahlins argues that whether the Kongo tradition of origin is verifiably 'true' or not is beside the point.[9] It needs to be taken seriously, Sahlins insists, because over time it has been taken with the utmost seriousness by the Kongo themselves. The 'myth' has served to locate the Kongo as a people in their own history, providing a crucial template for the understanding of historical change. We have seen this in Afonso's choice to present his own rise to power in a way that echoed the advent of Lukeni lua Nimi. Other recent scholarship has also sought to examine the deeper history of state-building in Africa by reconsidering traditions of origin in combination with evidence derived from the fields of archaeology and historical linguistics. The KongoKing project, based on archaeological fieldwork carried out in the Democratic Republic of the Congo (although unfortunately not in neighbouring Angola) between 2012 and 2016, is one such interdisciplinary endeavour. Its research team set out to explore the shape and dynam-ics of what they describe as the 'political space' of early Kongo; that is, changes in the degree of centralization – or decentralization – in the kingdom over time.[10] It seems likely that the historic king-dom emerged from the consolidation of several older polities, expanding first by negotiated alliances and then, after it had accu-mulated a degree of centralized power, through warfare. By the time of Afonso, hints about the process by which its constituent regions were incorporated could be detected in their political organi-zation and relationship with the royal court. Regions added to the emerging kingdom through alliance, such as Mbata, maintained a degree of autonomy and held a distinct voice in central politics, particularly in the election of kings. In contrast, conquered areas, such as Nsundi, were directly ruled by governors dispatched from the capital, Mbanza Kongo.

Yet differences in interpretation remain. One of the books that resulted from the KongoKing project includes chapters written by two leading scholars of Kongo, which offer strikingly different read-ings of the nature of that kingship. The anthropologist Wyatt MacGaffey questions the unproblematic identification of Kongo as a 'centralized kingdom' in 1480 and thereafter. Portuguese observers identified it so, MacGaffey suggests, because this is what they under-stood states to be. Yet political authority in Central Africa, he argues, worked quite differently: it was more diffuse and based less on 'instru-mental power' backed up by armed force than on the creative mobi-lization of spiritual forces.[11] The historian John Thornton disagrees, rejecting the view of the kingdom as largely a symbolic entity. 'While this situation may well have existed in the predecessor polities', Thornton argues, 'Kongo as seen in the earliest documents was a much more integrated polity that the early European visitors under-stood as a kingdom'.[12] 'The degree of centralization of authority and income', he writes elsewhere, 'was remarkable'.[13] Despite Afonso's mobilization of Christianity as a new form of ritual authority, this, too, was how he sought to portray his domains to the outside world.

What seems clear is that political authority was also based on Kongo's location and the ability to redistribute goods from a variety of ecological zones. Trade routes connecting regions to the north and east producing copper and raffia with those to the west and south producing salt and *nzimbu* shells used as currency shaped its territorial formation. By 1480, the realm extended over three contrasting ecological zones: a narrow, relatively dry savanna strip along the Atlantic coast in the west; a more fertile central region of rolling forested hills where the kingdom's capital and most densely populated districts were located; and escarpments reaching a height of nearly 5,000 ft (1,500 m) interspersed with valleys and riverbeds in the more thinly populated east. Kongo's prosperity was in part derived from the diversity of these regions, which yielded different resources and sustained a variety of craft production. It also sat at a crossroads of longer-distance trade routes that extended beyond the kingdom. An efficient system of agricultural production combined with tribute extracted from the provinces brought under its control by military expansion made it a wealthy land.[14]

Kinship groups called *makanda* (sing. *kanda*) and powerful ritual specialists concerned with the fertility of the land called *itomi* (sing. *kitomi*) animated Kongo's interwoven political and spiritual economies.[15] *Itomi* held spiritual, but also at times secular, power over a particular territory through their relationship with the *nkita*, the spirits attached to that land. *Makanda* are best understood as 'clans', whose members claimed descent from Lukeni lua Nimi and formed the aristocracy of the kingdom, the population of which was otherwise made up of free citizens of lower status and enslaved men and women.[16] Political power ultimately belonged to the king, who bestowed it on provincial rulers chosen from the *makanda* or on favoured clients based in clusters of population called *mbanza*, or towns. The local ruling elites of the *mbanza* benefited from the productive labour of surrounding rural dwellers, who were organized in kinship groups and inhabited small villages or *mabata*. Aside from the payment of taxes imposed by the centre and collected by the village leader, the *nkuluntu*, this rural population lived largely outside of the purview of the *mbanza*.

The land was also inhabited by ancestors, who, having departed from the known world to another realm, maintained intimate connections with their living descendants. A specific site in Mbanza Kongo known as the *ambiro* was where the presence of royal ancestors took concrete form. Material objects, including wooden figures called *iteke* (sing. *kiteke*) that Kongo and European written sources would describe as 'idols' or 'fetishes', and constructions described as 'temples' allowed people to interact with ancestral and nature spirits. Ritual specialists known as *inganga* (sing. *nganga*) possessed the training and knowledge to access and, to some extent, control and harness this range of spiritual forces, for example by ensnaring them in a *kiteke* or other kind of vessel.[17] An important category of such 'power objects' were *minkisi* (sing. *nkisi*). The word *nkisi* is acknowledged to be difficult to translate, as it included the idea of transcendent spiritual force as well as a wide range of ritual procedures and the material objects used in them. The most widely recognized form in Europe and North America among the many types of west Central African power objects is the *nkisi nkondi*, a type first documented in the late eighteenth century in regions peripheral to the core of the historical kingdom. A *nkisi nkondi* was typically an anthropomorphic wooden figure studded with assemblages of potent materials and ritually activated by having iron nails or blades driven into it by the *nganga*. In the late nineteenth and early twentieth centuries, the *nkisi nkondi* served as an instrument of resistance against European colonial conquest. As a result, many were forcibly seized and removed to Europe, where they served as objects of study in ethnological displays and learned societies, before being re-categorized as 'art'. Many remain in Western galleries and museums today. Such *minkisi*, MacGaffey has explained, organized social order and political power. In line with his analysis of the spiritual basis of political authority, he argues that, as elsewhere in Central Africa, 'to belong to the "kingdom", [rulers] acquired a title in exchange for tribute, and equipped oneself with appropriate power objects'.[18] Indeed, the extraordinary – and dangerous – nature of kingship and other political office can be equated with that of spiritual force: 'once initiated, the chief himself becomes a sort of human *n'kisi*'.[19]

An understanding of these fundamental political and cultural traits has emerged through close consideration of written documents, material objects and oral narratives, but are only imperfectly connected to Kongo's history before 1500. Testimonies dating from the moment of transition to the Christian period in the early sixteenth century, ethnographic information from people living in the twentieth and twenty-first centuries, and objects and images created in the aftermath of conversion afford only partial access to this deeper past. Perhaps the most eloquent traces of pre-1500 Kongo are therefore to be found in the role they played as the foundation on which King Afonso built the new Christian order. Afonso's recasting of the kingdom's political and spiritual structures served at the outset to legitimate his rule, and it would anchor the claims to legitimacy of the rulers that followed him in later centuries. It would also set the kingdom on a course unparalleled by any of its contemporaries in West Africa: that of a cosmopolitan realm intimately involved in the political, commercial and religious networks linking Africa, Europe and the Americas in a new interconnected Atlantic world.

KONGO IN THE CHRISTIAN ERA

Beginning in the era of João Nzinga a Nkuwu and Afonso Mvemba a Nzinga, and continuing over the next four centuries, the ruling elite of Kongo adopted and adapted a wide range of ideas, objects and practices – as well as considering and rejecting others – brought to the kingdom by its involvement in the networks of the Atlantic world. Established cultural forms mixed with these new elements to create a distinctive and enduring Kongo Christian culture. The kingdom was transformed on its own terms – or at least on those of its rulers – into a cosmopolitan realm anchored in Central Africa but engaged in dynamic dialogue with Europe and the Americas.[20]

If life and thought in the Kongo before 1500 only emerges in fragments and echoes, there is a wealth of sources for the kingdom's Christian era. Historians have made much use of the valuable written accounts by both Africans and Europeans. Recent research has focused too on the rich range of visual sources and Kongo material cultures. Between 1650 and 1750, for example, Capuchin and Franciscan friars active in Kongo and in Angola to the south painted a series of vivid watercolours portraying local peoples and customs. The friars hoped that these would serve as didactic tools for the training in Italy of future missionaries, ridding novices of their misconceptions and prejudices about Africa.[21] The paintings bring seventeenth- and eighteenth-century Central Africa dramatically to life. When approached critically, they enhance the established written and oral archives, conveying many of the complexities and ambiguities of a kingdom grappling with rapid and often tumultuous transformation.

Strikingly pictured, for instance, are enduring forms of political ceremony and regalia that emerged during the reign of Afonso. In one watercolour, made by the friar Bernardino Ignazio, a ceremonial dance features elite Kongo men dressed both as African warriors and as Christian knights, reenacting the transformation of the kingdom from heathen to Christian and affirming the legitimacy of its ruler (see pl. XII). The dance looks back to the ancestral figure of Afonso and his adoption of Christianity as an alternative source of royal legitimacy to that bestowed by indigenous spiritual forces. To the sound of drums, ivory horns and marimbas, Kongo warriors leap and wave their swords at the foot of a cross before a church, staging a mock battle that evokes Afonso's triumph on the battlefield. At their head, a local ruler kneels in front of a friar to receive his blessing. He wears distinctive Central African markers of status: a shoulder net, an *mpu* cap and a leg wrapper (likely made of prestigious fabric imported from overseas), together with a red cape embroidered with the emblem of the Catholic knights of the Order of Christ given by the Mwene Kongo to his vassals. He is, that is, a Kongo Christian aristocrat, whose insignia and pious demeanour embody the creative combinations and reinventions that underlay the kingdom's early modern culture.[22]

The friar has place of honour in the image, reflecting the importance of ordained Christian clergy in the circuits of Kongo political power. But it is the figure standing next to him, wrapped in a luminous white cloth, who had the most crucial sociopolitical and spiritual role in the proceedings. He belonged to the institution known in Portuguese as the *mestres da igreja* or 'masters of the Church'. These were members of the most elite circles of the kingdom, who, as children, received a literate education in Portuguese and Latin as well as training in church teachings, either from clerics or, more often, from older generations of *mestres*.[23] In part because of the obstacles Portugal put against it, a local ordained African clergy never emerged in Kongo.[24] The organization of the Church and the transmission of its rites and teachings remained firmly in the hands of the *mestres*, who taught children catechism, maintained churches, led prayers and assisted European missionaries in their evangelistic endeavours – including ensuring a respect for local Christian practices. They were, that is, the backbone of the Kongo Church, to whom the missionaries had to defer, and their position brought them considerable social status and financial gain. Tellingly, the *mestres* often appear in images from early modern Central Africa, standing next to visiting missionaries and holding a cane with a cross, wearing rosaries and with a white cloth draped over one shoulder. The Kongo Church emerged in the early sixteenth century through the efforts of Kongo-supported Portuguese secular clergy and would subsequently be bolstered by periodic missions by orders like the Capuchins and Jesuits – but it was largely thanks to the local *mestres* that the Catholic faith endured into the nineteenth century.[25]

In Bernardino Ignazio's watercolour, the ruler kneels in front of the friar and the *mestre*, but his gesture of respect is also directed to the church, cross and image of the Virgin behind them. Since the

time of Afonso, Christian churches outfitted with liturgical para-
phernalia and paintings imported from the workshops of Lisbon
and other parts of Europe were erected across Kongo. The imported
images were installed alongside textiles and objects crafted in established Central African styles. Raffia textiles with complex geometric
motifs cut into their pile, exquisitely carved ivories, stamped terra-
cottas and decorative metalwork all enhanced sacred interiors, creating similar combinations of texture, colour and design to those
displayed in royal palaces and deployed in courtly rituals.[26]

The dazzling display of motifs and hues in the local and imported
textiles, and in the metalwork, ivory and carvings by Kongo artists
that made up lay and religious ceremonial life in the kingdom,
appears in an illustration from Olfert Dapper's 1668 *Description of
Africa*.[27] This image, perhaps derived from drawings made by Dutch
artist Abraham Willaerts during his stay in Central Africa around
1641, takes us to an enclosed plaza prepared to host the ceremonies

The throne of the king of Kongo, from Olfert Dapper,
Naukeurige Beschrijvinge der Afrikaensche Gewesten (Amsterdam, 1668).

and rituals for the coronation of the Mwene Kongo Garcia II.[28] A European-style throne bearing the Kongo royal coat of arms sits on an elevated platform covered with a large carpet. Before the empty throne is a cushion holding the royal regalia: a gilded crown sent by the Pope as a gift, three bracelets – referring to the *malunga* armlet that symbolized the infinite fortitude of the kingdom and its monarch – and a bag holding a Papal bull. [29] Dignitaries with their distinctive tall hats and splendidly dressed in flowing lengths of textile and fashionable European leather boots stand to the left. Musicians and dancers to the right complete this tableau of the multisensory spectacle of Kongo ceremonial life.

In addition to images made by Europeans, locally crafted objects eloquently reflect the spiritual and political environment of the Christian kingdom. Copper-alloy (or brass) crucifixes called *nkangi kiditu*

LEFT A brass pendant of St Anthony of Padua, 16th to 19th century. Height 4 in. (10.2 cm). RIGHT A brass crucifix, possibly 18th century. Height 10¾ in. (27.3 cm). Both created by unknown Kongo artists.

(meaning 'Christ the Protector') displayed in houses, churches or about the body of the elite expressed the correlation between the narrative of the death and resurrection of Christ and Central African understandings of a cyclical passage between life and death. Figures of saints worn as pendants or displayed as statues mirrored, in their draped outfits and the crosses they bore, the appearance of Kongo Christian aristocrats, reinforcing the connections between Christianity, prestige and power. Crucifixes were also insignia of local political might and continued to be so into the twentieth century, when rulers of regions once part of the kingdom maintained them as the symbol of their authority. Churches, steeples and monumental crosses also rose over the compounds and plazas of the central places of the kingdom, first among which was the capital of Mbanza Kongo, also known by the end of the sixteenth century as São Salvador. By then, Mbanza Kongo's cathedral, some of its other churches and houses used by foreigners were built in stone and mortar or with white-plastered straw walls in the European manner, complementing established architectural technologies based on the use of wood and fibre. Despite being destroyed and rebuilt a number of times over the turbulent history of the kingdom, parts of the cathedral still stand in Mbanza Kongo in present-day northern Angola. In 2017, the site of the ancient capital was named a UNESCO World Heritage Site. 'More than anywhere in sub-Saharan Africa', the UNESCO website notes, the remains of Mbanza Kongo illustrate 'the profound changes caused by the introduction of Christianity'.[30]

The contrast between churches and the low-built compound houses was not merely a matter of height. Church façades and bell towers faced outwards towards open plazas and other public spaces, while traditional buildings faced inwards, surrounded by a series of fences that hid them from the outside. Only after passing through what European observers described as a labyrinthine set of corridors and doorways did visitors come face-to-face with the spectacle of houses constructed of interwoven planks of various hues and delicate designs. The intricate geometric patterns of houses and fences were

Chief Makosso-Tati with his *nkangi kiditu*,
photographed in Yenga, Angola, 1940–50.

designed to be in visual dialogue with similarly decorated textiles,
ivories and metalwork displayed, worn and held by the Kongo elite.
As suggested in the illustration from Dapper and attested in archaeological findings, luxury imports, such as textiles and ceramics from
Asia, Europe and the Americas, played an important role in creating
this rich visual assemblage.[31]

Kongo's cosmopolitan visual culture testifies to its connectivity
with the broader Atlantic world. Since the first contact with Portuguese
mariners in the 1480s, its monarchs sought to advance their political
agendas by dispatching ambassadors, writing letters and sending
gifts to Europe, in turn receiving envoys, missionaries, luxury goods
and new forms of knowledge. The result of these exchanges was the
recognition by the papacy and other European courts of Kongo's
status as an independent Christian kingdom. The game of diplomacy,
however, was a dangerous one. By the early seventeenth century,

Kongo had built an alliance with the Dutch against the Portuguese, who since 1575 were based at the kingdom's southern frontier in the colonial city of Luanda.[32] Dutch West India Company attacks forced a Portuguese retreat from the southern Atlantic for a few decades: the company occupied the northeastern provinces of Brazil in the 1630s and in 1641 seized Luanda. By the late 1640s, however, the Portuguese had fought back, retaking Luanda in 1648 and then ejecting the Dutch from Brazil in the 1650s. Portuguese-Brazilian forces and their African allies from the region of Angola then applied sustained military pressure on the kingdom until they inflicted a devastating defeat on Kongo at the Battle of Mbwila in 1665. Dozens of prominent Kongo leaders were killed, including the Mwene Kongo António I, whose decapitated head was taken back in triumph to Luanda, where it is said to have been deposited in the wall of the Church of Our Lady of Nazareth. This catastrophe was to mark another watershed in the history of the kingdom.

THE IMPACT OF THE ATLANTIC SLAVE TRADE

Diplomatic exchanges and Christian missions brought prized luxury goods to the Kongo region. Most exotic imports, however, came to the kingdom through its involvement in the Atlantic slave trade. As early as the 1520s, Kongo was exporting two to three thousand captives each year, most of whom were destined for harsh servitude on the sugar plantations created by the Portuguese on the island of São Tomé off the coast of Africa to the north. In 1526, Afonso wrote a series of letters to João III in Lisbon, explaining the deepening social crisis caused by the traffic. The king did not object to the institution of slavery per se. Rather, he was alarmed by the enslavement and trafficking of people who according to Kongo law were freeborn and had the right to remain so. Local and foreign slave traders, 'thieves and men of bad conscience', he wrote, were every day 'taking our natives, sons of the land and sons of our noblemen

and our vassals and our relatives'.[33] Afonso's objections to the trade
and his recognition of its destructive impact, however, came too late:
although he succeeded in confining slave exports to foreign captives
and those of his own subjects convicted of serious criminal offences,
the implacable wheels of Atlantic commerce were in motion.

The slave trade would continue to play a role in shaping the history of Kongo in the following centuries. As elsewhere on the west
coast of Africa, enslaved captives became the kingdom's main export
commodity, whose sale would become entangled with other key
factors in its history: relations with neighbouring states and with
European maritime powers, and the inability of the elective succession system to ensure peaceful transitions of royal power. The trafficking of enslaved people would increase in periods of political
instability, particularly during the civil war that engulfed the kingdom
in the second half of the seventeenth century. Participation in Atlantic
commerce may have provided the local elite with new forms of wealth,
material goods and insignia of authority, but these came at a high
cost, as they were obtained in exchange for men, women and children
captured not just from beyond the kingdom's frontiers but – despite
Afonso's efforts – from within Kongo itself.

The increasing encroachment of the trade in enslaved people had
complex and at times contradictory consequences for the Kongo
social order and the sovereignty of its king. Leading African mid-
dlemen not only derived great wealth from the trade, but also power:
the European firearms and militarized systems constructed to kidnap
and transport captives could also be mobilized to achieve political
ambitions. Whether established members of the local aristocracy or
ambitious upstarts, the merchandise they received in exchange for
captives was used to maintain or to forge political prominence and
legitimacy. Insignia, such as civet pelts or luxury foreign textiles,
which rulers once obtained through diplomatic channels, became
part of the package of goods that European slavers used to purchase
their human cargo.[34] In the first century and a half of Kongo's
embrace of Atlantic commerce, the slave trade at times threatened

but did not seriously undermine the stability of the monarchy. By the mid-seventeenth century, however, the accumulation of wealth and power by provincial rulers, in particular the self-styled princes of the coastal province of Soyo, led to rising claims of independence from the Mwene Kongo. These claims, combined with dynastic instability caused by recurring succession disputes at the centre, resulted in the outbreak of a prolonged period of civil war in the aftermath of the defeat at the hands of the Portuguese in 1665. By the early eighteenth century, the partially recentralized Kongo crown was able to reimpose a degree of control over the slave trade, while the surviving nobility that owned enslaved people benefited from the labour of the servile population absorbed into the local economy.[35] A century later, new forms of authority emerged around figures from outside the traditional ruling elite. These figures, in turn, sought to accumulate manpower, wealth and influence from the nineteenth-century Atlantic slave trade and would again pose a challenge to the kingdom's social and political order.[36]

THE FATE OF THE STATE

The history of Kongo in the era defined by its entanglement with the broader Atlantic world was a tumultuous one. Periods of political and social stability were followed by recurring outbreaks of instability and conflict. The long and effective reigns of Afonso (r. 1506–1542) and Garcia II (r. 1641–1660) bracketed a century and a half often considered to be the golden age of the kingdom. Even within this era, however, there were times of civil unrest and foreign invasion, notably the incursion in 1568 of the warlike 'Jaga' from outside of the kingdom's frontiers, which resulted in the destruction of Mbanza Kongo/São Salvador.[37] The alliance with the Dutch held much promise, but then came defeat by the resurgent Portuguese and the sustained violence and fragmentation of the civil wars. Political turbulence unfolded against a backdrop of ecological crisis, as recurring droughts combined with insecurity to cause food shortages and hardship. All of this led to a profound popular questioning of the political and spiritual order forged by Afonso. It is against this backdrop that the prophetic Antonian sect led by Beatriz Kimpa Vita emerged in the early 1700s. An elite woman raised in the Kongo Christian Church, Kimpa Vita declared herself to be an incarnation of St Anthony who sought to heal the social wounds inflicted by the civil wars. Every Friday, she explained, she died, returning to life on Sundays after having consulted God and the saints about the ailments of the world and their remedies. Attracting a large popular following, Kimpa Vita's anti-European teachings and rituals appeared for a while to offer an alternative to the Kongo Christian orthodoxy. Eventually, however, conservative forces prevailed and in 1706 she was burned at the stake as a heretic, along with her newborn baby. A more orthodox reading of Catholicism – one wedded to established political hierarchy – can be seen to have won out against the popular synthesis of Christian and indigenous belief. Paradoxically, however, the deep roots of Kongo Christianity can be measured by the role it played in movements such as Antonianism or in initiation associations, such as *kimpasi*.[38]

While the Kongo kings had initially found in Christianity a powerful ideological glue against centrifugal forces, clan politics also gained prominence from the late seventeenth century.[39] A degree of stability returned in 1709 with the restoration of a centralized monarchy based on an agreement to rotate the succession between the different royal lineages or *makanda*. The restored monarchs successfully reaffirmed their connection to Afonso and the sacred character of Christian kingship extolled during his reign. Yet the nature of their sovereignty had changed. Although the king exercised a symbolic power over the outlying provinces, he could not control them in real terms. Rather, the court at Mbanza Kongo sought to extend ideological legitimacy to the provincial rulers, whose authority in turn depended upon upholding the symbolic structure of the kingdom.[40] From the mid-eighteenth century, 'entrepreneurial nobles' began to transform the political landscape, creating new *makanda* by claiming territory and gathering a mixture of free and unfree populations under their authority. This change in political ideology would shape later oral traditions, which were increasingly structured around the histories of specific clans.[41] Some historians have written of the kingdom's 'decline', although others, as MacGaffey points out, argue that 'it had reverted to something like the structure it had had in 1480, when the Mwene Kongo was *primus inter pares* in a collection of rival principalities or 'districts', and government was more a matter of ritual affiliation than of administration'.[42]

KONGO IN THE AMERICAS

Despite increasing limitations to royal power within the frontiers of the realm, the aura of the Mwene Kongo transcended frontiers not only in Central Africa, but also in the wider Atlantic world beyond. Men and women of Central African origin or descent drew upon the idea of Kongo kingship to carve a degree of independent social space in the slave societies of the Americas. The Catholic Church played a central role in this regard, offering a setting familiar to enslaved Kongolese, to those more distantly acquainted with the Christian kingdom, and to their descendants. Close to half of all Africans transported to the Americas during the course of the Atlantic slave trade came from Kongo, Angola and elsewhere in Central Africa. As early as the opening decades of the sixteenth century, enslaved Central Africans were creating associations in the orbit of the Church in Portugal and Spain, a practice that subsequently emerged in the colonies of the Americas. These Catholic fraternities in Brazil and elsewhere elected a king – and sometimes a queen – of 'Congo', together with a court of office-holders whose titles seemingly mimicked those of their European oppressors but in fact looked back to those of Mbanza Kongo. The memory of Afonso and of the annual ritual re-enactment of his famous victory against his heathen enemies animated similar mock battles staged in enslaved and free African diasporic communities of the Americas.[43]

An image from the late eighteenth century depicts the pageantry surrounding a king and queen of Congo elected by the African population, both enslaved and liberated, in slavery-era Brazil (see pl. XI). Wearing a crown, coat, cape and leg wrapper, the king walks solemnly in procession under a crimson umbrella. We can recognize the fine clothing, animated poses and musical instrumentation – here an Iberian-style guitar is added to the African marimba – from the image painted on the other side of the Atlantic just a few decades earlier. The depiction of this Afro-Brazilian ceremony points to the reach of the idea of Kongo kingship across space and time in the Black Atlantic. From Brazil to Cuba, Haiti and even to Albany in New York, people in the diaspora forged a social world that drew in part on memories of Central Africa.[44] As 'subjects of the King of Congo', enslaved Africans found the means to endure servitude and, as has been documented in Haiti, to rise up against slavery in the age of revolution that would sweep across the Atlantic world.[45] In the twenty-first century, men and women across the Americas continue to make a social, spiritual and artistic home for themselves through the pageantry of Kongo kingship and the ritual power that underpinned it.[46]

KONGO IN THE NINETEENTH
AND TWENTIETH CENTURIES

The alternating system established in 1709, by which competing royal *makanda* shared the Kongo crown, fell apart in the 1770s. From then into the first half of the nineteenth century, a succession of kings no longer associated with the dynastic lineage of Afonso took up the throne. They nonetheless continued to draw from the symbolic toolbox of sixteenth-century Christian kingship to affirm their sovereignty in the face of an increasing threat from the Portuguese colony of Angola to the south. Internal instability also resulted from the increasing ability of low-level nobles to carve out domains within the kingdom, and of non-aristocratic merchants to create new *makanda* based on commercial wealth.[47] Meanwhile, the powerful and wealthy coastal province of Soyo continued to drift further from Kongo's grasp and to extend its reach north of the Congo River. Although the kingdom's domains were much reduced, it continued to function as a structure of governance and Mbanza Kongo remained a vital spiritual and cultural centre.[48] Kongo's long experience with international trade, diplomacy and Christianity put its elite in a strong position to negotiate the mid-nineteenth-century transition from an economy based on the slave trade to one based on the export of the so-called legitimate commodities of ivory and rubber.

In 1859, King Pedro V (r. 1859–1891) secured the throne of Kongo by allying himself with the Portuguese, just as some of his predecessors had done before him. Pedro saw himself as a successor of Afonso and imprinted his own correspondence with a wax seal bearing the kingdom's sixteenth-century coat of arms.[49] As part of the negotiations, however, Pedro signed an act of vassalage – and his subsequent letters would also bear the insignia of the Portuguese empire.[50] This 1860 treaty began the Kongo's long incorporation into Portuguese Angola – a process that Portugal would pursue with new resolve from 1885 following the Berlin Conference, which stipulated that European powers had to demonstrate 'effective occupation' of a territory to claim it as a possession. The rubber boom and the development of new cash crops also finally made the occupation financially viable for the Portuguese, who exercised their control over the region through the crown at Mbanza Kongo. By the early twentieth century, Portugal had achieved a goal it had sought for many centuries: the integration of the Kongo heartland into colonial Angola. Closer to the Congo River, meanwhile, the northern provinces of the kingdom became part of Leopold II's Congo Free State (from 1908, the Belgian Congo).

As elsewhere in Africa, colonial conquest did not mean cultural or political annihilation. Its sovereignty as an independent kingdom may have been terminated and its domains partitioned, but the Kongo region survived European rule and its peoples continue today to maintain an identity that draws on memories of a glorious past. Indeed, it has been argued that it was in the twentieth century that Kongo became a distinct group identity, defined around a nationalist conception of the Kikongo language and situated in the politics of managing colonial rule.[51] This was particularly the case in the Belgian Congo. As anti-colonial nationalist movements belatedly emerged in the 1950s, the Association des Bakongo (ABAKO), a cultural organization that became a political party, called on all the heirs of Kongo dia Ntotila – another name for Mbanza Kongo, now across the border in Angola – to join forces.[52] ABAKO members strongly associated themselves with the historical kingdom and even referred to the movement's leader Joseph Kasavubu as their 'king'. Popular mobilization against Belgian rule first emerged in the

A dramatic photograph captures Ambroise Boimbo snatching the sword of King Baudouin of Belgium on 29 June 1960.

Kikongo-speaking region of Bas-Congo adjacent to the colonial capital of Léopoldville, and in 1960 Kasavubu, sharing power with Patrice Lumumba as prime minister, would become the first president of the newly independent Congo.

But it is in a more modest capacity that one of the heirs of the Kongo kingdom made modern history. On 29 June 1960, King Baudouin of Belgium was driven through the streets of Léopoldville (now Kinshasa) on his way to the ceremony that would inaugurate the independence of the Congo. En route, one Ambroise Boimbo, a member of ABAKO, seized the opportunity to perform a transition of power of another kind.[53] In an iconic gesture, Boimbo leapt from the crowd and snatched Baudouin's sword. The weapon in hand, he twirled and jumped into the air, seemingly in a performance of the martial dance staged by his ancestors to claim legitimacy and assert power. Boimbo's dramatic act of *lèse-majesté* has generally left commentators perplexed. Seen from the perspective of the *longue durée* of Kongo's history, however, the meaning of his gesture is perhaps less obscure. Like the great Christian king Afonso, Ambroise Boimbo made Kongo history anew by appropriating an exotic emblem of power and transforming it into a potent local symbol. By doing so, he made independence Congo's own.

N

SOUTH SUDAN

THE
DEMOCRATIC
REPUBLIC
OF CONGO

River

Nile

Lake Kyoga

Lake Albert

BUNYORO

UGANDA

BUSOGA

KENYA

TOORO

Kampala

BUGANDA

Lake
Edward

Lake
George

NKORE

Lake Victoria–
Nyanza

KARAGWE

Lake
Kivu

RWANDA

RWANDA

BUHAYA

BURUNDI

BURUNDI

TANZANIA

Lake
Tanganyika

0   100   200 kilometres
0   50   100 miles

**BUGANDA AND
THE GREAT LAKES REGION**

– – – – –   Present-day international frontier

CHAPTER 6

BUGANDA

John Parker

Buganda is the archetypal East African kingdom. Located on the northwestern shore of Lake Victoria-Nyanza in present-day Uganda, it is one of the few great kingdoms in the continent to have given its name to an existing nation of which it is part. Indeed, Buganda's position within twentieth-century Uganda – first the British colony and then, since its independence in 1962, the modern country – has been central to an understanding of its history. That history extends deep into the past: the centralized state probably began to take shape from around 1600 CE, but its roots can be traced to social and economic developments that unfolded for many centuries before that. Yet it was Buganda's acquisition as the prize possession in Britain's emerging East African empire in the 1890s that created the conditions for a remarkable flowering of research into the kingdom and production of knowledge about its past. As elsewhere in colonial-era Africa, much of this scholarship was produced by Europeans, for whom the existence of a powerful and sophisticated kingdom in a bucolic land at the heart of the continent provoked intense interest. The most notable contributions, however, came from African scholars, in particular the Ganda politician and Christian modernizer Apolo Kaggwa (1869–1927), who, in the opening decades of the twentieth century, published a sequence of books in the Luganda language on the history and culture of his people. The most famous is *Basekabaka be Buganda* (The Kings of Buganda), a dynastic chronicle which first appeared in 1901, but Kaggwa's work also included studies of Ganda customs, *Mpiza za Baganda* (1905), and of clans, *Bika bya Baganda* (1912). These inspired similar intellectual projects in the neighbouring kingdoms of Uganda, particularly Buganda's historical rival Bunyoro, as well as in other Bantu-speaking kingdoms of the Great Lakes region, such as Belgian-ruled Rwanda and Burundi. The oral traditions recorded in this pioneering local scholarship would in turn be mobilized as evidence for the long history of kingship and effective state-building by a new generation of professional scholars from the 1960s. As Jean-Pierre Chrétien writes in his authoritative survey of its history, the region, and Buganda in particular, 'became and remained a site for theoretical debates on African political systems'.[1]

This chapter is about the history of Buganda, but it is also about the ways in which that history has been perceived, interpreted and contested – by outside observers and by the Ganda people themselves.[2] Far from remaining theoretical, debates about the nature of the political system of Buganda and the other kingdoms of the region have had a profound and sometimes devastating impact on its more recent history. The Great Lakes region at the equatorial heart of the continent may have appeared bucolic to colonizing Europeans – Winston Churchill famously described Uganda as 'the pearl of Africa' – but its descent into extreme violence from the 1970s was in part a result of political conflict rooted in distorted perceptions of the past. The brutal military dictatorship of Idi Amin in the 1970s and the civil war of the early 1980s plunged Uganda into turmoil, but worse was to follow when recurrent conflict between Hutu and Tutsi groups in neighbouring Rwanda escalated in 1994 into the genocidal killing of an estimated 800,000 people. This conflict then spilled over into the eastern part of what is now the Democratic Republic of the Congo, where ongoing violence has resulted in an even greater loss of life. Debates about historical political systems – over the nature of power; over who 'belongs' and who does not – have therefore been of enormous consequence. The role of violence in Buganda's history has played an important part in these debates: was the kingdom an impressively governed and orderly bureaucratic state, or was it in essence an aggressively militarized, predatory despotism? Either way, the study of Buganda's past has in many ways dominated that of the broader region – although Rwanda too has attracted considerable attention, mainly from scholars writing in French. Indeed, in a recent analysis, Richard Reid has set out to 'de-centre' Uganda's history from its established focus on the great kingdom.[3] In order to begin to understand that history, let us turn to Buganda's location in the lakeside environment and to how its explosive nineteenth-century encounter with the world beyond shaped the production of knowledge about its past.

BUGANDA IN THE GREAT LAKES

Buganda was one of a great many kingdoms forged over time by Bantu-speaking peoples in the region that by the middle of the nineteenth century became known to the outside world as the Great Lakes. This geographical designation was a European one, coined by Victorian-era explorers striving to fill in the 'blank spaces' on maps of the interior of Africa and to locate the source of the River Nile. That most of the lakes were named after members of the British royal family speaks volumes about the lasting imprint of the encounter between African societies and European imperialism in the region. Lakes Albert, George, Edward, Kivu and Tanganyika run north–south in an 800-mile (1,300-km) chain along Africa's Rift Valley, today forming the frontier between the Democratic Republic of the Congo to the west and Uganda, Rwanda, Burundi and Tanzania to the east. To their east lies the vast Lake Victoria or, to add the name given to it in the Kiswahili language of the East African coast, Victoria-Nyanza. Local societies, of course, had their own names for the lakes: the Nyoro and Tooro people, for example, called Lake Edward Mwitanzige ('locust killer') and the Ganda called Lake Victoria Nnalubaale (the 'mother of *lubaale*', spirits or gods). As the English explorer John

Hanning Speke would learn on his visit to Buganda in 1862, the Nile does indeed flow north from Victoria-Nyanza, into Lake Kyoga and then curling into Lake Edward before heading north on its long journey to the Mediterranean through South Sudan, Sudan and Egypt. It was in the relatively high-altitude, well-watered and fertile zone between the lakes that language communities ancestral to those speaking the region's various Bantu languages gradually took shape over the first millennium CE.

It was its perceived isolation from the outside world that drew Speke and other Victorian explorers to Buganda and contributed to the somewhat mystical aura that hung over the kingdom in early European accounts. It is certainly the case that the states and societies of the region were among the last to be drawn into the networks of long-distance trade that were extending across Africa: small amounts of exotic goods, such as cloth and tableware, began to arrive in the late eighteenth century, but it was not until the 1840s and 1850s that the first caravans of Arab and Swahili traders from Zanzibar and elsewhere on the east coast reached Buganda. Yet the

Kabaka Mutesa receives the British explorers Speke and Grant in 1862, from John Hanning Speke, *Journey of the Discovery of the Source of the Nile* (Edinburgh, 1863).

region had been an important cultural crossroads for thousands of years, a zone of interaction where the movement from the west of peoples speaking ancestral Bantu languages crossed that of those speaking Nilotic languages from the north. Its complex topography and rainfall patterns also gave rise to a wide variation in local ecologies, which, in contrast to West Africa, resulted in the interspersal of pastoralism and agriculture. It would be these two farming systems, together with the use of iron and, for those communities located along the lakeshores, fishing that would provide the basis for increasing social complexity and, in time, state-building. For the drier zones in the north and west of the region, cattle-keeping was the main economic activity. Agriculture predominated on the well-watered shores of Victoria-Nyanza, where one food crop would come to dominate all others: the banana. If, as historians have argued, distinctive 'pastoralist ideologies' that associated cattle-keeping with political authority emerged in some areas, then the humble banana was the material foundation on which Ganda society was built.[4] It was a foundation, moreover, with a distinctly gendered form: Buganda's banana gardens were exclusively the responsibility of women, whose labour has been seen to have enabled men to focus on other tasks: 'fishing, exchange and war'.[5]

'Isolation' may well be in the eye of the beholder, but Buganda's belated encounter with agents of the outside world certainly impacted on the study of its past in one crucial respect: a complete absence of written records before 1862. In contrast with the Sudanic zone of West Africa, where accounts of Arab geographers and travellers date back to the ninth century and the Timbuktu Chronicle tradition to the seventeenth century, historians of this region are more dependent upon alternative sources of evidence: archaeology, comparative ethnography, oral traditions and historical linguistics. Unfortunately, archaeological evidence too is limited, having been degraded by the humid environment of the lakeshore. As in the Bantu-speaking region of equatorial Central Africa to the west, however, linguistic evidence has proven to be fruitful in efforts to understand the deep past. The

Engraving of the capital of Buganda, with banana groves visible behind the fence
neatly lining the main thoroughfare to the royal palace, from H. M. Stanley,
Though the Dark Continent (London, 1878).

methodology is complex and contested, but, in short, the chronology
of language change can be estimated by comparing the range of different words used for the same things or concepts in the various
branches of the Bantu language family. Let us take as an example the
point about cattle and bananas. 'Cattle had been part of the legacy
of Great Lakes food systems from very early on', David Schoenbrun
explains, 'and the span of time between the development of a breed-
ing taxonomy and a color taxonomy is fully two millennia'. Following
its arrival from Southeast Asia, in contrast, the vocabulary associated
with the banana developed much faster, 'with no more than 600 years
separating the innovation of the first varietals from the development
of generics and plantation terms'.[6] Yet these different rates of language change harmonized around the years 1000 to 1200 CE, with
the sudden explosion of different words to describe the colour of
cows and for the varieties, cultivation and preparation of bananas.
The 'language archive' indicates that specialized pastoralism and
intensive banana farming were taking shape. Rhiannon Stephens

has recently applied this methodology to explore the history of motherhood among speakers of the North Nyanza branch of Bantu, the ancestral speech community of the Ganda and their Soga neighbours across the Nile to the east. Ideologies of motherhood and other forms of gender identity, like the growing of bananas, would have an important impact on the history of Buganda.[7]

Yet the perceptions of outsiders mattered. Speke and other visitors to the court of the *kabaka* or king of Buganda, Mutesa (r. *c.* 1856–1884), were suitably impressed by the efficient governance and good order of the kingdom – exemplified for many by the broad, straight and carefully maintained roads that radiated out from the royal capital and connected the palaces within it. Mutesa and his *nnamasole* or 'queen mother', Muganzirwaza, occupied separate palace complexes atop adjacent hills and the broad avenue connecting them was the capital's most important thoroughfare – a vivid indication of the gendered balance of political power. Such positive assessment was tempered, however, by alarm at Mutesa's volatile temperament and the frequent outbursts of coercive violence in the shape of large-scale executions, cruel mutilations and random killings. As in the West African kingdom of Asante, nineteenth-century European visitors had trouble reconciling these apparent contradictions, although the general conclusion was that the Ganda were a strikingly gifted people and their kingdom a model of good – if despotic – governance. After visiting Mutesa in 1875, the Welsh-born American newspaperman Henry Morton Stanley – whose career as an explorer of Africa was also characterized by outbursts of murderous violence – issued an urgent call for missionaries to administer the gospel to what he regarded as a sophisticated people ripe for the benefits of Christian modernity. By the end of the decade, both Catholic and Protestant organizations had responded to this call and the rapid embrace of Christianity, particularly among young men attached to the royal court, only served to reinforce the special status of Buganda in the eyes of Europeans. Violence and a collapse into civil war would follow. When that political disorder subsided in the late 1890s,

however, it was the Protestant faction of literate Christian modern-
izers who emerged, in alliance with British imperial forces, in control
of the kingdom. That faction of so-called *basomi* or 'readers' would
also seek to assert its control over Buganda's past: one of its leaders
was the kingdom's *katikkiro* or 'prime minister', Apolo Kaggwa.

THE KINGS OF BUGANDA

Buganda's written history effectively began with Apolo Kaggwa.
First published as *Ekitabo kya Bakabaka be Buganda* (The Book of
the Kings of Buganda) in London in 1901, his major work subsequently appeared in a second edition as *Basekabaka be Buganda* (The
Former [or perhaps better, 'Exalted'] Kings of Buganda) in 1912 and
in a third edition with '*na be Bunyoro, na be Koki, na be Toro, na be
Nkole*' ('and of Bunyoro, and of Koki, and of Toro, and of Nkole')
added to the title in 1927. In 1971 – the year that Idi Amin's military
coup brought an end to the opening phase of Uganda's postcolonial
history – it appeared in an annotated English translation by
M. S. M. Kiwanuka as the first volume in a series of 'Historical Texts
of Eastern and Central Africa'. Kiwanuka's own history of Buganda,
for which *Basekabaka* was the most important single source, appeared
the same year.[8] Kaggwa's was far from the only work on the history
and culture of the kingdom by Ganda scholars in the early colonial
period: much other material appeared in its aftermath, often in missionary publications like the Catholic Church's journal *Munno*, established in 1910.[9] Neither was he the first to record in writing the
dynastic history of Buganda in the form of a list of the kingdom's
rulers: starting with Speke in 1862 and Stanley in 1875, five such king
lists had appeared by the time Kaggwa began collecting oral traditions in the 1890s. Yet his body of work was the most authoritative
and influential: 'by the 1950s', Christopher Wrigley observed, 'there
were copies of Kaggwa's book in most villages, and it would have
been hard for an outsider to go behind or beyond it'.[10] Except for

the Bible, *Basekabaka* was certainly the most read book in Buganda and its author became one of colonial Africa's most famous intellectuals and 'cultural brokers', of a stature comparable to that in Nigeria of the pioneering Yoruba historian Rev. Samuel Johnson. Much of the subsequent vernacular-language scholarship on neighbouring kingdoms as well as later writing on Buganda by professional historians has, in one way or another, been an attempt to respond to his foundational work.

Kaggwa's scholarship has a fascinating intellectual genesis and political context. The great-grandson of a leading provincial chief of the Grasshopper clan, he was one of the ambitious young 'pages' at the court of *kabaka* Mutesa drawn to missionary teaching and the literacy it offered. Emerging in the late 1880s as the leader of the victorious Protestant or 'English' faction in the tumultuous four-way struggle between Protestant, Catholic, Muslim and traditionalist political rivals, he was appointed *katikkiro* and in 1900 was the leading local negotiator and signatory of the so-called Uganda Agreement, which established the terms for British colonial rule. These terms were highly favourable to Buganda – or at least to what would become its land-owning elite – and it can be argued that Kaggwa's reconstruction of an ancient and glorious dynastic history was a key part of his project to secure for the kingdom as best a deal as possible within the new colonial order. Kaggwa was also prompted to begin his collection of historical traditions by his close collaborator Rev. John Roscoe, an Anglican missionary who produced a parallel body of ethnographic writing on Ganda society. Roscoe was a disciple of the doyen of early British anthropology, Sir James Frazer, whose ideas on the nature of 'divine kingship' in the classical world, Africa and elsewhere – including material derived from Kaggwa and Roscoe – were set out in his famous compendium *The Golden Bough* (which began to appear in 1911–15). In contrast to Egyptian pharaohs, *kabakas* were not divine kings or gods incarnate. Neither did the Ganda practise the ritual regicide that lay at the heart of Frazer's theories, which would soon fall out of favour in anthropological circles. Like

many kings in Africa and beyond, however, they did embody important sacred attributes: forms of ideological or so-called creative power,
which were entangled with the 'instrumental' power derived from
coercive force. 'The Kabaka of Buganda was not only a bureaucratic
and political instrument in the evolution of centralized polities',
Benjamin Ray argues, 'but also an ideological creation, the embodi-
ment of a symbol, expressed most significantly in the royal myths
and rituals recorded by Kaggwa and Roscoe'.[11]

The evidence suggests that the ideology of kingship in the Great
Lakes region began to take shape long before the forging of centralized polities. Kaggwa identified thirty remembered *kabakas*, beginning with Kintu, the first man to be sent down to earth by God, and
ending with Mutesa, who we know from other evidence to have taken
power around 1856. Aside from noting the arrival of Speke in 1862,
however, he was unable to provide any dates before 1867. That was
the year that Mutesa, influenced by Muslim Arab and Swahili traders, first kept the fast during the Islamic month of Ramadan, which
enabled Kaggwa to date the events of the remainder of his reign by
subsequent fasts ('At the end of his seventh Ramadhan, Mutesa went
to Kabojja to build a capital ...').[12] Deeper chronology would come
later: on the basis of the traditions associated with each *kabaka* collected by Kaggwa, Kiwanuka determined that the dynastic genealogy
spanned nineteen generations, which at an average of thirty years
per generation enabled him to estimate the regnal dates down to the
appearance of Kintu in the early fourteenth century. Further evidence
has enabled some of these dates to be modified, although there is a
growing consensus among historians that only those from the mid-
seventeenth century, at the earliest, should be considered reliable.
It was during the reign of the powerful *kabaka* Ssekamaanya (whose
regnal dates Kaggwa gives as 1584–1614) that Wrigley identifies 'a
profound change in the nature of kingship'. 'Here', he writes, 'we
do seem to be approaching the threshold of history' – meaning history in the Western sense, based on written records and defined ideas
of cause and effect.[13] In his study of the Nyiginya kingdom of Rwanda,

Jan Vansina is even more cautious, declining to offer any firm dates before the accession of King Mimambwe Sentabyo in 1796 – which can be identified by a concurrent eclipse. Rejecting the chronology suggested by the Rwandan court scholar Alexis Kagame in his *Inganji Kalinga* (1943–47), Vansina argues that the kingdom, in line with others of the Great Lakes region, 'was probably founded around 1650, almost six centuries after the 1091 date proposed by Kagame'.[14]

Before then, historical time shades into mythological time. This is not to say that myths of origin should be dismissed as simply 'made up'. Rather, it is to argue that they require close and critical analysis; only then can they yield the profound and often contested meanings embedded within them. As Ray demonstrates, it is precisely in myths and rituals that the ideological essence of Ganda kingship resides. To record these traditions in the 1890s, Kaggwa turned to the elderly guardians of the so-called royal jawbone shrines, where the disarticulated jawbones and preserved umbilical cords of each *kabaka* were kept as mnemonics – memory devices – for their reigns.[15] Later scholars looked too to the elaborate ceremonies associated with the installation of the *kabaka*, during which, Ray writes, the kingship was 'reconstituted through a series of rites in which the new king and chiefs enacted the founding deeds of the early kings'. These ritual performances therefore also acted as key mnemonic devices; indeed, 'Ganda accounts of the founding of the kingship are based almost entirely on the installation rites'.[16] That may be so, but historical linguistics provides further important evidence for the emergence in deep time of ideas of royal authority. As early as the middle of the first millennium, Schoenbrun has shown, speakers of West Nyanza Bantu (from which North Nyanza and then Luganda would evolve) developed two key suffix nouns related to hereditary power: *-kama* or 'king' and *-langira* or 'hereditary royal'. The word *-kama* was derived from an earlier verb meaning 'to milk' or 'to squeeze', while *-langira* came from a verb meaning 'to report', 'to announce' or 'to prophesize'. Thus, the latter can be seen to describe sacred or 'creative' power, while the former more closely represents 'instrumental' power

– although whether the symbol of a king as a milker of cows should be taken to mean his role as a provider of sustenance to his people or his ability to squeeze wealth from them is a matter of interpretation. Given the ambivalence with which historical kings were regarded by their own people, it may be that it means both.[17]

That the Ganda royal line should begin with Kintu, the primordial first man, is unsurprising. A typical wandering 'stranger king' – a heroic figure who arrives from another realm bringing a more advanced sense of cultural order – Kintu was said by Kaggwa to have founded the kingdom following his defeat of Bemba the Snake, an established despotic ruler whose python-like attributes are suggestive of a time when human culture was only partially removed from an anarchic and threatening nature. Like Kagame's dynastic genealogy of Rwanda extending back to 1091, it can also be read as an expression of Buganda's later status as a dominant regional power: in his analysis of the tension between kingship and clans in Ganda history, Neil Kodesh suggests that the story of Kintu and Bemba may have been incorporated into the dynastic narrative only in the eighteenth century, as part of a strengthening of royal authority.[18] It would accumulate yet another layer of interpretation in the mid-nineteenth century. On being told of his arrival as a conquering hero, Muslim traders readily associated Kintu with the biblical (and Quranic) figure of Ham, the son of Noah sent into exile for looking upon his father's nakedness and held to be the progenitor of the African race. Ham would also lend his name to the Hamitic Hypothesis, the pernicious Eurocentric notion that any degree of sophistication in African society must have been due to the influence of a superior lighter-skinned 'race' from the north, Ethiopia perhaps, or Egypt. First developed with regards to Buganda by Speke following his visit in 1862, this racist fantasy would continue to influence European thinking about East Africa throughout the colonial era – including, catastrophically, in Rwanda and Burundi, where Belgian rulers perceived and treated Tutsi aristocrats as a superior 'Nilo-Hamitic' ruling elite.

Yet Buganda was neither the first nor, initially, the most powerful kingdom in the region. To the north lay an older state, Kitara, said to have been ruled by a dynasty known as the Chwezi (or Bacwezi) and to have established an extensive, if loosely articulated, imperial influence over a wide area of grasslands. The Chwezi would subsequently 'disappear', swept aside by a new dynasty founded by another conquering stranger king named Rukidi. Rukidi's appearance from the north is suggestive of the gradual southward movement of Nilotic-speaking Luo peoples along the Nile and, indeed, his new Bito dynasty is remembered in oral tradition as arising from a Luo 'conquest' of established Bantu-speaking communities. Archaeological and linguistic evidence suggests that these processes might be dated to the fifteenth or sixteenth centuries. The nature of Kitara is complicated, however, by the reappearance of the Chwezi as an influential spirit cult, which continues to exist in the Great Lakes today. Were the Chwezi a dynasty of kings who were deified as ancestral spirits, or a family of spirits who in oral traditions were reconstituted as founding kings? Historians differ on this point.[19] Either way, it was from the Bito dynasty that a new kingdom would emerge by around 1600: Bunyoro.

Bunyoro is Buganda's 'significant other', and vice versa: bitter rivals for regional dominance, whose military expansionism tended to come at the other's expense and whose mutual antipathy would extend into the twentieth century. In response to Kaggwa's work and the Ganda ruling elite's deal with the British, from the 1920s Nyoro writers – including the *mukama* or king himself – would construct the kingdom's own increasingly elaborated dynastic history. This project culminated in court historian John Nyakatura's *Ky'Abakama ba Bunyoro-Kitara* (1947), 'The Kings of Bunyoro-Kitara', which, as the title suggests, sought to establish the kingdom as the inheritor of the legacy of the ancient empire of Kitara and the deified Chwezi.[20] According to Nyakatura, the third remembered *kabaka*, Kimera, was Rukidi's younger twin brother, sent to rule over what was then the small vassal kingdom of Buganda. Be that as it may, Bunyoro was certainly the more dominant kingdom until the dramatic expansion of Ganda power in the eighteenth century. 'Buganda was on the receiving end of some devastating attacks', Reid writes, 'and had to learn quickly – perhaps by emulating the Nyoro themselves – in order to even survive as an autonomous political unit'.[21]

CLANS AND KINGS

It will be apparent by now that the dynastic king lists and associated oral traditions of the Great Lakes kingdoms are complex and often contested historical texts. The recording of royal traditions by pioneering local scholars, such as Kaggwa, Kagame and Nyakatura, has provided later generations of historians with an extensive body of rich source material, but it is one that has clearly been shaped by past political circumstance and reshaped by the twentieth-century collision with colonial rule and the forging of 'a newly literate world'.[22] The density and complexity of Buganda's oral and written archive has also opened the history of the kingdom to an interesting range of interpretations, as scholars have sought to move beyond the state-centred frame of 'dynastic time' as set out by Kaggwa and then Kiwanuka. Let us now consider the broad historical development of Buganda from its emergence as a centralized state in the seventeenth century to its encounter with the disruptive forces of the world beyond in the 1850s. What can be said about the changing nature of kingship and its relationship with Ganda society in those two hundred years?

There is general agreement among historians that at the heart of Buganda's history lies a tension between clans and kings. The institution of kingship, most would argue, represented a rupture from an older form of social organization and belonging based on membership of kinship groups called *bika* or 'clans'. Despite his avowedly royalist perspective, Kaggwa recognized this by turning his attention in the years after the Uganda Agreement of 1900 to clans, publishing *Bika bya Baganda* in 1912. Each of the forty or more *bika* was named after its unique animal or vegetable emblem and membership tended to be dispersed across the Ganda region, although each had a recognized home territory with lands or *bataka* managed by office-holding 'chiefs' and secured by the burial of its dead within those boundaries. *Ensi engula mirambo*, a well-known maxim, ran: 'land is acquired (or 'humanized') through tombs'.[23] Far from being an archaic institution overtaken by the rise of centralized state authority, moreover, clanship continued to play a crucial role in governance. Powerful *bataka* chiefs occupied designated offices at the royal capital: one important example was the office of *mugema*, held by the head of the Vervet Monkey clan and of the province of Busiro, which contained the graves of deceased kings. Responsible for the installation of the *kabaka*, it was the *mugema* who placed a bark cloth and calf skin on his shoulders with the words, 'I am your father, you are my child. Through all the ages, from your ancestor Kimera, I am your father'.[24] The authority of the *bika* was also asserted through the office of queen mother or *nnamasole*. Because the royal family itself had no clan and stood above the *bika*, the *nnamasole* was the most powerful 'commoner' in the kingdom and tended to come from one of a select group of leading clans – the influence of which she would further bolster. That both clan leaders and women exercised a degree of constitutional authority is an important step in an emerging understanding that Ganda political power was somewhat more 'diffuse' than has hitherto been thought. As Stephens points out, the title of *kabaka* embraced three offices: the *kabaka* himself, the *nnamasole* and the *lubuga* or 'queen sister'.[25]

The expansion of the kingdom can therefore be viewed as a two-pronged process: territorial enlargement, mostly by military means and generally at the expense of neighbouring Bunyoro and Busoga; and the enlargement of royal authority over clans, shrines, healing centres and other institutions of Ganda society. Tellingly, at his installation in 1884, Mutesa's successor Mwanga was instructed by the *mugema* to 'fight your enemies and conquer Buganda'.[26] The oral traditions associated with the reigns of successive *kabakas* have allowed historians to identify crucial moments in this twin political project. For Wrigley, an early indication of an increase in royal power was the killing by *kabaka* Ssekamaanya (meaning 'the Violent') of Nankere, a chief responsible for the rite of *okukulu kwa kabaka*, 'the growing up of the king'. Required to give up a son to be stabbed to death by Ssekamaanya's designated successor, Nankere incurred the king's wrath by refusing to do so and offering instead a bullock for ritual slaughter. For this he paid with his life. If this episode did indeed occur as the 'historical horizon' was beginning to come into view in the early seventeenth century, it demonstrates, Wrigley argues, that 'the old rituals were losing their power and those who conducted them were no longer sacrosanct'.[27] It is an indication, too, of the crucial role of ritual violence in making the king a sort of 'sacred monster', unburdened by the rules governing ordinary people: the *okukulu* rites would continue to be the final act in a *kabaka*'s installation into the nineteenth century. We will return to this in more detail below.

At this point, Buganda was still a tiny kingdom or 'micro-state' centred on its Busiro heartland, 15 miles (24 km) northwest of present-day Kampala. It was in the second half of the seventeenth century, under the leadership of *kabakas* Kateregga (r. c. 1640–c. 1670) and Mutebi (r. c. 1670–c. 1700), that its militarized territorial enlargement began. Valuable cattle-grazing lands were acquired and defeated local clan leaders were replaced by royal appointees, often the generals who led the campaigns. A further period of military expansion took place under *kabaka* Mawanda (r. c. 1730–c. 1760), which carried the frontier of the kingdom eastwards to the Nile. Of equal significance was the creation under Mawanda and his successor Namugala (r. c. 1760–c. 1790) of a new class of chiefs, the *batongole*, appointed by the king and answering directly to him. Known as the 'king's men', the *batongole* have been seen by some historians to represent the beginning of the more bureaucratic form of government that so impressed nineteenth-century European observers. As with the West African kingdom of Asante in the same period, however, Buganda looks less like a bureaucratic state than it does a 'patrimonial' one; that is, with an administration staffed by aristocratic appointees. 'The core of social organization was military', John Iliffe writes, and 'territorial conquest was changing a clan society into a militarized state with patrimonial offices'.[28]

Namugala is also notable for instituting the elaborate royal installation rites at Buddo in southern Busiro, which all subsequent kings would undergo and which would be observed and recorded by Kaggwa and other scholars. The new ceremony has been seen to represent a key development in the historical tug of war between Ganda clanship and kingship, shifting the focus of installation from the clan estate at Bakka Hill to the north – the site of the older *okukulu kwa kabaka* – to the royal domain of Buddo Hill. There, with the heads of the nearby Civet Cat, Frog, Colobus Monkey and Mushroom clans now excluded, the rites were focused on a symbolic 'battle of the reeds' re-enacting Kintu's defeat of Bemba, the veneration of the mortal remains of the diviner Buddo, who had facilitated Namugala's rise to power, and the final investiture of the *kabaka* and *lubuga* on an anthill seen to be the seat of the spirit or *lubaale*, Kibuuka. In a recent reinterpretation, however, Kodesh reads the evidence somewhat differently. It was as part of these new installation rites, he suggests, that Kintu was transformed in the dynastic narrative into the first *kabaka* and Kibuuka into a great 'national' war god. Rather than being a strategy to marginalize existing forms of ritual and clan power, the rites sought 'to direct the authority embedded in public healing networks toward the support of an increasingly ambitious royal center'.[29] From a perspective 'beyond the royal gaze', Kodesh concludes, priests, spirit mediums, healers and clan leaders remained crucial to Ganda society, all serving to shape local identities in ways that were often more profound than those achieved by centralized state power.

VIOLENCE

The use of violence has been a crucial tool of state-building in every part of the world, Africa included. Whether real or threatened, or whether directed militarily at outside enemies or by the state at its 'own' people, coercive force has throughout history been central to an understanding of political power. In a recent and wide-ranging dissection of the idea of kingship, the historical anthropologists David Graeber and Marshall Sahlins propose that a fundamental definition of sovereignty – 'that which makes one a sovereign' – would be 'the right to carry out arbitrary violence with impunity'.[30] Graeber and Sahlins's discussion of what kingship is and how it functions goes far beyond violence; indeed, it makes a compelling case for a critical re-engagement with older anthropological ideas of the essentially sacred nature of kings in Africa and elsewhere. In line with many scholars of Africa who have begun to downplay the historical role of coercive or 'instrumental' power relative to non-coercive or 'creative' power, they argue that the importance of warfare in forging and governing states may well have been exaggerated, including in indigenous oral traditions: 'some of what passes for "conquest" in tradition or the scholarly literature consists of usurpation of the previous regime rather than violence against the native population'.[31] Yet violence, both real and symbolic, remains crucial to any understanding of the history of the Great Lakes region. Buganda was far from the only highly militarized and aggressively expansionist kingdom to take shape from the seventeenth century: neighbouring Rwanda was another, and in West Africa such authoritarian 'fiscal-military' states also took shape in the increasingly violent era of the Atlantic slave trade. It has, however, been perceived – by others but, more importantly, also by itself – as distinctively violent; a state where the sovereignty of its kings rested squarely on an ability 'to fight your enemies and conquer Buganda'.

The danger here for the historian is of mistakenly being 'led by the sources', whether oral traditions, which exalt military prowess and the awesome power of the *kabaka*, or accounts of nineteenth-century European visitors, which do the same, with an added racialized twist of African 'savagery'. Recent efforts to shift the history of Buganda away from the perspective of its royal court and to stress instead more diffuse forms of authority that resided in broader society have been useful in qualifying the image of the kingdom as being a militarized predator. Holly Hanson's book on the mutual obligations that bound Ganda state and society is one example, opening with the arresting sentence: 'When people in Buganda thought about power, they spoke about love'. Ceremonial exchange and intense expressions of affection were central to the Ganda practice of power, Hanson argues. Yet, 'the vocabulary of love in governance accommodated ruthless violence, as nineteenth-century subjects knelt down to thank the king for the privilege of being stripped of their chiefships' or for 'being sentenced to death on the king's whim'.[32] Historical change is important here, too, as there is every indication that the culture of violence and predation in Buganda had reached a peak by the mid-nineteenth century, when it became entangled with Mutesa's volatile personality. Hanson argues that an older, gentler tradition of mutual obligation within communities was overlaid by the expansion of centralized state power. Whereas others have regarded the creation of the *batongole* chiefs as marking the beginnings of a modernizing bureaucratic regime, she interprets it more negatively: as a partial unravelling of the bonds of mutual obligation.

Neither was it just Nyoro and Soga enemies or supposed Ganda malefactors who found themselves on the receiving end of punitive state violence. The royal family itself appears to have been riven by murderous and often patricidal rivalry. Kaggwa's chronicle reveals that of the eight or nine *kabakas* who ruled in the eighteenth century, no fewer than seven were murdered by princely usurpers. Namugala's reforms can be seen as an attempt to restore stability after a particularly tumultuous sequence of regicides, and he himself succeeded in avoiding assassination – but only by abdicating in favour of his brother Kyabaggu, whom he feared was plotting against him. Kyabaggu was in turn to die at the hand of his son, around 1790. 'The increased power of the monarchy appears to have created an unstable situation', Ray comments, with some understatement.[33] This situation was finally taken in hand by *kabaka* Ssemakookiro (r. c. 1800–1812), 'probably the ablest and most ruthless of all Buganda's rulers', whose actions marked 'a decisive moment in the consolidation of the state'.[34] Ssemakookiro's solution was the systematic liquidation of all the royal princes except for his designated successor and one or two other favoured sons. This practice would be repeated at those points in the cycle of succession when the number of princes and other potential rival claimants had again built up to dangerous levels: following his succession around 1830, *kabaka* Ssuuna had sixty of his brothers killed to protect his grown-up sons. Buganda appears to have found a solution to a problem that plagued many kingdoms in Africa: bitterly contested and violently disruptive royal succession. Indeed, of the five principal nineteenth-century *kabakas*, all died of ostensibly natural causes. Stability, however, had come at a great cost in royal lives: the ruling family, Wrigley reflects, 'had made singularly poor use of the biological advantage conferred by unlimited access to the most beautiful and fertile women both of Buganda and of neighbouring countries'. 'Or perhaps it could be said that it had sacrificed its genetic interests to the good of the kingdom.'[35] For Ray, Ssemakookiro's brutal cull enabled the nineteenth-century *kabakas* to become 'a law unto themselves and turned Buganda into an ordered despotism'.[36]

It was this 'ordered despotism' that in turn impressed and appalled Speke and other European visitors to Mutesa's court in the 1860s and 1870s. Buganda may have reached its territorial apogee under Kamaanya (r. c. 1812–1830), the last of its great warrior kings, but the militarization of political culture continued under his successor Ssuuna (r. c. 1830–1856) and then Mutesa.[37] Vansina identifies a similar trajectory in Rwanda, culminating in an 'unrelenting rise of a tide of terror', which spread from the royal court to engulf the kingdom in the reign of Mutesa's contemporary, Rwabugiri (r. 1867–1895).[38] The power of kingship in the Great Lakes region, it appears, had reached its height, symbolized by the possession of great dynastic war drums: *mujaguzo* in Buganda, *bagendanwa* in Nkore or *kalinga* in Rwanda (which gave Alexis Kagame the title of his royal chronicle, *Inganji Kalinga*, 'Triumphant Kalinga'). Like the pounding dynastic drums that called the kingdom to war (see pl. XIV), royal violence had both a practical and a symbolic role. It was not only an expression of the king's authority; it was what *made* him a king. The *kabaka*, Ray writes, 'was likened to the queen termite that … devoured the termites of her colony, to the blacksmith's forge that melts iron in order to mold it, and to a hammer that crushes what it hits'.[39] This awesome and at times arbitrary power over life and death, moreover, appears not only to have been tolerated, but also applauded by ordinary people as only fitting for 'their' king. As Wrigley alludes to in his reflection on the wasted reproductive capacity of royal wives, power was also projected by the accumulation of increasingly ostentatious numbers of women – including enslaved female war captives redistributed to chiefs as part of the ideology of mutual obligation. Indeed, by the nineteenth century, the capture of women may have been becoming an increasingly important aspect of organized violence.[40] 'The Europeans who arrived in the 1860s saw, above all, aristocracies in power', Chrétien writes. What escaped them 'was how this institution ultimately took root in the popular imagination. The abuses of the powerful were revealed, but not the motives for why people supported them.'[41]

Despite the impressive accumulation of coercive power, however, the *kabakas* never fully succeeded in freeing themselves from the underlying skeins of authority that resided in clans, shrines and the sacred realm – if that was indeed their goal. Ssemakookiro's ruthless reform of the system of succession may have ended the alarming sequence of regicides, but the point that the nineteenth-century *kabakas* all died of 'natural' causes rather than being killed by their own sons needs some qualification. According to Kaggwa, Ssemakookiro died of an illness sent by the ghost of a prominent healer whom he had murdered. His successor Kamaanya was also killed by a ghost, that of his murdered son Nakibinge, acting in concert with the *lubaale* Mukasa, the god of Lake Victoria-Nyanza. Then Ssuuna, after declaring himself to be a *lubaale* on earth, was struck down by lightning sent by the *lubaale* Kiwanuka. He survived – although would die of smallpox allegedly caused by his refusal to take the advice of the priest of Mukasa's fellow *lubaale*, Nnede. Finally, Mutesa died in 1884 after a prolonged venereal infection, said to have been the result either of the ghostly vengeance of a murdered wife or because he confiscated the office of *mugema* from the Vervet Monkey clan. The *kabakas*, the oral traditions therefore suggest, still answered for their actions to the great *lubaale* and paid for the crime of hubris and for overreaching their authority with their own lives.[42]

NINETEENTH-CENTURY ENCOUNTERS

Buganda's encounter with the world beyond the Great Lakes region was a tumultuous one. It began with the arrival in 1844 of a group of Arab and/or Swahili traders from the island of Zanzibar, the headquarters of the Sultan of Oman's domains on the east coast of Africa. The Omanis had been insinuating themselves for some decades into the coastal Swahili city-states and the long-distance trade routes that extended from them into the interior, seeking to tap into the growing demand for two lucrative export commodities: enslaved captives and ivory. The result was widespread disruption and violence, as new sources of mercantile wealth and the firearms it could purchase offered ambitious warlords a route to political power. The expansion of slave-raiding, moreover, led to escalating predation and insecurity. As Iliffe writes, 'changes occupying centuries in western Africa were compressed into decades in the east'.[43] The established concentration of centralized power at first insulated

Buganda from such disruption. Indeed, the main commodities offered for sale by the coastal traders, cloth and firearms, were readily embraced by the royal court and aristocratic elite. Following his accession around 1856, Mutesa was also drawn to another innovative resource carried by the Zanzibari trading caravans: Islam. Motivated in part by the ongoing tension between royal power and the clan-based authority of the *lubaale*, the *kabaka* actively encouraged his court officials and pages to read the Quran and to practise Islam. By the late 1860s he had ordered the construction of a mosque in his capital, encouraged the wearing of imported cloth instead of the traditional bark cloth and, as we have seen, began himself to observe Muslim prayers and Ramadan fasts. Mutesa also staged a dramatic intervention into royal funerary practices by disinterring the remains of up to ten of his predecessors from their tombs in Busiro, reuniting their skeletons with the removed jawbones and reinterring them in a new mausoleum under his control; it was as part of this process that he launched his attack on the Vervet Monkey clan's control of the office of *mugema*. There is every indication that the *kabaka* was mobilizing Islam as a new weapon in the project of consolidating dynastic power.

In 1876, however, Mutesa deviated from this path, executing some seventy Muslim converts, who had dared to defy him on matters of Islamic principle, and stepping back from his own public profession of the faith. By the end of the decade, the religious landscape became yet more complicated with the arrival of Anglican evangelists of the Church Missionary Society and then Catholic White Fathers. Both missionary organizations soon began to attract converts, principally from the ranks of the young *bagalagala* or 'pages' who staffed the lower echelons of the royal court. Mutesa remained aloof from Christianity, although hoped that his European connections might prove valuable in countering a renewed threat from the old enemy, Bunyoro. Bunyoro too had been drawn into the expanding tentacles of long-distance trade – not, initially, from the east coast but from the north, in the form of Turco-Egyptian merchants and slave raiders who had pushed down the Nile from Khartoum into present-day South Sudan. For *mukama* Kabalega of Bunyoro (r. *c.* 1870–1899), this encounter offered one thing of great importance: guns. Briefly, Kabalega enjoyed great success, using his new weaponry to reassert control over his own chiefs and going on the offensive against Buganda in the 1870s and 1880s. While Buganda collapsed into civil war in the late 1880s, Bunyoro reasserted its ancient status as the leading regional power. 'In terms of political consolidation', Iliffe writes, 'Bunyoro was East Africa's chief beneficiary from nineteenth-century trade'.[44]

Mutesa died in 1884, his mortal remains interred, intact, in a new royal mausoleum at Kasubi, as he had specified. In the years that followed, things fell apart. Succeeding his father at about the age of eighteen, *kabaka* Mwanga had neither the experience nor the character to manage the escalating tensions generated by a combination of rapid social change and external threat. In 1886, anxious about the ambitions of the Christian *busomi* or 'readers', Mwanga followed established royal precedent by staging a large-scale display of punitive violence, executing some forty of them. He then sought to coopt and unite the emerging factions of Protestant, Catholic and Muslim converts by dragooning them into regiments of gunmen and deploying them against increasingly recalcitrant clan chiefs. Instead, they turned on the *kabaka*, overthrowing him in 1888. The three groups then began fighting among themselves and against a fourth, 'traditionalist' religious faction, which continued to revere the *lubaale*. As elsewhere in the continent, the effort on the part of the kingdom's rulers to contain the forces unleashed by rapid social change and to 'rearm' the state in the face of escalating external threat was ineffective. Yet from the chaos of the late 1880s and early 1890s would emerge a new kind of Ganda leadership: a literate modernizing elite, willing and able – with British assistance – to seize the moment and take the kingdom forward into the twentieth century.

The second half of the nineteenth century is the most intensively studied period in Buganda's history. The question remains, however,

An early 20th-century photograph of the Kasubi royal mausoleum in Kampala.

whether the sequence of events culminating in the imposition of British rule in 1894 is best seen as resulting from long-gestating internal processes or the sudden, devastating impact of external pressures. Like most historiographical issues, there is no definitive answer to this question, although as more becomes known about the deeper past of the kingdom, the more historians have been able to trace lines of continuity across time. This shift in emphasis has also been encouraged by a disinclination to privilege colonial conquest as the key watershed in Africa's long history. As Hanson points out, the upheaval of the 1880s and 1890s has been seen by Ganda observers and later historians alike 'as a "religious revolution" in which modernizing Ganda Christians and Muslims toppled paganism and then fought each other to make Buganda Catholic, Protestant, or Muslim'. Yet these sectarian identities were only one dimension of the conflict, she argues; it was also 'a Ganda expression of the collapse of social institutions that affected all of eastern Africa as a consequence of the trade in ivory and slaves'.[45] This is not quite right: Rwanda strictly excluded trade caravans from the coast, but also experienced dramatic social transformation and political violence in the late nineteenth century, generated by an intensifying contest between aristocratic lineages and dynastic rule, and resulting in a deepening divide between the Hutu and Tutsi social categories.[46] Might Buganda's crisis too have been a new manifestation of a longer contest between the historical project of kingship and the broader society over which it sought to impose itself? If so, it was a contest that would continue to take new forms in the twentieth century.

BUGANDA INTO UGANDA

Buganda's subjugation by the British impacted in different ways on the kingdom and its people. Its history as a sovereign state was over and the once awesome power of the *kabaka* was extinguished: in 1897, the British deposed the rebellious Mwanga for the last time and replaced him with his infant son Daudi Cwa, who ruled as a figure-head, initially with Kaggwa and two other leading Christian power brokers as regents, until his death in 1939 (see pl. XIII). For many ordinary Ganda, the opening decades of colonial rule were a time of great stress, one of increasingly heavy labour demands, social disruption and recurring epidemics of sleeping sickness. The entire Great Lakes region, Chrétien writes, underwent 'a true ecological and demographic crisis between 1890 and 1930'.[47] Yet for those 'readers' and progressive chiefs who at the turn of the century stepped forward as the legitimate inheritors of the kingdom, colonial overrule held much promise. The terms of that overrule were set out in 1900 in the Uganda Agreement – the incoming British adopting the Kiswahili name for the kingdom and for the larger colony of which it became a part. Within Buganda, the agreement enabled the privatization of land, turning estates that had previously been managed by office-holders into the inheritable personal property of the chief who happened to be holding office at the time. The result was the emergence of a male land-owning elite, which then turned itself into a class of capitalist cotton-growers. Beyond its frontiers, the neighbouring kingdoms of Bunyoro, Nkore, Tooro and Busoga were subjected to a progressive

'Gandaization' of their political systems. This was particularly galling for the Nyoro, the heirs of the ancient Kitara kingdom. The disputed frontier zone between the two kingdoms – which contained the Nyoro royal tombs associated with the Chwezi cult and therefore a key link to its past – was handed to Buganda. The loss of these counties rankled for many decades and would provoke the creative effort to reconstruct Bunyoro's dynastic history. After a brief Nyoro resurgence under *mukama* Kabalega, Buganda had reasserted itself with British assistance as the dominant regional power.

Meanwhile, colonial-era ethnographic scholarship stressed the rational, 'bureaucratic' element in Ganda governance: the idea of the *batongole* as 'the king's men'.[48] As European colonial rule entered its terminal phase in the years after the Second World War, however, Buganda's status as the core of Uganda was called into question. The prospect of being submerged in an independent Uganda divided Ganda society and rising political agitation prompted the British in 1953 temporarily to deport *kabaka* Edward Mutesa II (r. 1939–1966). Just as he was being reconstituted as a constitutional monarch, the king emerged as the symbol of a reinvigorated Ganda political identity. In the run-up to independence in 1962, royalists formed the Kabaka Yekka party, 'The King Alone', which campaigned to separate the kingdom from Uganda. That was not to happen, and in 1966 Mutesa II was again sent into exile, this time by the postcolonial government of Milton Obote. The following year, Buganda and the other kingdoms were formally abolished. They would remain so until 1993, when all except Nkore were once again restored and their kings constitutionally designated as 'cultural leaders' by the National Liberation Movement regime of President Yoweri Museveni.

The ideology of kingship in Buganda and elsewhere in the Great Lakes region, therefore, has endured. The colonial and then the postcolonial state may have stripped away its coercive capabilities, but the result is that present-day kings may well bear some resemblance to those of ancient times: not militarized predators but 'architects of consensus', concerned above all with community well-being.

Indeed, the return of kingship to Uganda in 1993–95 created what Chrétien describes as a 'restoration fever', which swept through not only the historic kingdoms but also, despite some initial popular resistance, through regions without monarchical traditions. In Nyoro, this was accompanied by renewed public veneration of the ancient Chwezi spirits; here and elsewhere, Chrétien observes, what above all was revived was 'the honor of the ancient rituals'.[49] The importance of royal rituals and tombs as sites of historical memory and collective identity was again thrown into relief when in 2010 Mutesa's mausoleum at Kasubi was destroyed by fire, an event that provoked widespread anguish in Buganda. As elsewhere in Africa, Buganda's twentieth- and twenty-first-century history has seen a fundamental shift in the historical contest between centralized state power, on the one hand, and more creative and diffuse forms of authority, on the other: in short, the royal dynasty and the kingdom it created has become part of civil society. The precise terms of that contest in the deeper past will continue to occupy Uganda's historians for many years to come.

CHAPTER 7

FROM HAUSA KINGDOMS
TO THE SOKOTO CALIPHATE

Muhammadu Mustapha Gwadabe

With a long history of state-building, urban development and cultural creativity, the Hausa region of West Africa is one of the most populous and well-studied parts of the continent. Occupying the central section of the Sudanic savanna zone between the Niger River to the west and Lake Chad to the east, *kasar Hausa* or 'Hausaland' today is encompassed by northern Nigeria and the southern parts of the Republic of Niger. In that historic heartland and in West Africa beyond, up to 40 million people speak Hausa as their mother tongue, and perhaps another 20 million as a second tongue, making it one of the continent's most important languages.[1] Over the course of the last millennium, what would emerge as *kasar Hausa* experienced a gradual process of political, economic and cultural evolution, resulting in features such as walled cities, a dynamic economy based on agriculture, craft production and trade, and political institutions characterized by powerful kings and sophisticated courtly cultures. The region's city-states developed impressive military capabilities and a cultural ethos of the heroic mounted warrior, which not only shaped conflict between them, but also allowed for further territorial expansion. For a long time, Hausaland was little known to the outside world, forming something of a decentralized frontier between the more powerful kingdoms of Kanem-Borno to the east and Gao to the west. Yet by the sixteenth century, the region had emerged as a key crossroads of trans-Saharan trade routes and those extending

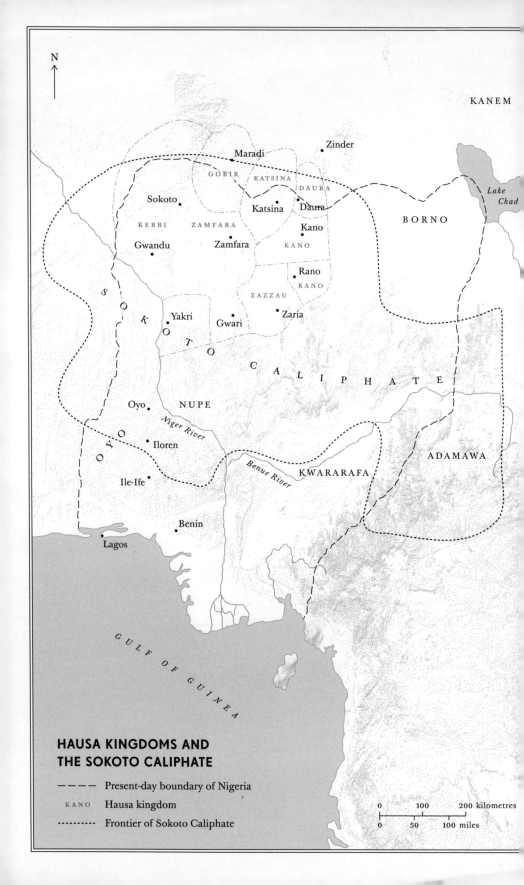

N

KANEM

Zinder

Maradi

GOBIR

KATSINA

DAURA

Sokoto

Katsina

Daura

KEBBI

ZAMFARA

Kano

BORNO

Lake
Chad

Gwandu

Zamfara

KANO

S

O

K

O

Yakri

Gwari

RANO

Rano

ZAZZAU

Zaria

T

O

C

A

L

I

P

H

A

T

E

NUPE

Oyo

Niger River

Iloren

O

Y

O

Benue River

KWARARAFA

ADAMAWA

Ile-Ife

Benin

Lagos

G

U

L

F

O

F

G

U

I

N

E

A

HAUSA KINGDOMS AND
THE SOKOTO CALIPHATE

– – – – Present-day boundary of Nigeria

KANO   Hausa kingdom

· · · · · · Frontier of Sokoto Caliphate

0   100   200 kilometres

0   50   100 miles

across the savanna zone to the south of the desert. The leading Hausa kingdoms, first Katsina, Kano and Zazzau and subsequently Zamfara, Gobir and Kebbi, had begun collectively to forge a distinctive identity and an influence in the wider region. That influence would further be enhanced by the collapse in 1591 of Songhay, which had expanded from its heartland of Gao to become the last of the sequence of great imperial states in the western Sudan (see chapter 2). Despite recurrent military conflict between – and sometimes within – the Hausa kingdoms, the following centuries witnessed ongoing economic prosperity, demographic growth and the deepening influence of Islam.[2]

By the end of the eighteenth century, however, first Gobir and then the other Hausa states faced a growing challenge from a militant Islamic reform movement that sought to purify the faith and, ultimately, to overthrow what it regarded as a decadent and corrupt ruling elite. Led by the charismatic cleric Shaikh 'Uthman ibn Fudi, or, as he is usually known in Hausa, Shehu 'Uthman Dan Fodio (1754–1817), the jihad that erupted in 1804 resulted in the unification of the kingdoms into nineteenth-century Africa's largest and most impressive state, the Sokoto Caliphate. One of the most dramatic events in the continent's modern history, it is also one of the best documented – albeit largely from the perspective of the triumphant reformers. Literate in Arabic, the leadership of the movement were, as one historian has described, 'inveterate writers' and left an extensive body of literature.[3] This included two authoritative histories of the uprising by 'Uthman Dan Fodio's son Muhammad Bello and his brother 'Abdullahi. The emergence and subsequent history of the Sokoto Caliphate has therefore attracted intensive study, notably from generations of Nigerian scholars in the country's leading universities.[4] As a project of state-building, 'Uthman Dan Fodio's movement is also one of the few in African history that sought to overthrow an established system of kingship and replace it with a radically new form of governance. Indeed, as one of its pioneering historians has written, 'the movement is as central to West African history as is, for example, the French Revolution to Europe'.[5] As with that revolution, to understand it we need to explore the deeper past of *kasar Hausa*. This chapter therefore examines the emergence and growth of the Hausa kingdoms and the processes that led to the transformation of their established political structure into a powerful Islamic emirate.

THE FOUNDATION OF THE HAUSA KINGDOMS

Early state-building in what would become the Hausa-speaking region took shape in an ecological zone endowed with extensive tracts of fertile land. This generated agricultural prosperity and provided a place of refuge for waves of immigrants seeking to establish viable communities.[6] 'Hausa origins are a mystery', John Iliffe admits in his history of Africa.[7] The Hausa language belongs to the Chadic branch of the family of Afroasiatic languages spoken across North Africa and the Sahara region, which has prompted speculation that its ancestral speakers may in the deep past have retreated south in the face of desertification. Recent reconsideration of the linguistic evidence, however, has cast doubt on such a definitive north–south movement.[8] Be that as it may, the savanna environment of the central Sudan would enable an emergent ruling class to assert control over a relatively dense population and its agricultural production. The region was also characterized by abundant deposits of iron ore, which made it an important centre of metallurgy in West Africa. These factors laid the foundation for the enlargement of social scale and the establishment of political entities, perhaps as far back as the tenth century CE. Local society does not appear yet to have been known as 'Hausa' – a term that appears in the written record only in the early seventeenth century. Arabic sources point to the emergence of two broad cultural zones: one in the northern part of the region identified by observers from North Africa as 'Habasha' (a term usually associated with Ethiopia, but the origin, perhaps, of the word Hausa) and the other to the south known as 'Mbau'. Settlement appears often to have been focused on granite outcrops like Dala Hill in the city of Kano, identified by archaeologists as an early site of ironworking (see pl. xv). Small polities, in turn, developed around a sacred sovereign or shrine. Indeed, these could be one and the same thing: as Murray Last writes, 'in some cases the "shrine" was not a particular place or object but the sacred person of a particular individual elevated to the kingship'.[9]

Written sources for the region, however, are few and far between, as the initial focus of trans-Saharan trade in the central Sudan was on the kingdom of Gao on the Niger River to the west and the kingdom of Kanem near Lake Chad to the east. In contrast, the exchange networks of the proto-Hausa states appear to have been more localized. As a result, Islam was to make a relatively late impact on the Hausa, who remained little known to medieval North African traders and Arab geographers. Yet oral traditions – many of which were later written down in locally produced Arabic texts – record various versions of the process by which kingdoms took shape in the Mbau region. The most famous of such works and a crucial source for the history of the Hausa region is the so-called *Kano Chronicle*, an anonymous manuscript probably compiled in the late nineteenth century but drawing on oral traditions and written sources dating back to the seventeenth century.[10] The best-known tradition of origin is the story of Bayajidda, which recounts how the eponymous culture hero travelled from Baghdad via Egypt to Kanem and on to the Hausa state of Daura, where he married the queen. Their son Bauwo then had three pairs of sons by three wives, each of which went on to found six of the seven 'true' Hausa kingdoms, the *Hausa Bakwai*: Daura, Kano, Zazzau, Gobir, Katsina and Rano (the identity of the seventh kingdom varies).[11] Bayajidda's origins can be described as a 'historical metaphor', reflecting a widespread desire on the part of Muslims on the frontiers of the *dar al-Islam*, 'the abode of Islam', to connect their communities to the heartland of the faith. His connection to Kanem, moreover, can be read as a prototypical transfer of statecraft from a more established and powerful neighbouring kingdom. Like other myths of origin, Last writes, 'the historical ideas

which must have given it credence to its first audiences are significant'.[12] Likewise, the 'Song of Baugada' – the founding king of Kano
– tells of diverse waves of immigrant groups fleeing famine and
discord to settle in the increasingly prosperous kingdom.

These processes of economic expansion and the development of
kingship are likely to have unfolded gradually between the eleventh
and the fifteenth centuries. The structure of long-distance trade also
shifted, as so-called Juula or Wangara merchants from the domains
of the Mali Empire (in Hausa, 'Wangarawa') extended their far-flung
commercial networks into the Hausa savanna. From the other direction, the region was also brought into closer contact with Kanem
following the relocation of its ruling Saifawa dynasty to Borno,
southwest of Lake Chad, around the fourteenth century. The writings
of the Andalusian-born North African diplomat al-Hasan al-Wazzan
(also known as Leo Africanus) indicate that by the time he visited
the region in the early sixteenth century, the Hausa city-states were
fully fledged kingdoms. By that time, too, Mali had been eclipsed
by the rising power of Songhay, the capital of which at Gao lay on
the frontier of *kasar Hausa*. Although these early Hausa states were
independent from one another, a regional system developed that
linked all of them together, sometimes in economic cooperation but
at other times in conflict. Localized developments within the Hausa
communities interacted with long-distance trade to generate population growth, economic expansion and the emergence of sophisticated
statecraft, all of which drew scholars, merchants and other immigrants
into the region.

The collapse of the Songhay Empire in the aftermath of its defeat
by a Moroccan army that crossed the Sahara in 1591 was a watershed
in the history of West Africa. The end of the 'imperial tradition' in
the western Sudan had important historical ramifications for the
Hausa region to its east. The Moroccan victory at the Battle of Tondibi
was not simply a result of military superiority provided by the firearms carried by its battle-hardened army: it was also due to the
growing weakness of imperial Songhay's administrative machinery.

Songhay military resistance continued until 1595, when its last ruler, Askia Nuh, was killed and his vast domains declared to be a province of Morocco. Yet Morocco's ruler, Sultan al-Mansur, was unable to impose effective authority or to establish order in his West African empire, which led to the rise of regional warlords and recurring violence. The Tuareg of the Sahara, the Fulbe and the Bamana of Segu and the so-called Arma (the remnants of the Moroccan army) fought against each other for control of the region. The great trading and scholarly cities of Timbuktu, Gao and Jenne along the Niger River entered a period of decline. This chaotic situation led to a disruption in economic activity in the western Sudan and in trans-Saharan trade. The established trading system, which sent gold, enslaved people and other commodities northwards across the desert, moreover, began to be diverted southwards to the Atlantic coast, where first the Portuguese and then other European maritime powers established commercial outposts. Despite – or perhaps because of – this dislocation, it was in the seventeenth century that the Hausa states asserted their independence and began to flourish.

The disorder following the collapse of Songhay served to redirect the activities of merchants and scholars eastwards to the relatively peaceful and prosperous Hausa region. The original *Hausa Bakwai* together with the more recently established kingdoms of Zamfara and Kebbi were all independent and at various stages of socio-economic and political development. One thing they had in common was an administrative system called *sarauta*. Celebrated in the *Kano Chronicle*, *sarauta* was essentially a structure of titled office-holders appointed by the king or *sarki(n)* (pl. *sarakana*). As a broader system of governance, however, it can be seen to have included 'the building of walled capital towns like Kano and Katsina, the appointment of titled administrators (often on Bornoan lines), the import of more powerful war-horses, systematic slave-raiding among Niger-Congo speakers to the south, recurrent warfare among the new kingdoms, the adoption of Islam by the ruling class alongside indigenous religious practices, and urban domination of the countryside'.[13] In Kano, this sophisticated structure included the offices of Galadima, the closest advisor or *wazir* of the *sarki*; the Maidawaki, the commander of the cavalry or 'master of the horse'; and the Sarkin Kasuwa, who oversaw the city's great Kurmi central market.[14]

Advances in military technology, on the one hand, and trade in enslaved people and territorial expansion, on the other, were closely connected. As early as the turn of the fifteenth century, John Hunwick writes, 'Kano is said to have acquired mail coats, iron helmets and quilted "armour" (*lifidi* in Hausa from the Arabic *libd*), probably through Borno and ultimately from Egypt'.[15] While captives could be exchanged for more horses, many others were absorbed into local economies as agricultural and urban workers. Trusted enslaved individuals, including eunuchs, could also be appointed under the *sarauta* system as office-holders; the *Kano Chronicle* associates this practice with Kano's powerful *sarki* Muhammad Rumfa (r. 1463–1499), whose 'twelve innovations' were also said to have included the founding of the Kurmi market, the celebration of the festival of Eid al-Fitr at the end of the Ramadan fast and the custom of *kulle*, the seclusion or purdah of women.[16]

As Muhammad Rumfa's name indicates, individual Hausa rulers, or in some cases entire royal families, had also begun to convert to Islam. The kings of the two most powerful and prosperous states, Katsina and Kano, appear to have been the first to do so in the fifteenth century. Islam is recorded as coming both from Borno to the east and from Songhay to the west, carried along the trade routes of the Wangarawa merchant diaspora. Adherence to the new faith on the part of the ruling elite, however, continued to exist alongside indigenous belief and practice, based on the established spirits of the land. The two could also fuse together into a 'syncretic' whole: some of the spirits of the *bori* cult, for example, came to have distinctively Muslim names, demonstrating 'how deeply Islam had taken root in the local society on Hausa terms'.[17] This tendency was condemned by visiting Arab and Berber clerics, notably the jurist Shaikh al-Maghili, from Tlemcen in present-day Algeria. Travelling to Kano during the reign of Muhammad Rumfa, al-Maghili warned the king against letting the 'pagan' Hausa – who would come to be known by the Hausa term *Maguzawa* (i.e. *magi* or 'magicians') – 'contaminate the Muslims through contact with them in the markets and elsewhere'.[18] Yet the slow and uneven expansion of Islam was a key factor in the evolution of the region. Islam offered a new legal system as well as new methods of funding the states through the collection of taxes from subject populations. All of this created a climate that attracted further Islamic scholars and enabled the spread of literacy, the production of books and the development of new administrative skills. These arrivals included Fulbe (or Fulani) clerics, scholarly representatives of an expansive network of pastoralist peoples originally from the region of Senegambia. The Fulbe, as we will see, would play a decisive role in the Islamic reform movement of the eighteenth and nineteenth centuries.

Economic progress and state expansion produced determined rulers who consolidated a virile Hausa political culture. The kingdom of Zazzau (or Zaria) extended its borders as far as the Nupe and Kwararafa kingdoms to the south. Kano too had an effective government and dynamic economy. Yet it was Katsina that most directly benefited from the defeat of Songhay. Due to its location, the kingdom had been connected since the fifteenth century to Agades (in present-day Niger), resulting in the emergence of a large Hausa community in the desert-side city. With the collapse of Songhay, Katsina emerged as the new terminus of the caravan route extending from Tripoli through the Saharan oases of Ghadames and Ghat and on to Agades. Seventeenth-century Katsina was therefore the first of the kingdoms to attract significant numbers of traders and Islamic scholars, emerging as the region's leading commercial and educational centre. The kingdom had already expanded southwards into Yauri during the reign of Aliyu Karya Giwa (r. 1419–1431) and maintained its dominance there until the rise of Kebbi. As a result, Katsina became caught up in the rivalry between Gao, with its remnant of Songhay power, and Kanem-Borno. Closer to home, it also faced challenges to its position from Gobir and Kano. To meet this challenge, Katsina sought friendship from the non-Hausa states of Hadejia and Nupe.

Kano also sought to consolidate its position in the region following the demise of Songhay. Kano's economic dynamism appears to have been emerging as early as the late fourteenth century, resulting in the creation of a distinctively open society receptive to new cultures and commodities, and therefore attractive to incoming migrants with a variety of skills and occupations. It also became a key link in the network of long-distance trade within West Africa, by which Kukawa and Wadai in the east were linked to Timbuktu on the Niger Bend, and Hausaland to Nupe and the Yoruba region to the south and beyond to the Akan region of present-day Ghana. It was from the Akan forest that gold and kola nuts began to be traded through Kano. By the late sixteenth century, a visiting merchant from Ragusa (present-day Dubrovnik in Croatia) reported that Kano should be ranked alongside Fes in Morocco and Cairo in Egypt as one of Africa's great trading cities.[19] As at Katsina and Kebbi, the city's imposing walls had been rebuilt and enlarged in the sixteenth century. Kano too constructed a new *casbah* or citadel – where it was part, Last writes, 'of a skillful attempt to institute ... a new, independent kingship, with novel privileges, regalia, and ritual'.[20] Communities of immigrants, including from North Africa, continued to settle and establish commercial activities in the city. This economic success served to enhance royal power in Kano and led to the creation of increasingly elaborate forms of governance and territorial control. The kingdom was divided into districts, each of which was then governed at a local level by ruling houses with defined political responsibilities.[21]

The founding of permanent, walled capital cities or *birni* is also apparent in Zazzau, on the southern frontiers of the Hausa region. There, the construction of walls around Birnin Zaria was recorded in oral histories as being directed by the legendary Queen Amina. Indeed, as R. A. Adeleye notes, 'her name is associated with a widely dispersed activity of wall building all over the Hausa states and beyond'.[22] In the nineteenth century, the ruler of the Sokoto Caliphate Muhammad Bello would write that Amina of Zazzau was 'the first to whom power was given over the Hausa states'. Although her remembered status as 'the first Hausa empire builder' is questionable, Adeleye considers that there is enough evidence to show that she was a historic figure, likely to have reigned in the fifteenth century. Zaria's walls (called, as elsewhere, the *Ganuwar Amina*), however, may have been built during the reign of Sarkin Zazzau Bakwa (r. *c.* 1492–1522).[23] Either way, such striking urban development marked a distinctive landmark in the history of the region.

A gateway in the city walls of Kano, photographed in the mid-20th century.

Zazzau's achievement was also the result of military pressure exerted by neighbouring Kano, which had the effect of uniting the various settlements in its realm in their loyalty to the *sarki*. In the mid-fifteenth century, moreover, Sarkin Muhammadu Rabbo (r. 1456–1481) accepted Islam, which led to the further settlement of Muslim merchants in Birnin Zaria. Zazzau entered a period of prosperity and prominence in the region. This appears to have continued into the post-Songhay seventeenth century, as the kingdom continued to benefit from its connections to the south of Hausaland. Commodities flowed from the forest region via Zazzau into the expanding market-places of Hausaland: these included tribute payments of kola nuts and enslaved eunuchs from the Nupe kingdom.[24]

The kingdoms of Kebbi, Zamfara and Gobir also consolidated their power in the western half of *kasar Hausa*, balancing the established Katsina-Kano-Zazzau axis in the east. Kebbi was the first to rise to prominence, emerging in the sixteenth century as a bulwark against Songhay encroachment under the leadership of its assertive king Kanta Kotal, whom other Hausa states appear to have acknowledged as an overlord and paid tribute. Following Kanta Kotal's death in battle against Katsina in 1555, however, Kebbi's dominance began to wane, allowing its vassal states, notably Zamfara and Gobir, to assert their own independence. Here, too, the presence of Islam began to deepen: Sarkin Zamfara Aliyu is reported to have built many mosques in his capital and in outlying villages.[25] By the mid-eighteenth century, it was Gobir's turn to be in the ascendancy. Yet recurring military conflict between the kingdoms was putting a strain on finances and on the relationship between the ruling elite (*masu sarauta*) and the ruled (*talakawa*). Sarkin Kano Muhammad Sharefa Dan Dadi (r. 1703–1731) was remembered as imposing seven different taxes on his subjects, including one on the families of brides on their marriage and another on transactions in the Kurmi market – 'all of which', the *Kano Chronicle* recorded, 'were robbery'.[26] The Hausa *sarakana* may have begun to style themselves also as Muslim *emir*s – some of whom themselves sought to purify the faith – but the deepening reach of Islam in both town and countryside meant that the faith would become a vehicle for rising popular discontent.

THE RISE OF ISLAMIC REFORMISM

Historians have given much thought to the reasons for the emergence in the late eighteenth century of the populist reform movement led by Shehu 'Uthman Dan Fodio, which exploded into an armed jihad that overthrew the Hausa kingdoms and forged the Sokoto Caliphate.[27] Was the rise and ultimate triumph of the movement the result of the coherence of its Islamic ideology or of a deterioration in the established *sarauta* system of dynastic rule? How crucial was the inspirational leadership of the Shehu and his commanders in relation to underlying social and economic factors? Aside from being a religious struggle, did the movement also have an ethnic dimension? Was it, that is, essentially an uprising of Fulbe pastoralists against an urban-based Hausa order? Finally, how 'revolutionary' was the resulting confederation, ruled from the new capital city that gave it its name, Sokoto? Did the victorious clerics retain their ideological vigour and purity, or was their movement ultimately absorbed into the long-established culture of the defeated Hausa kingdoms? To what extent, in other words, 'does the Caliphate represent a new political order?'[28]

The first point to make in addressing these questions is that although the creation of the Sokoto Caliphate was the most dramatic example of an Islamic reform movement seizing political power in African history, it was not the only one. As elsewhere on the frontiers of the Islamic world, the question for Muslims of how best to live with non-Muslims had long been a challenging one, open to a range of interpretations. This was the case whether the Muslims in question were a minority community under the suzerainty of 'pagan' kings, or whether they were aristocratic converts to Islam who themselves ruled over non-Muslim populations. Despite the admonitions of puritanical clerics such as al-Maghili, the tendency in West Africa was for toleration and cohabitation. This worked both ways: whether they held political power or not, small Muslim communities residing in islands of urban cosmopolitanism had little choice but to come to terms with the sea of traditional religion that surrounded them. As conversion to Islam grew, however, this so-called quietist approach – which assumed that the faith would in time prevail due to its inherent superiority – began to be challenged by more militant ideologies that sought to speed up the process. Such militancy underlay the rise, as early as the eleventh century, of the Almoravid movement among the nomadic Sanhaja Berber peoples of the western Sahara, who swept out of the desert to conquer Morocco and much of Muslim Spain. South of the Sahara, populist Islamic reformism gained political momentum from the late seventeenth century, first in the western Sahara in a movement known as Sharr Bubba, then in the Futa Jalon region of present-day Guinea in the 1720s and in Futa Toro in Senegal in the 1760s. In both Futa Jalon and Futa Toro the prime movers were Fulbe clerics, whose call for jihad led to the overthrow of non-Muslim dynasties and the creation of Islamic imamates.[29]

If these movements represented a first phase of Islamic reformism in West Africa, then those in Hausaland in the 1790s and 1800s and in the kingdom of Masina on the middle Niger River in the 1810s and 1820s were the second phase. There was, however, a crucial difference: the targets of the latter were themselves Muslims. There were certainly questions over just how devout the Hausa kings were, but they ruled over a realm widely recognized as being part of the *dar al-Islam*. The fundamental fault line that took shape was one that mapped a debate over adherence to the faith onto a growing rural–urban divide: in the words of Last, the uprising was 'dominated by a rural populist revolt against the Muslims of the cities'.[30] It was also characterized by an anxiety on the part of 'Uthman Dan Fodio and other leading reformers to demonstrate the legitimacy of their cause, giving rise to the large body of so-called apologetic literature, which often looked to the early history of Islam as a precedent.

Despite recurrent warfare, there is every indication of ongoing dynamism in the various sectors of the Hausaland economy: grain agriculture, pastoralism and long-distance trade – including the export of enslaved captives across the Sahara to Tripoli. Yet rising popular discontent was generated by a decline in the administrative efficiency of dynastic rule and a perception that the actions of the established ruling elites were contrary to the principles of social justice.[31] In Gobir, as in Kano, increased taxation caused widespread resentment. State impositions simply became too burdensome for subject populations, who began to resent the luxurious lifestyles of the large royal family. The result was escalating social tension. Gobir was also faced with external threats in the shape of recurrent conflicts with Katsina and with the Tuaregs of the Aïr Mountains in the desert to the north. Three of Gobir's kings lost their lives during these wars, undermining the kingdom's military capacity and political stability. This led to a loss of confidence in the established dynastic rulers on the part of the common people, the *talakawa*, many of whom turned to the *ulama* or Islamic scholars for inspiration and leadership.

The situation in Katsina was no better, particularly during the reign of Sarkin Katsina Gozo (r. 1796–1801). Gozo himself was something of a reformer: his policies of refusing to follow established practices because they were against *shari'a* law annoyed the more traditionalist section of the ruling class. These practices included the funerary rituals of the new king stepping over the corpse of his deceased predecessor, the sacrifice of a black bull and the use of the blood to anoint the new king, and his seclusion in the palace for seven days. The resulting rift threatened to tear the political fabric of Katsina apart. As in Gobir, the ruling elite was also perceived as exerting undue pressure on the *talakawa*, which contributed to escalating social tension. One prince, Bakin Wake, was accused of exhibiting overbearing tendencies that involved turning people into beasts of burden. Threats of secession followed from the chiefs of Gozaki and Maska, two regions that had a long history of loyalty to Katsina. It was at this point that the *ulama* class came into the picture, preaching in support of rebellion against the state. In Kano, too, rulers subjected the population to repressive policies. By the reign of Sarkin Kano Kambari (r. 1731–1743) taxation was seen as so harsh that many Arab settlers chose to abandon the city for Katsina. As a result, the Kano economy declined, leading to military incursions by Borno, as well as internal disorder that escalated into civil war. Ignoring these challenges, the ruling class continued with their ostentatious lifestyles supported by government coffers.

Despite the spread of Islam, established beliefs and practices, in particular rituals associated with *bori*, a spirit possession cult, continued to be widespread. Concerned Muslim *ulama* saw such rituals not only as encouraged by a policy of religious tolerance, but also practised by the ruling elites themselves. Hodi Dan Tarana, for example, son of Sarkin Kebbi Suleiman (r. 1783–1803), is said to have been an ardent patron of 'pagan' beliefs, or *tsafi*, although Suleiman's other children were devout Muslims. In Kebbi, relations between the ruling elite and the subject population were not initially as pronounced as elsewhere. Yet tension emerged following the death of Suleiman and his succession by Hodi Dan Tarana, when Kebbi too became fertile ground for the revolutionary preaching of the local *ulama* led by Usman Mussa. These increasing pressures appear to be absent only in Zamfara, where a deep hostility towards Gobir served to align the kingdom with the rising reformist movement. Indeed, it was from among the Dakkawa of Zamfara that Dan Fodio recruited many of his early supporters.[32]

Shehu 'Uthman Dan Fodio was the dominant figure to emerge from this situation of escalating unease across Hausaland. Born in 1754 at Maratta in western Gobir (present-day Niger), Dan Fodio was descended from a distinguished line of Fulbe scholars of the Torenke family, originally from Futa Toro.[33] Becoming a *shaikh* of the Qadiriyya *sufi* brotherhood and acquiring fluency in Arabic, Hausa and the Tuareg language of Tamacheq in addition to his native Fulfulde, he forged a reputation as a learned and charismatic preacher. In 1781, he was employed as an advisor to Sarkin Gobir Bawa and as a tutor to the royal family in the capital of Alkalawa. These were established roles for leading members of the Islamic *ulama*, although the Shehu remained an outsider rather than an urban 'court cleric' and in his later writings would denounce scholars who associated themselves with kings. By the late 1780s, he sought to secure special privileges for Gobir's Muslims: the right to wear distinctive dress (turbans for men and veils for women), exemption from taxation and the freedom to proselytize and make converts. These privileges were granted, although clearly represented a threat to royal authority: Bawa himself commented with alarm that 'there would be only a village head, not a king, of Gobir after him'.[34] Following Bawa's death around 1790, however, the privileges were rescinded. The new Sarkin Gobir, Nafana, decreed that all preaching in the kingdom, except by the Shehu alone, was prohibited, that there were to be no more conversions to Islam, and that those who had converted were to return to their former religion. This prompted Dan Fodio and his followers to withdraw from Alkalawa into the countryside at Degel, where they sought to create an autonomous 'Muslim space' beyond royal power.

'Uthman Dan Fodio's withdrawal from the royal court back to his rural homeland marked the opening of a more militant phase in his movement. Such a withdrawal, or *hijra*, consciously mirrored the relocation of the Prophet Muhammad and his followers from Mecca to Medina at the dawn of the Islamic age in the year 662 CE (or in the Islamic calendar, 1 AH). Rejecting the attempt by Nafana to reimpose taxation and other 'caste' restrictions on the Muslim community, he decided that his followers should arm themselves and prepare for the 'jihad of the sword'. Their enemy was a dynastic elite now condemned as illegitimate on account of its continued adherence to elements of indigenous religion. 'The government of a country is the government of its King without question', the Shehu wrote in 1811, in justification of the move to armed revolt. 'There is no dispute that the Hausa Kings worshipped many places of idols, and trees, and rocks, and sacrificed to them. This constitutes Unbelief, according to the general opinion.'[35] Despite their self-identification as Muslims, the kings were condemned by the Islamic movement as *habe*, a derogatory Fulbe term for 'pagan'. Growing opposition to the established order was mobilized by Dan Fodio, who interpreted the deteriorating conditions in Hausaland as the result of a decadent elite that had lost touch with the faith it professed. By early 1804, attacks by Gobir forces led to the further withdrawal of the growing community from Degel to Gudu, a strategic location on the frontier with Kebbi, where the Shehu was joined by other scholars and their zealous followers from across the Hausa region. The banner of jihad was unfurled and war had begun: the call for reform had become revolution.

THE ESTABLISHMENT OF THE SOKOTO CALIPHATE

The initial military struggle between 'Uthman Dan Fodio's movement and the kingdom of Gobir was focused on the valley of the Rima River, where Gobir, Kebbi and Zamfara had long confronted one another in campaigns of territorial expansion. Katsina, Kano, Zazzau and the other Hausa kingdoms were also drawn into the conflict, as the Shehu distributed flags among his network of pupils, which symbolized his authorization for them to revolt against the corrupt rulers of their own areas. For some years the outcome of the struggle hung in the balance: Gobir's troops were well armed and the capital strongly defended, although Dan Fodio's Fulbe-dominated forces were more mobile and complemented by disgruntled Hausa peasants and Tuareg nomads. In 1808, Dan Fodio won a resounding military victory, driving the Sarkin Gobir into exile and the following year founding a new capital at Sokoto.

Victory over Gobir was followed by that in other parts of Hausaland. In Katsina, the assassination of Gozo created a vacuum, which the scholarly class exploited, overthrowing the ruling dynasty. In Kano, the various clan heads reached out to Dan Fodio and a flag was given to the Sullubawa clan to lead the jihad. From his head-quarters at Danyahiya, Sarkin Kano Alwali attempted to defend his territory, but could not stand the challenge of the Danbazawa clan on the eastern frontiers. The final defeat of Kano and the death of Alwali came at the battle of Burum-Burum, which marked the end of the ancient dynasty and the incorporation of its powerful army into the Islamic forces.[36] In Kebbi, as in Katsina, it was a succession dispute that gave an opening to the reform movement, while in Zamfara the effects of the struggle in Gobir created the conditions that toppled dynastic rule. Beyond the core Hausa region, the military struggle continued into the 1810s, as new emirates were forged on the frontiers of Borno in the east and south into Nupe and Oyo, and into Adamawa in present-day Cameroon. A crucial point was reached in 1812, when Dan Fodio stood back from the struggle and entrusted the renewed *dar al-Islam* to his son Muhammad Bello and his brother 'Abdullahi. The former took responsibility for the eastern emirates from the new capital of Sokoto, while the latter oversaw the western emirates from Gwandu. The Shehu's death five years later created something of a constitutional crisis, which was resolved when he was succeeded as Commander of the Faithful, *Amir al-Mu'minin* – or in Hausa, *Sarkin Musulmi* – by Muhammad Bello. At that point, it is appropriate to speak of the vast domain as a caliphate, consciously modelled on the original Islamic state forged by the successors of the Prophet Muhammad.

The forging of the Sokoto Caliphate marked the end of the estab-lished Hausa dynasties, now designated as *habe* and consigned to a pre-Islamic past of *jahilliya* or ignorance. Ruled in two sectors from the joint capitals of Sokoto and Gwandu, the confederation at its height was composed of thirty emirates and extended over an area of some 250,000 sq. miles (650,000 sq. km). The vision of a renewed and purified Muslim space, however, did not go unchallenged. The most notable resistance came from the ancient kingdom of Borno, where the attempt to carry the 'sword of truth' further to the east was checked by forces led by the charismatic scholar Shaikh Muhammad al-Kanemi. Having turned back Sokoto's military advance, al-Kanemi then engaged Dan Fodio and Muhammad Bello in a sequence of Arabic letters in which he questioned the theological justification of their movement. Suggesting that their jihad was more an effort to extend Fulbe ethnic power than to champion Islam, he argued too 'that the religious sins of the Borno people did not constitute unbelief and should be corrected by internal exhortation and not war'.[37] There was some justification for this first critique: despite the attraction of the Shehu's movement for many disgruntled Hausa and Tuareg, Last argues that some 80 per cent of the movement's core followers were Fulbe and that in the course of the conflict the revolutionary army became more and not less dominated by Fulbe warriors.[38] As for the second, it points to the ongoing existence of an alternative and equally valid interpretation of the *dar al-Islam* in the West African savanna.

If Dan Fodio's movement was indeed dominated by stern Fulbe pastoralists – fighting men, as Iliffe describes them, 'hostile to cities, governments and taxes' – then it quickly needed to formulate ways to administer the huge domain under its sway according to the norms of Islamic governance.[39] That it rose to this challenge was in large part due to the outstanding leadership of Muhammad Bello, who from 1817 to his death in 1837 succeeded in suppressing ongoing opposition to the new state and constructing an enduring system of rule. Power at the centre was dominated by the Shehu's family and its close advisors, notably Bello's brother-in-law Gidado, who became his *wazir*. Yet the system was a federal one, in which considerable autonomy was retained by the thirty emirates, most of which were ruled by the descendants of the local Fulbe clerics who had responded to the call to jihad. Effective governance was underpinned by literacy, the rule of law and by the historical model of the original Islamic caliphate, which provided what amounted to a written constitution. 'Such authority', Iliffe writes, 'was lacking in even the most sophis-ticated of Africa's pre-literate states. Sokoto, for once in Africa, was a government of laws and not of men.'[40] On matters of taxation, for example, all the levies imposed by the old regimes were abolished and replaced by ones sanctioned by Islam and specified in the constitution. Unlike in the past, the emirs kept their distance from the state treasuries. Literacy was further extended, moreover, by the creation of a Quranic education system and by the writing of the vernacular Hausa and Fulfulde languages as *ajami*; that is, in Arabic script.[41] Education for elite women was championed by the Shehu's daughter, and Bello's sister, Nana Asma'u (1793–1864), who had actively participated in the jihad and became a noted poet. Nana Asma'u aimed also to purify the *bori* possession cult – often dominated by women, including those who were enslaved – but rather than condemning it outright, recognized its Islamic elements and its efficacy in solving everyday problems and anxieties. 'It is in no small part because of her efforts', David Robinson writes, 'that Islam has become so deeply imbedded in the culture of Hausaland'.[42]

Despite the deepening of Islam, however, *bori* persisted. So too did other strongly rooted aspects of Hausa culture, both in the political and in the popular realm. Indeed, like other austere zealots throughout the history of Islam in Africa and beyond, Dan Fodio's Fulbe warriors were gradually absorbed into the urban Hausa culture they sought to overthrow. Many would intermarry with Hausa women, come to speak Hausa and readily adjust to the comforts of city life. Contrary to the stated wishes of the Shehu, the emirates also adopted the established hierarchy of noble titles. The result, it can be argued, was the consolidation rather than the overthrow of the *sarauta* system.[43] Ironically, it may have been this process of enculturation that underlay the stability of the caliphate and in turn led to further economic dynamism. Not only did the cities of Hausaland supplant Timbuktu in terms of Islamic scholarship, they also became the nodal points of one of the most prosperous regions in Africa. Agriculture, local trade and trans-Saharan commerce all continued to flourish, while Kano emerged as the continent's leading centre of textile manufacture, famous for its indigo-dyed cloth. By the mid-nineteenth century, European travellers began to be drawn to this great walled city, and their accounts add a new body of historical sources to those written by the reformers. 'Kano has been sounding in my ears now for more than one year', Heinrich Barth wrote on his approach in 1851; 'it has been one of the great objects of our journey as the central point of commerce, as a great store-house of information, and as the point whence more distant regions might be most successfully attempted. At length, after nearly a year's exertions, I had reached it.'[44]

Prosperity, of course, was not spread evenly throughout all social classes. Slavery had long been a feature of Hausa society, but it expanded dramatically in the nineteenth century as non-Islamic peoples on the frontiers of the state – who could legally be enslaved due to their status as 'pagans' – were subjected to brutal raids each dry season by the caliphate's mounted warriors. Some of these captives were exported across the Sahara to North Africa and the Islamic world beyond, but most were absorbed into the domestic economy, often living in agricultural slave villages or plantations (*rinji*) owned by Fulbe aristocrats or Hausa merchants. Others supported the urban lifestyles of their owners as domestic servants, artisans, soldiers

An indigo-dyed *riga* (men's robe) from the Hausa region of northern Nigeria. The embroidered designs in silk thread are drawn from the corpus of Islamic imagery and include the classic 'eight knives' and spiral 'drum' motifs, both designed to protect the wearer from malign influence.

'View of Kano from Dala', from Heinrich Barth, *Travels and Discoveries in North and Central Africa*, vol. 2 (London, 1857).

and concubines. The proximity of the enslaved to their masters coupled with their rights as enshrined in Islamic law offered some protection and at least the possibility of a degree of social mobility across the generations or even a lifetime. Yet historians estimate that by the end of the nineteenth century, a considerable proportion of the population was enslaved. As elsewhere in the continent, the institution lingered on well into the twentieth century, as incoming British colonial administrators were unwilling to interfere too drastically with the property rights of aristocratic ruling elites.[45]

CONCLUSION

The forging of the Sokoto Caliphate was arguably the most impressive project of state-building in Africa in the period after the collapse of Songhay in 1591. In contrast with the rise of other expansionist kingdoms in the era of the Atlantic slave trade, moreover, its origins were largely internal. Shehu 'Uthman Dan Fodio was certainly aware of efforts to revive Islamic governance in the wider world, including in the new emirates of Futa Jalon and Futa Toro to the west, but, as Iliffe writes, 'the *jihad* resulted chiefly from the contradictions that the steady growth of Islam created within the Hausa states'.[46] The roots of the caliphate, that is to say, lie in large part in the deeper history of the Hausa region. Much of that early history is speculative and can be reconstructed only in outline using a combination of archaeological and linguistic evidence. Between the fourteenth and the sixteenth centuries, *kasar Hausa* begins to emerge more clearly from the historical record. It may be that the region's earlier 'isolation' between Gao and Borno was simply the result of a lack of knowledge on the part of traders and geographers looking across the Sahara from North Africa. Be that as it may, by the sixteenth century, and more so with the end of Songhay hegemony, the Hausa kingdoms came to occupy a key crossroads in the Sudanic zone to the south of the desert. The deepening of Islam was far from the only cause of contradiction in their distinctive system of governance. *Sarauta* can be seen as a sophisticated form of statecraft designed in part to manage a prosperous regional economy: the Hausa kingdoms, Adeleye writes, 'were organized to promote exchange'.[47] Yet their ruling elites were also aggressively militaristic, prone to internecine warfare and, ultimately, overbearing and exploitative in their relationship with their subjects, the *talakawa*. By the late eighteenth century, a rising popular demand for change was increasingly expressed in the idioms of a purified Islam.

The vast Islamic confederation that emerged also had its contradictions. Many historians have portrayed the caliphate as having an initial 'golden age' under the leadership of Muhammad Bello, after which a degree of progressive deterioration in the system of governance can be detected. Barth's valuable account of his journey in the 1850s gives an impression of mounting disarray due to political conflicts within many of the emirates, while by the 1870s, the balance of power between the central government at Sokoto and the outlying emirates was beginning to weigh towards the latter. Yet it might be argued that the complex problems thrown up by the effort to apply Islamic principles to so vast a domain were still being worked out when, in the closing decades of the century, the caliphate came under increasing pressure from European imperialism. This pressure was initially applied by the Royal Niger Company, a commercial venture to which Britain subcontracted the management of its interests in what would become the colony of Southern Nigeria. As commercial 'spheres of influence' escalated in the 1890s into the full-blown Scramble for Africa, however, Britain, France and Germany competed to extend their rule into the West African interior. In the end, it was Britain that took the lion's share of the caliphate, declaring a pro-tectorate over a territory dubbed Northern Nigeria in 1900. Two years later, the *khalifa* Attahiru Dan Ahmadu rejected, in the name of Islam, overtures from the commander of British forces, Frederick Lugard, to submit to colonial rule. In 1903, Kano and then Sokoto were finally subdued; fleeing eastwards, 'claiming he had begun a *hajj* (pilgrimage to Mecca), though his movements more resembled *hijra* (flight from infidels)', Attahiru was killed by the pursuing British forces.[48]

If the political culture of the Hausa kingdoms can be seen to have survived in a new guise within the framework of the Sokoto Caliphate, then so too did the resulting 'Hausa-Fulani' order outsee British colonial rule between 1903 and the independence of Nigeria in 1960. Indeed, that ruling order was in many ways deliberately supported by Lugard, under whose governorship the protectorate of Northern Nigeria became the testing ground for the transfer of the British style of 'indirect rule' from India to Africa. Lugard found in the Fulbe emirs just the sort of authoritarian and con-servative aristocrats he could do business with, so took advantage of the sophisticated administrative and tax-collecting apparatus they presided over, by largely keeping it in place. The caliphate was formally abolished and the *khalifa* redesignated as a secular 'sultan' but, as Lugard declared, 'every Sultan and Emir will rule over people as of old time'.[49] Other aspects of Sokoto's precolonial social hierarchy were also retained, notably slavery and the subordination and seclusion of women. So too was the network of Quranic education and the system of Islamic law, which continued to function alongside colonial law and was in some areas extended to residual non-Muslim communities. The Sokoto Caliphate no longer existed as a sovereign state and in 1960 its core territories in turn became absorbed into the new nation of Nigeria. Yet British overrule had done much to preserve the authority and the autonomy of the Islamic ruling elite, which would re-emerge – supported by the demographic weight of northern Nigeria – as a key player in the often bitterly contested political struggles and religious conflicts of the era of independence.

CHAPTER 8

THE AKAN FOREST KINGDOM
OF ASANTE

John Parker

On 19 May 1817, Asantehene Osei Tutu Kwame welcomed for the
first time a British diplomatic mission to his capital, Kumasi. The
envoys and their African retinue had set out four weeks earlier from
Cape Coast Castle, a fortified outpost on the seashore of the Gulf
of Guinea, which from the mid-seventeenth century to 1807 had
served as the headquarters of Britain's slave-trading operations in
West Africa. Making its way through the tropical forest up one of
the eight 'great roads' radiating from Kumasi to the outer reaches
of Asante's imperial domains, the mission was instructed to halt at
a town 30 miles (48 km) short of the capital while Osei Tutu Kwame
presided over what it understood to be 'the King's fetish week'.[1]
This was the six-day period leading up to *akwasidae*, one of the two
solemn *adae* ceremonies held in every forty-two-day cycle of the
Asante calendar, during which the king withdrew from public gaze
into the confines of his palace to commune with his ancestors and
thereby ensure the well-being of the *Asanteman*, 'the Asante nation'.
Following an early-morning visit to the royal mausoleum containing
the bones of his hallowed predecessors, he would then re-enter the
public realm on what was deemed to be a particularly auspicious
day for the conduct of diplomatic and other state business. It was
on the afternoon of that day that the four British envoys were permitted to enter Kumasi. Emerging from the forest and the neat
patchwork of agricultural settlements surrounding the capital, they

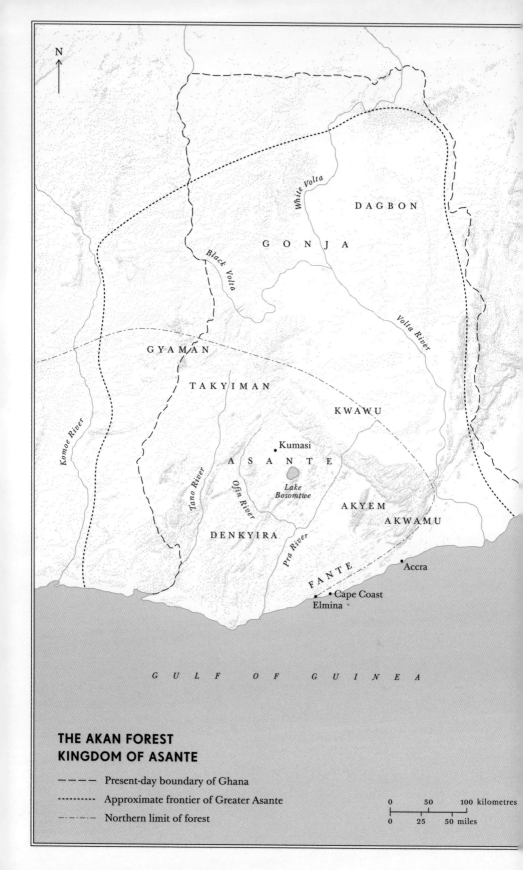

N

White Volta

Black Volta

Volta River

Komoe River

Tano River

Ofin River

Pra River

DAGBON

GONJA

GYAMAN

TAKYIMAN

KWAWU

ASANTE

• Kumasi

Lake
Bosomtwe

AKYEM

AKWAMU

DENKYIRA

FANTE

• Accra

• Cape Coast
Elmina •

GULF   OF   GUINEA

**THE AKAN FOREST
KINGDOM OF ASANTE**

– – – – Present-day boundary of Ghana

• • • • • • Approximate frontier of Greater Asante

– · – · – Northern limit of forest

| 0 | 50 | 100 kilometres |

| 0 | 25 | 50 miles |

XI A watercolour by Carlos Julião depicting the so-called Black King Festival in Brazil, from *Riscos illuminados de figurinhos de brancos e negros dos uzos do Rio de Janeiro e Serro do Frio*, late 18th century.

XII Christian encounter in the kingdom of Kongo, as depicted in a watercolour by the Capuchin friar Bernardino Ignazio titled 'The missionary gives his blessing to the Mani during Sangamento'. From the manuscript *Missione in prattica. Padri cappuccini ne' Regni di Congo, Angola, et adiacenti* in the Biblioteca Civica Centrale, Turin, c. 1750.

XIII Apolo Kaggwa (second from right) and Kabaka Daudi Cwa of Buganda.

XIV The royal drums of Buganda.

XV Dala Hill, the ancient epicentre of the city of Kano in northern Nigeria.

XVI Two pages from a small manuscript book (*c.* 3 × 3 in. or 8 × 8 cm) from the Hausa region, late 17th to early 18th century. Written in Arabic, the text on the folio to the left concerns the measurement of time. The folio to the right has the names of the Prophet Muhammad and three of the four 'rightly guided' caliphs set inside a circular design: a symbol often displayed in the palaces of Hausa kings as a sign of royal authority.

XVII 'Captain in his war dress', from T. Edward Bowdich, *Mission from Cape Coast Castle to Ashantee* (London, 1819). Although the 'captain' is depicted carrying a spear, his distinctive eagle-feather and gilded ram's horn headdress suggest that he was in fact one of the royal sword bearers or *afenasoafo* observed by Bowdich on his entry into the Asante capital Kumasi on 19 May 1817.

XVIII 'The King's Sleeping Room', from T. Edward Bowdich, *Mission from Cape Coast Castle to Ashantee* (London, 1819). Bowdich's drawing captures the stunning use in Asante architecture of red- and white-painted clay decorated with geometrical shapes in low relief. Two palace attendants play the board game *warri*, and next to the tree stand two metal bowls placed in forked branches: the ubiquitous protective household shrine or *nyame dua* ('God's tree').

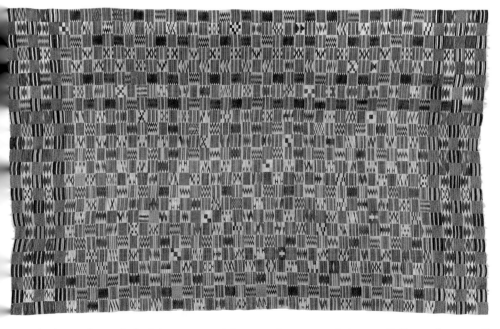

XIX An Asante *kente* cloth of the most prestigious type known as *adwinasa* or 'fullness of ornament' and in the classic design called *sika futura*, 'gold dust'. 5 ft 10½ in. × 5 ft 11 in. (1.79 × 1.8 m).

XX A detail from 'The First Day of the Yam Custom', from T. Edward Bowdich, *Mission from Cape Coast Castle to Ashantee* (London, 1819). Asantehene Osei Tutu Kwame, seated under the red umbrella with the gilded elephant finial and with the Golden Stool held aloft to his right, hosts the British envoys on the *odwira fomemene* of 6 September 1817.

XXI The Zulu king Cetshwayo depicted boarding a surfboat that will carry him out to HMS *Natal* and into exile on 4 September 1879. From the *Illustrated London News*, 18 October 1879.

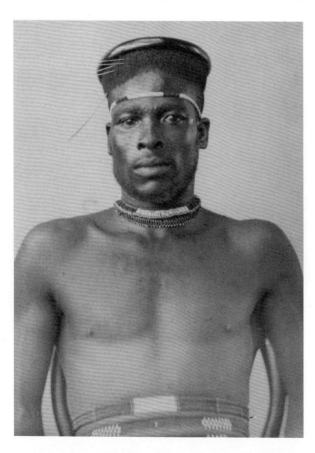

XXII A photograph titled 'Zulu man with an *isicoco c.* 1879', from the collection of Queen Victoria.

were astounded by the spectacular choreographed display that enveloped them.

'Upwards of 5000 people, the greater part warriors, met us with awful bursts of martial music, discordant only in its mixture; for horns, drums, rattles, and gong-gongs were all exerted with a zeal bordering on phrenzy, to subdue us by the first impression', one of their number, T. Edward Bowdich, wrote (see pl. XVII). 'The smoke which encircled us from the incessant discharges of musquetry, confined our glimpses to the foreground; and we were halted whilst the captains performed their Pyrrhic dance, in the centre of a circle formed by their warriors; where a confusion of flags, English, Dutch, and Danish, were waved and flourished in all directions.' Inching their way through the thronging mass of dignitaries and townspeople, the party 'passed through a very broad street, about a quarter of a mile long, to the market place'.

Our observations ... had taught us to conceive a spectacle far exceeding our original expectations; but they had not prepared us for the extent and display of the scene which here burst upon us: an area of nearly a mile in circumference was crowded with magnificence and novelty. The king, his tributaries, and captains, were resplendent in the distance, surrounded by attendants of every description, fronted by a mass of warriors which seemed to make our approach impervious. The sun was reflected, with a glare scarcely more supportable than the heat, from the massy [i.e. solid] gold ornaments, which glistened in every direction. More than a hundred bands burst at once on our arrival, with the peculiar airs of the several chiefs ....
At least a hundred large umbrellas, or canopies, which could shelter thirty persons, were sprung up and down by the bearers with brilliant effect, being made of scarlet, yellow, and the most shewy cloths and silks, and crowned on the top with crescents, pelicans, elephants, barrels, and arms and swords of gold ....
The prolonged flourishes of the horns, a deafening tumult

of drums ... announced that we approached the king: we
were already passing the principal officers of his household;
the chamberlain, the gold horn blower, the captain of the
messengers, the captain for royal executions, the captain of the
market, the keeper of the royal burial ground, and the master
of the bands, sat surrounded by a retinue and splendor which
bespoke the dignity and importance of their offices.[2]

Finally, Bowdich and his companions made their way into the presence of the waiting Asantehene.

His deportment first excited my attention; native dignity in
princes we are pleased to call barbarous was a curious spectacle:
his manners were majestic, yet courteous ... he wore a fillet
of aggry beads round his temples, a necklace of gold cockspur
shells ... his bracelets were the richest mixtures of beads and
gold, and his fingers covered in rings; his cloth was of a dark
green silk ... and his ancle strings of gold ornaments of the
most delicate workmanship ... he wore a pair of gold castanets
on his fingers and thumb, which he clapped to enforce silence.
The belts of the guards behind his chair, were cased in gold,
and covered with small jaw bones of the same metal; the
elephants tails, waving like a small cloud before him, were
spangled with gold, and large plumes of feathers were
flourished amid them. His eunuch presided over these
attendants ... [and] the royal stool, entirely cased in gold, was
displayed under a splendid umbrella ....[3]

The description goes on. As day turned to night, the vast reception
continued by torchlight 'and it was long before we were at liberty
to retire'. Bowdich estimated the total number of warriors alone in
attendance at thirty thousand.

The British effort to secure a treaty governing commercial and
political relations with Asante failed. For the remainder of the nineteenth century the two powers would be drawn into a series of

recurring confrontations, until in 1896 the kingdom was occupied by the British, at the height of the European conquest and partition of Africa. Five years later, in the aftermath of a final, futile war of resistance, it was annexed to the older Gold Coast Colony. In 1957, the Gold Coast – with the Asante kingdom at its centre – became the independent nation of Ghana. The 1817 mission may have come to nothing, but Bowdich's account, published two years later as *Mission from Cape Coast Castle to Ashantee*, represented the start of an enduring fascination with the great forest kingdom on the part of outside observers. Founded in the late seventeenth century, Asante would become the most powerful and prominent of what a recent study has called 'fiscal-military states' in West Africa.[4] The rise of Oyo, Asante, Dahomey and Segu represented a new phase of militarized state-building after the fall of the Songhay Empire in 1591, and the expansion of the Atlantic slave trade marked the end of the 'medieval' period and the opening of an increasingly volatile 'modern' era in West Africa's history. Asante was renowned for its fabulous wealth, and Bowdich leaves no doubt as to what that wealth was based on: gold. Heir to the tradition of West African gold production, which in the medieval period had supplied the precious metal to the trans-Saharan trade and from the fifteenth century had drawn acquisitive Europeans to the Atlantic coast, Asante entered world history as an alluring kingdom of gold. By the reign of Osei Tutu Kwame (r. 1804–1823), it was at its peak in terms of wealth, military prowess and imperial reach. The nature of the kingship that emerged from and presided over this wealth in gold is the subject of this chapter.

The extracts quoted above from the description of the entry of the 1817 mission into Kumasi contain important clues to the nature of Asante statecraft. Kingship was based on the accumulation of wealth derived from forest agriculture and gold production, and was reinforced by military prowess and an elaborate and sophisticated government apparatus. It was also enshrined by spiritual power. As Bowdich observed, the Asantehene devoted a large amount of time and effort attending to the spiritual realm: for a start, for twelve days of every forty-two-day *adaduanan* or monthly cycle he was sequestered within his palace in the company of his departed ancestors. He also presided over a host of other ritual observations, performances and sacrifices, including the great Odwira festival, which served on an annual basis to recapitulate the historic project of Asante kingship. To what extent can Asante be seen to conform to the model of 'sacred' kingship as set out by the historical anthropologists David Graeber and Marshall Sahlins in their recent book, *On Kings*?[5] This question lurks behind much debate among historians of Asante. Pioneering research tended to emphasize Asante's material base, the complex structures of its office-holding elite and the bureaucratization of its government.[6] Subsequent studies have been critical of this approach, exploring instead the ways in which political power was entangled with the spiritual realm and how the state sought to assert control over belief and knowledge in society.[7] One thing is clear: while Asante at its height possessed formidable coercive or 'instrumental' power, it also possessed a dazzling array of ideological or 'creative' powers and the ability to project them.[8] Its dynastic rulers were masterful performers of power. Before we consider this debate, let us first turn to the origins of the Asante kingdom and of the wider Akan culture from which it emerged.

AKAN ORIGINS

If written European accounts like that of Bowdich are important for understanding Asante in its nineteenth-century heyday, for the deeper history of the Akan peoples we must turn to another type of source: oral traditions. Passed down from generation to generation by the Akan and their fellow Twi-speaking Bono neighbours on the northern fringes of the forest, oral traditions took a variety of forms: *adomanko-masem*, myths of the creation of human culture; *atetesem*, stories of ancient migrations and the formation of settled communities; and *abakosem*, subsequent histories focused on the emergence of political

authority. Enshrined in the music of the state drummers, hornblow-
ers and praise singers described by Bowdich, these understandings
of the past began to be written down with the rise of literacy on the
Gold Coast from the mid-nineteenth century. One written version
was produced in 1907 by Asantehene Agyeman Prempeh (r. 1888–
1931), who had been deposed by the British in 1896 and exiled to
the Seychelles. Based on the deep knowledge of Agyeman Prempeh's
mother, the Asantehemaa (or 'Queen Mother') Yaa Kyaa, who had
accompanied him into exile, *The History of Ashanti Kings and the Whole
Country Itself* sets down the early history of the kingdom's ruling
Oyoko ruling dynasty. It is the earliest authoritative version of Asante
origins and perhaps the first example of history writing in English
by any African ruler.

'After the beginning of the world', when 'the thing to do is hunting', the *History of Ashanti Kings* opens, a hunter went into the forest
and was told by a honey badger that people were about to arrive on
earth. Soon after, a gold chain descended from the sky, down which
climbed a herald, a woman bearing a stool and then Ankyewa Nyame,
the ancestress of the Oyoko lineage, or *abusua*.[9] Ankyewa Nyame
settled at a place called Asantemanso, where other people emerged
from holes in the ground to join her and where, over the ensuing
three generations, the Oyoko built up their numbers and began to
formulate the rudiments of the social order. In search of new living
space, they then moved to nearby Kokofu and, under the leadership
of Oti Akenten, on to Kwaman, where they used gold to purchase
land from its original female owner and founded the settlement of
Kumasi, 'under (*ase*) the *kum* tree'. 'The protohistoric period', the
pioneering historian of Asante, Ivor Wilks, writes, 'is giving way to
the historic; Oti Akenten was succeeded by Obiri Yeboa, and Obiri
Yeboa by Osei Tutu, first Asantehene, whose death in 1717 is reported
in contemporary European sources'.[10]

Wilks used this and similar traditions from other lineages as
evidence that the transition from hunting and gathering to agriculture
in the forest may have happened as late as the fifteenth or sixteenth

century. Faced with the formidable challenge of carving out a settled society in the dense rainforest, he argued, the Akan exchanged the one valuable commodity they produced, gold, for the one thing they needed to clear away enough tree cover and tropical vegetation to establish an agrarian economy: people. Yams, the original staple crop in the forest, were later supplemented by new foodstuffs acquired from the Americas in the so-called Columbian Exchange: cassava and maize. Wilks's interpretation came to be known as the 'big bang' theory of Akan origins, on the basis that the formation of farming communities and kingdoms in the forest, far from happening in the deep primordial past, occurred rapidly and in conjunction with the emergence of the modern global economy. Exchanging gold for enslaved labour, first from the savanna region to the north and sub-sequently from Portuguese mariners who arrived on the Atlantic coast in the 1470s, entrepreneurial 'big men' (or, in Twi, *abirempon*) forged agricultural and gold-mining 'estates', which then coalesced into early kingdoms. From the outset, that is to argue, Akan states were characterized by a powerful ethos of accumulation – *sika sene, biribi ansen bio* declares one of many proverbs that reflect on the importance of monetary wealth: 'gold (or money) is beyond every-thing; nothing is beyond that'. Another ubiquitous maxim addressed the process by which enslaved captives and free settlers were incor-porated into expanding local society: *obi nkyere obi ase*, 'one does not disclose the origins of another'. Yet this sought to disguise an underlying reality: that the emerging states were also hierarchical and inegalitarian.[11]

The 'big bang' theory of Akan origins has not gone unchallenged. Recent archaeological excavations of earthwork sites in southern Ghana and elsewhere in West Africa dating back to the late first millennium CE point to an alternative hypothesis: that the forest zone had been widely settled by concentrations of iron-using cultiva-tors prior to the advent of Atlantic commerce.[12] Analysis of coins minted in Tunis and Libya, moreover, indicates that gold exports from the region were arriving in North Africa as early as the ninth century.[13] Emerging evidence for a longer time frame for the economic transformations that gave rise to the Akan *oman* (pl. *aman*) or state, however, need not detract from the crucial importance of oral histories in preserving local understandings of the origin and nature of society and of kingship. The underlying 'meaning' of the first people descending from the sky or up from the ground, for example, is that they came from nowhere else; they were, that is, the original masters of the land. This identity was further encapsulated in the word Akan itself, which has connotations of a 'first and foremost' and culturally superior people. The *akanman piesie nnum*, the five remembered 'firstborn' towns that formed the cradle of the Akan peoples, were all located in a basin between the Pra and Ofin rivers that was less than 80 miles (130 km) in diameter. The *abirempon* who mobilized wealth in land, gold and people, to emerge as the historical *amanhene* of the resulting states (the Twi suffix *hene* indicating 'ruler of'), were therefore not the classic 'stranger kings' that we see

Osei Agyeman Prempeh II (r. 1931–1970) seated next to – and slightly below – the *sika dwa kofi* or Golden Stool on the day of his restoration as Asantehene by the British colonial authorities on 31 January 1935.

elsewhere in the continent: heroic wanderers who arrive from another place or realm bearing the gift of a more sophisticated culture. Kingship was an indigenous development, symbolized, in the same way as European 'thrones', by stools, like the one that preceded Ankyewa Nyame down the golden chain at the dawn of time. At the turn of the eighteenth century, another stool was said to have descended from the skies to confer political authority on the ruler of a powerful new military alliance. This was the *sika dwa kofi*, the Golden Stool – the hallowed object that Bowdich saw displayed 'under a splendid umbrella' on 19 May 1817, and which for the Asante enshrined the *sunsum* or very 'soul' of the nation.

OSA NTI FO

Early Akan state formation clearly preceded the arrival of the Portuguese in the 1470s on what became known as the Gold Coast. Yet the advent of Atlantic commerce would have a profound impact on the region. The Portuguese and their northern European maritime rivals were quite aware that the forest hinterland was ruled over by 'kings', a political landscape captured in the first detailed map of the interior produced by a Dutch cartographer in 1629. By then, a century and a half of maritime trade had reoriented the Akan away from their established connections to the Malian-dominated world to the north, and towards the expanding Atlantic economy. The remainder of the seventeenth century was a time of dramatic political change: by the 1660s, two expansionist Akan states, Denkyira in the Ofin-Pra River Basin and Akwamu to the east, had risen to a position of dominance in their respective regions. Following the eclipse of the Portuguese by the early seventeenth century, both kingdoms supplied gold and, increasingly, enslaved captives to the growing number of Dutch, English and Danish forts on the coast (hence the flags of these trading nations noted by Bowdich in Kumasi in 1817). In exchange, Denkyira and Akwamu imported firearms and other European commodities to expand their military capacity and reinforce centralized political power. The small 'estate' of Kwaman centred on the settlement of Kumasi was one of many which found itself under the sway of Denkyira, forced to pay a yearly tribute to its swaggering, gun-bearing rulers. Chafing under the terms of this tributary status, the upstart *Kumasifo* (the suffix *fo* meaning 'the people of') began to forge local alliances and to accumulate the resources – human, technological and ritual – needed to overthrow Denkyira.

The *History of Ashanti Kings* takes up the story. It records how the kingdom was forged by the combined genius of two men: Osei Tutu, the *omanhene* of Kumasi, and Komfo Anokye, a famed ritual specialist or 'priest' (*okomfo*). Osei Tutu was the nephew of Oti Akenten and his successor Obiri Yeboa; his mother was Manu, the granddaughter of Birempona Piese, who was in turn the daughter of the Oyoko ancestress Ankyewa Nyame. This genealogy underlines that although Asante would be ruled by men, women played a fundamental role in the functioning of state and society, as the Akan are a matrilineal people who define kinship and trace succession through the female line. In order to guarantee the annual tribute, the Denkyirahene Boamponsem demanded that Oti Akenten send one of his family as a hostage: that hostage was Osei Tutu, who, following mutual accusations of sexual transgression, fled back to Kumasi before seeking refuge in the Akwamu kingdom to the east. It is at this point that Komfo Anokye enters the narrative, escorting Osei Tutu to and from safety in Akwamu and, following the latter's succession as the *omanhene* of Kumasi, mobilizing ritual power in support of his military campaigns. As Wilks notes, the broad thrust of events in the 1690s is confirmed by the written records of Europeans on the Gold Coast, whose imports of firearms were keenly sought by the competing forces in the forest interior. In the words of the pioneering nineteenth-century African historian of the Gold Coast, Rev. Carl Reindorf, Osei Tutu's sojourns in the militarized kingdoms of Denkyira and Akwamu provided him with 'the opportunity of acquiring the politics of the two principal powers then existing'.[14]

If this 'politics' can be summed up as the organization of the
Akan kingdoms along military lines, then it was underpinned by the
miraculous feats of Komfo Anokye. Indeed, while the Oyoko tradition of the final epochal battle against Denkyirahene Ntim Gyakari
notes the importance of gunpowder technology, it places greater
emphasis on the prowess of Komfo Anokye's magical arsenal in
overcoming the numerically superior forces of their enemy. The
'principal wonders done by the prophet Annochi' included turning
himself into a woman and making love with Ntim Gyakari in order
to sap his opponent's martial strength and, emblematically, demonstrating mastery over the forest environment once the battle had
commenced. 'When they reached a place called Féyiasi', the *History
of Ashanti Kings* records, 'Annochi said "I am going to see the enemy"
so he and his son Japa climbed a tree and the footsteps of Annochi
and his son could [i.e. can] still be seen all along the tree where his
feet touched'.

> On his return Annochi said, They are too numerous so you
> (Ossai) and all your men must come and hid[e] yourself behind
> this tree and because a single volley of the enemy will crushed
> [*sic*] you all. And so the Ashantis hid themselves behind the said
> tree and it was said that as soon as the enemy fired, the tree
> enlarged ... itself and all the balls stucked [*sic*] to the tree but as
> soon as the Ashantis fired the tree became small and the balls
> killed the enemy. The balls of the enemy could [i.e. can] still be
> seen in the tree.[15]

The Denkyira army was vanquished and Ntim Gyakari killed: 'through
the genius of Annochi the Ashantis ... became the leading nation
over all the largest countries around it'. In late 1701, news reached
the Dutch on the Gold Coast that 'the Assjanteese' – the first appearance of the word in the written record – 'had a complete victory over
the Dinquirase', who were 'forced to fly before those, whom they
not long before thought no better than their Slaves, and themselves
now being sold as Slaves'.[16] The etymology is uncertain, but the

Kumasi-led military alliance appears to have taken its name from the Twi phrase *osa nti fo*, the 'because of war people'.

Following (or in some accounts, preceding) the defeat of Denkyira, Komfo Anokye further demonstrated his ability to harness powerful spiritual forces by presiding over the creation of the Golden Stool. The *History of Ashanti Kings* does not mention this seminal event, but various versions were recorded in Asante in the early twentieth century; details differ, but all agree that the stool was designed as the hallowed ur-symbol of the new kingdom. 'Anotchi told the Ashanti that if this stool was taken or destroyed', the colonial-era ethnographer R. S. Rattray was informed, 'then, just as a man sickens and dies whose *sunsum* during life has wandered away or has been injured ... so would the Ashanti nation sicken and lose its vitality and power'.[17] One informant told Rattray that Komfo Anokye drew the wooden core of the stool down from the sky and onto the knees of the waiting Osei Tutu; another, Anokye's descendant and successor as Agonahene, Kwadwo Apao, however, said that it was carved on earth, like any stool or *akonnwa*. Either way, Komfo Anokye inserted a range of potent 'medicines' into the stool, including the spirit of a sacrificial victim: according to Kwadwo Apao, Anokye 'struck him upon the head, and he disappeared into the Stool'.[18] It was then encased in gold and hung with seven bells, which Anokye said 'represented the seven Kings who would all be powerful; after whose time the power of Ashanti would wane'.[19] The stool would subsequently be decorated with golden effigies of the decapitated head of Ntim Gyakari and other great kings defeated in the course of Asante's military campaigns – striking symbols of the implacable power and ethos of accumulation of the expansionist state.

EMPIRE STATE

The Golden Stool enshrined the status of Kumasi as *primus inter pares*, first among equals, in the military alliance of neighbouring kingdoms that came together in the 1690s under the leadership of Osei Tutu. These original territorial divisions of Asante were collectively known as the *amantoo*, the most significant of which were further defined as the *ka naman nnum*, 'the five *aman* of the first rank': Dwaben, Kokofu, Bekwai and Nsuta, which were also ruled by branches of the Oyoko matriclan, and Mampon, whose kings were from the Beretuo clan. All five were within a 30-mile (48-km) radius of Kumasi, so the core of the new kingdom – what historians often refer to as 'metropolitan Asante' – was relatively compact. Mampon, with its unique 'silver stool', was generally regarded – and certainly regarded itself – as the leading *oman* after Kumasi: the Mamponhene Boahen Anantuo had led the Asante army in 1701 and his successors continued to hold the office of Asante Kontihene or supreme military commander. Each *amantoo* kingdom retained its own *omanhene* and a considerable degree of autonomy in terms of military organization, taxation and finance, law and ritual affairs. These realms, however, were all firmly articulated to the royal court of the Asantehene. The legal system, for example, included the right of ultimate appeal to the tribunal of the Asantehene – who, visitors to Kumasi observed, spent a great deal of time adjudicating such cases. In the spiritual realm, each *oman* held its own annual Odwira festival, but only after the *omanhene* and his court had renewed their allegiance to the Asantehene by attending the great Odwira in Kumasi. Indeed, it was Odwira that functioned as the crucial mechanism binding the constituent kingdoms to the centre; its ritual focus was not the Golden Stool, but an older *suman* or talisman called Apafram, said to have been acquired from the domains of Akwamu. Once Osei Tutu had mastered Apafram's fearsome powers, the *History of Ashanti Kings* explains, he reported its existence 'through all his districts and countries and told them that a day once in a year will be appointed for every one under Ashanti Kingdom to celebrate the suman'.[20]

Looking back to the precolonial past from the vantage point of the 1920s, when the British regime had effectively dismantled Asante and was governing its constituent *aman* as separate 'native states',

Rattray was full of praise for what he saw as the constitutional genius of this confederation. Fifty years later, Wilks too stressed the rationality and effectiveness of Asante government, albeit with a greater emphasis on the central organs of power in Kumasi and the dizzying complexity of its ranks of office-holders. Yet the constitutional balance between the Asantehene, on the one hand, and the *amanhene* of the other core kingdoms, on the other, would remain a matter of recurring dispute throughout Asante history. Mampon and Dwaben had a notably uneasy relationship with centralized authority, the latter rising in open rebellion against Kumasi overrule in the 1830s and again in the 1870s. Neither was conflict within the Oyoko ruling dynasty itself uncommon: succession to the Golden Stool was sometimes violently contested (albeit less so than in many African kingdoms) and of the twelve Asantehenes who ruled in the precolonial period, four were overthrown or 'destooled'. These problems were in part a result of Asante's expansive ambitions. By the middle of the eighteenth century, it extended far beyond its original forest heartland: to quote Wilks, 'Kumasi, from being in effect only the senior of the *amantoo*, found itself the metropolis of a large and sprawling empire'.[21]

The creation of what the Ghanaian anthropologist Kwame Arhin dubbed 'Greater Asante' was largely the result of a series of well-executed military campaigns led by Osei Tutu's successor as Asantehene, Opoku Ware (r. *c.* 1720–1750).[22] Osei Tutu had successfully mopped up remaining Denkyira resistance early in his reign, but in 1717 was killed fighting against the Akyem kingdoms to the southeast. Following this setback, Opoku Ware's armies overran the Bono kingdom of Takyiman to the northwest in 1722–23, defeated and imposed tributary relations on the savanna kingdom of Gonja in 1732–33 and the Bono kingdom of Gyaman in 1740, and then in 1742 overran the recalcitrant Akyem before sweeping down to Accra and the eastern Gold Coast. A further campaign into the savanna resulted in tributary relations being imposed upon Gonja's neighbour, the Mossi kingdom of Dagbon. Despite periodic interventions to quell local unrest, the following reigns of Kusi Obodom (r. 1750–1764), Osei Kwadwo (r. 1764–1777) and Osei Kwame (r. 1777–1803) were characterized by a shift from imperial expansion to consolidation. Sustained militarism would not reappear until the opening decades of the nineteenth century, when Osei Tutu Kwame invaded the Fante region of the central Gold Coast on three occasions and then in 1819 secured victory over the rebellious Gyamanhene Kwadwo Adinkra on the northwest frontier. It was to sort out conflicts of jurisdiction in the Fante coastal towns arising from the former that the British mission travelled to Kumasi in 1817, by which time Asante had reached the apogee of its territorial expansion. The skulls of Kwadwo Adinkra and other defeated kings joined that of Ntim Gyakari in the royal mausoleum in the Bantama ward of Kumasi, from where they were brought out each Odwira as a mnemonic for the kingdom's military prowess.[23]

Asante was no longer simply a forest kingdom. It encompassed a diversity of non-Akan peoples on the Gold Coast to the south and in the grasslands to the north, while by the late eighteenth century, Kumasi had a substantial community of resident Muslims from the tributary savanna states and beyond. If military campaigns were often triggered by a desire to enforce obedience on unstable frontiers, then the maintenance of these new domains also had a clear economic rationale, in that they furthered the founding ethos of accumulation forged in the struggle against the encircling forest. Expansion to the coast secured access to the European forts, which by the eighteenth century were increasingly oriented towards purchasing captives for the Atlantic slave trade, while tribute in kind (including yearly quotas of enslaved people) flowed in from Gonja and Dagbon. Kumasi's Muslim community, meanwhile, was engaged in commodity trade with the broader Sudanic zone, including the lucrative export of kola nuts, a mild stimulant popular in Hausaland and elsewhere where Islam discouraged the consumption of alcohol. Muslim clerics also acquired great prestige in Kumasi for their mastery of literacy, their access through prayer and the Quran of 'the great God', and their production of much-sought-after protective talismans that incorporated Quranic script. 'I know that book (the Koran) is strong, and I like it because it is the book of the great God; it does good for me, and therefore I love the people that read it', Osei Tutu Kwame said to Joseph Dupuis, who in 1820 led a second British mission to Kumasi.[24] Indeed, Dupuis's Muslim informants in Kumasi reported that Osei Tutu Kwame's predecessor, Osei Kwame, demonstrated an 'inclination to establish the Korannic law for the civil code of the empire' – one factor that led to his overthrow and execution in 1803 by forces led by his ascribed mother, Asantehemaa Konadu Yaadom.[25]

Wilks made much of what he called the 'northern factor' in Asante history and of the contribution of Muslim literate skills to the bureaucratization of central government beginning in the reign of Osei Kwadwo in the 1760s and 1770s. In response to Asante's increasing size and complexity, he argued, Osei Kwadwo sought to subvert the power of Kumasi's hereditary chiefs and 'the transfer of the functions of government to a new class of officials controlled by the king and charged with the administration of the affairs of the empire'.[26] What Wilks described as a 'Kwadwoan revolution in government' – thus drawing a parallel with the well-known 'Tudor revolution in government' in sixteenth-century England – was carried forward by Osei Kwame and Osei Tutu Kwame, until by the early nineteenth century, in Kumasi at least, 'the preponderance of the old aristocracy in political affairs was completely shattered'.[27] The management of financial affairs, provincial administration, state-controlled trade, the great roads and other branches of government, Wilks argued, passed to an emergent class of appointed office-holders, whose posts were formalized in the creation of new stools and whose skills were often passed down from father to son rather than via the dominant matrilineal line of succession. Contributing to increasing administrative efficiency was a distinctly 'pluralistic' concept of Asante sovereignty, encapsulated for Wilks in the coexistence of the *sika dwa kofi*, the Golden Stool (symbolizing the exercise of political power), with the *sika mena*, the Golden Elephant Tail (symbolizing fiscal appro-priation), and the *sika akuma*, the Golden Axe (symbolizing dispute resolution, with the threat of military intervention). By the nineteenth century, he argued, there were even incipient political parties repre-senting the ideals of militarism versus mercantilism. 'Asante was not, as it were, a one-party state', Wilks concluded. 'It was a multi-party state under a monarch who was subject to criticism and vulnerable to removal from office'.[28]

Wilks's interpretation of the nature of the Asante kingdom has been questioned by other historians. It was, his critics have argued, very much a product of the times in which it was formulated: the opening phase of African independence in the 1960s and 1970s, when nationalist leaders and historians sympathetic to their cause sought to recover the glories of the continent's past obscured by racist colo-nial rule and to demonstrate that contemporary nation-building represented the renewal of a longer history of statecraft. Wilks, one wrote, sought systematically 'to describe and interpret Asante society in terms of categories transferred from the European experience'.[29] The problem with his approach was that it tended, inadvertently or otherwise, to make Asante look too much like an incipient European-style state. In common with other powerful and authoritarian 'fiscal-military' kingdoms, it did indeed develop a sophisticated and effective administrative apparatus, but the argument that it underwent a bureaucratic revolution is difficult to sustain. 'This bureaucracy', John Iliffe writes in his authoritative survey of African history, 'like Buganda's, was patrimonial: it grew from the royal household, remained subject to the king's favour, became in part hereditary, and earned no regular salaries'.[30] Wilks's analysis of the well-documented ritualized killing of enslaved captives and others at the funerals of the wealthy and powerful as well as during the *adae* and Odwira celebrations has also generated debate. Such slayings, he insisted, were either voluntary or, more commonly, were judicial punishments – an argument that served 'to assimilate the practice of human sacrifice in Asante to a recognizable European custom'.[31]

As T. C. McCaskie, Wilks's most trenchant critic, has pointed out, this view of history 'has no real place for ideas'.[32] The structures of knowledge and belief by which African peoples interpreted the world and their lived experience of it, that is to argue, need to be taken seriously – even if those ideas, as was the case with the practice of human sacrifice, might make for uncomfortable reading. Let us therefore examine the nature of Asante kingship in a bit more detail and consider how royal power was shaped and projected by ideas, beliefs and expressive ideologies.

ASANTE KINGSHIP

In her book *African Kingdoms* (1977), the anthropologist Lucy Mair posed a fundamental question: how were individuals able to make themselves kings?[33] Published shortly after Wilks's monumental *Asante in the Nineteenth Century* (1975), Mair drew on the detail he provided on the Asante political order and located it in a continent-wide comparative perspective. Expressing some early unease with Wilks's bureaucratic interpretation, Mair came to a different con-clusion on the nature of sovereignty in Africa: that while kingship was often reinforced by coercive power and developed highly effec-tive institutions of government, it emerged from and remained underpinned by spiritual power. Subsequent research has pursued this insight, which is in no way limited to the history of dynastic rule in Africa: 'claims to divine power', Sahlins reminds us, 'have been the raison d'être of political power throughout the greater part of human history'.[34] It lies at the heart of McCaskie's extensive body of work on Asante, which, departing from Wilks's emphasis on the structure of office-holding and governance, explores the ways in which the kingdom sought to impose control over society by shaping to its own ends the entangled terrains of knowledge, belief and historical memory.[35] Like Graeber and Sahlins in *On Kings*, McCaskie is more interested in the tension between coercion and consent at the heart of dynastic rule and with the ways in which kings sought to secure 'privileged access to the divine sources of prosperity and life itself'.[36]

None of this is to argue that the Asantehene was a 'divine king'. Neither, as we have seen, was he the descendant of a primordial stranger king who arrived from another place to instigate royal power. Yet the office of Akan *omanhene* did have many sacred attributes: the king's health and vitality were very much bound up with those of the kingdom, and his person was bound – and to some degree his mobility constrained – by a multitude of complex taboos.[37] Embedded within oral historics is a great deal of evidence pointing to the origins of the *oman* as a 'cosmic polity' and of its ruler as an essentially sacral figure concerned above all with the promotion of life, fertility and increase. All of this stands in contrast to Wilks's thesis of state formation as being propelled by *abirempon* or entrepreneurial 'big men', who carved agrarian estates from the forest and, particularly when they got hold of guns from the coast, turned them into *aman* and themselves into warrior kings. Yet these processes need not be seen as incompatible; indeed, they were likely to have been mutually constitutive. As the *History of Ashanti Kings* makes clear, military prowess was perceived in large part in 'supernatural' terms. So too was agricultural fecundity: at the heart of the ritual performances of Odwira was the Asantehene's role in presiding over the production of the new season's yam crop. Indeed, Bowdich, who attended Odwira in 1817, thought this aspect so important that he mistakenly dubbed it the Yam Custom.

Asante was forged and its power extended on the battlefield, and the identity of the Asantehene was from the outset that of a warrior king. This posed a problem, one collector of oral traditions was told in the 1940s, because traditionally the Akan *omanhene* 'must on no account come in contact with death' and 'in the olden days he did not go to war nor did he attend a funeral or visit the burial ground or Mausoleum of the royal deceased'. 'The death taboo was partly abolished when the Asante kingdom was founded, and the first

Asantehene preferred to remain a warrior chief', although the body and soul of the king was at all times – in peace as well as in war – heavily protected from mystical threat by an array of physical talismans and ritual enactments.[38] In life and in afterlife, the reputation of successive Asantehenes in large part rested on their military achievements, with subsequent incumbents of the Golden Stool struggling to attain the heights of Osei Tutu and Opoku Ware: *Osei ne Opoku*, seen as the twin pillars of the Oyoko dynasty. Thus, Opoku Ware's successor, the elderly and reportedly gentle Kusi Obodom, was remembered as an ineffective military leader, whose inconclusive clash with Dahomey resulted in many casualties and a shortage of enemy prisoners to sacrifice in order 'to appease the shades of the great captains who fell in the war'.[39] A fierce military culture extended down through society: carrying a gun to war was fundamental to attaining the status of full manhood, and every warrior in Asante's formidable citizen army wore a *kapo*, an iron bracelet forged from the barrel of a gun.

The ethos of militarism also created an imperative for newly enstooled Asantehenes to prove their worth – not least in the eyes of their departed predecessors – by going to war. When this resulted in great victories, as in the campaigns mounted by Opoku Ware and by Osei Tutu Kwame, this set a triumphant tone for the new reign and exemplified the role of the king as *ogyefo*, 'the one who takes'. Armies returned to Kumasi groaning with booty and with large retinues of captives, many of whom in the eighteenth century were sold on to the European slave traders on the Gold Coast. When the outcome was less successful, the result was dismay, dissent and, in the cases of Kusi Obodom in 1764 and Kofi Kakari in 1874, destoolment. Neither was it just aggrieved subjects and the lingering animosity of the spirits of fallen war captains needing propitiation: the incumbent of the Golden Stool needed too to manage his own predecessors, sternly looking on from *asamando*, the afterworld. This unrelenting need to reassure the royal dead was the focus of the cycle of *adae* celebrations. It is also apparent from the many telling references to them in recorded conversations that various visitors to Kumasi had with Osei Tutu Kwame and with his successor Kwaku Dua Panin (r. 1834–1867). Not only were departed rulers seen to be not fully 'dead' at all, but the living Asantehene saw himself as one with them: in a revealing observation, Bowdich noted that 'the King always spoke of the acts of his ancestors as his own'.[40] This recounting of history focused on a seamless evolution of royal power can be seen as a crucial element in what McCaskie sees as the kingdom's 'hegemonic project': a powerful ideological statement that encapsulates its efforts 'to authorize the "continuous present" of the Asante experience'.[41] Like the marking of the *adaduanan* calendar by the *adae* ceremonies, it was a way of imposing dynastic control over time itself.

How successful was this hegemonic project? It certainly helped that Asante was prosperous and the state well financed. It emerged from the only part of Africa where rich agricultural and mineral resources coincided, while eighteenth-century exports of enslaved people further bolstered state revenues by bringing yet more gold into its coffers. If military service was crucial to the notion of manhood, then success in wealth creation also brought prestige and public acclaim. Indeed, the state encouraged and applauded individual accumulation: all men of substance carried a set of scales and an array of brass gold weights, *mbramo* (sing. *abramo*), with which to weigh gold dust. Millions of *mbramo* were produced over the centuries, many in intriguing figurative form, and count as one of the glories of Akan artistic achievement. As Iliffe points out, 'even Asante and Dahomey, the most authoritarian eighteenth-century trading states, operated mixed economies in which chiefs and private merchants exported alongside official traders'.[42] Yet, ultimately, wealth flowed upwards: the key fiscal mechanism for this was death duties, which ensured that a significant proportion of self-acquired wealth in the form of gold dust would pass at the end of life into the Asantehene's 'great chest'. This rigorously enforced power of appropriation was symbolized by the Golden Elephant Tail, the *sika mena*;

the right to carry an elephant-tail switch, moreover, was granted to those individual accumulators who had demonstrated outstanding success in wealth creation. The elephant as the mightiest of forest animals therefore came to symbolize the historic project of carving wealth from the forest environment and the resulting economic contract between state and society: that the Asantehene, as the guardian of culture and of well-being, was the ultimate recipient of that wealth.

There is no doubt that Asante, like Dahomey, was authoritarian. The Asantehene wielded great power, including a monopoly over the exercise of (or delegation of) capital punishment, and although legal disputes brought before his tribunal were carefully considered, in the end, his word was law. There has been some debate over the extent of that authoritarianism: Wilks tended to stress the checks and balances of the political system, arguing that the Asantehene ruled as a 'king in council', advised by the leading Kumasi chiefs and the rulers of the *amantoo* beyond. He alone had the authority, however, to create new stools and to award loyalty with appointments to them, standing at the centre of a dense network of patronage dedicated to the amplification of royal power. A key issue for historians is how royal sovereignty was shaped by the tension between state and society. This was a matter that attracted the attention of the pioneering Black British missionary T. B. Freeman. As head of the Methodist mission on the Gold Coast, Freeman visited Kumasi a number of times in the 1830s and 1840s and, despite being dismayed about the practice of human sacrifice, had a good relationship with Asantehene Kwaku Dua Panin, whom he regarded 'as doubtless one

A brass gold weight or *abramo* in the form of a stool, the key symbol of Akan royal authority. Height 1 in. (2.5 cm).

of the wisest and most prudent men who have occupied the throne'.[43] While he was in no doubt that Kwaku Dua Panin wielded 'despotic' power, Freeman was struck by the way in which his subjects freely acknowledged that power as a way of maintaining a degree of 'aristocratic independence' from it. 'The despotism of Ashantee is that of the Forest Country, and that of Dahomey of the Open Country', he reflected.

> In Ashantee the despotism is more open, and sustained as such, by the peculiar prejudices, manners and customs of the people than is seen in Dahomey. Indeed the Ashantees seem to pride themselves in the cruel and sanguinary despotism of their government; and hence as the King of Ashantee parades the streets of his Capital on the great Custom Days the women crying his strong names add 'long may you live and be strong to kill us at your pleasure', and the masses of the men seem to take delight in the horrid scenes of cruelty which too often transpire, as though they would say 'Our King is a great despot and kills us as he pleases ....'[44]

The same sentiment was expressed in the horn call of Manwerehene Kwasi Brantuo, made by his retainers on elephant tusk instruments in commemoration of his elevation to a position of authority and wealth by Kwaku Dua Panin: *Me tiri ne me kon wura Asantehene*, the vocalized call rang out; 'the Asantehene owns my head and my neck'.[45] There is evidence here and elsewhere that the state's hegemonic project was indeed a successful one.

KUMASI

One problem with writing the history of Africa is that written sources are often focused on kings and royal cities, together with the elite office-holders and the trade attracted to them. This is the case with respect to Asante, where nineteenth-century visitors, such as Bowdich and Freeman, were closely monitored and largely restricted to Kumasi. Their observations of the kingdom were therefore made from its centre rather than its periphery, a perspective that subsequent historical scholarship has found difficult to escape. Oral traditions too tend to amplify royal power: the *History of Ashanti Kings* has much to say about the former but little about the latter. Yet there can be no doubt that Kumasi did play a dominant and distinctive role at the heart of the Asante imperial system. It was '*Osei ne Opoku kuro*', Osei Tutu's and Opoku Ware's 'village', dominated by the royal court and its massed ranks of functionaries, by the organs of central government and by 'lavish public performances of ritual that exhibited and reinforced the authority of the Golden Stool'.[46] Surrounded by a penumbra of agricultural settlements and specialist craft villages producing pottery, woodwork and, most famously, the stunningly designed *kente* cloth (see pl. XIX), the city stood apart, its wide principal thoroughfares – each named, and overseen by a designated captain – connecting seventy-seven named wards. Its role was underscored by the dominance of a distinctive architectural style first recorded by Bowdich: the *odampan*, or open-fronted residence, on the verandah of which – in full public view – office-holders transacted government business. Freeman too was impressed with the 'taste displayed in the erection and in the cleanliness and order of their establishments', embossed with striking geometric designs in polished red clay and including indoor toilets (see pl. XVIII).[47] Kumasi was a place of excitement and opportunity, a magnet for ambitious young men from the provinces. Yet for those who failed to secure or who lost elite patronage, it could also be an unforgiving place of insecurity and danger: the historical record contains many accounts of the spectacular rise and the calamitous fall of individual fortunes.

At the heart of Kumasi, around which much of the life of the city revolved, lay the extensive royal palace. Its work was, in part, government. Yet, in common with all royal families, equally important was the work of reproducing itself, both in human and ideological terms. Thus, the Asantehene's retinue of wives – notionally 3,333, as set down in the sacred laws of Komfo Anokye, but in reality anything from several dozen to several hundred – occupied quarters secluded from public gaze and presided over by *adabraafo*, the royal eunuchs. The ethos of accumulation, then, extended to the accumulation of women. The palace was also devoted to the task of amplifying the sacred persona of the king, who was served by a vast retinue of *nhenkwaa*, mostly male royal servants: *akyeame*, spokesmen or 'linguists'; *adumfo*, executioners; *akrafo*, 'soul washers', the guardians of the royal soul; *nkonnwasoafo*, stool carriers; *afenasoafo*, sword bearers (see pl. XVII); *fotosanfo*, gold weighers; *ahoprafo*, elephant-tail bearers, who swept away evil forces from around the king; *nseniefo*, heralds; *asokwafo*, horn blowers; *nsumankwaafo*, specialists in medicines and talismans; and many more. Governed by intricate codes of etiquette and housed in the city's various wards, this army of servants can be seen as an extension of the king's body itself, as he moved through 'the landscape of his own public being'.[48] The aim of many status-conscious young men drawn to the capital was to be recruited to these retinues, Freeman noting the swaggering conduct of even the most menial palace serv-ants. The identity of the various classes of *nhenkwaa* was underscored by their responsibility for and display of the vast array of royal regalia: the 'massy gold ornaments' that bedazzled Bowdich in 1817. This sumptuous material culture served further to project royal power; in an extraordinary demonstration of the renewal of that power, the gold regalia was melted down each year in preparation for the Odwira festival and reworked into new and more innovative forms. As Bowdich noted, 'this is a piece of state policy very imposing on the populace, and the tributary chiefs who pay but an annual visit'.[49]

It was Odwira that encapsulated the essence of Asante kingship. If the British envoys were amazed by their welcome into Kumasi, then their experience of the annual celebration four months later was even more overwhelming. Bowdich captures something of the spectacle and sensory overload of Odwira in his famous drawing titled 'The First Day of the Yam Custom' (see pl. XX), which depicts the scene on *odwira fomemene*, Saturday, 6 September 1817, when the

Asantehene presided over a huge public assembly welcoming all those who, the day before, had poured into the city from the surrounding provinces. Odwira was indeed partly a harvest festival, celebrating the arrival of the new-season yam crop as a symbol of the triumph of forest agriculture. Yet it was far more than that: in essence a ritual of purification (*dwira*: to cleanse or purify), it encompassed a multitude of complex ceremonial performances directed towards the affirmation of the role of the living Asantehene and his departed ancestors as the guardians and arbiters of the received cultural and political order. It was, that is, the manifestation of a dynastic cult, which rehearsed the forging of the kingdom and the acquisition of the Apafram *suman* by Osei Tutu. Thus, the scene depicted by Bowdich took place at *apremoso*, 'the place of cannons', so called because mounted there were the European cannons supposedly captured from the defeated Denkyira army in 1701. Neither were accounts of the spectacular visual and sonic onslaught of *odwira fomemene* simply the result of overwhelmed European observers: they were specifically designed to fill the sensory horizons of all the participants and to generate a 'participatory and communal catharsis on terms defined and orchestrated by the state'.[50]

NINETEENTH-CENTURY TRANSITIONS

Asante's fortunes fluctuated in the nineteenth century. Under Osei Tutu Kwame, it rode out the impact of the abolition of the Atlantic slave trade, absorbing more captives into the local economy and redirecting its efforts towards the expanding trade in kola nuts to the north. The inability to resolve the nagging problems of sovereignty on the Gold Coast, however, led to escalating tensions with the British and their local African allies. These culminated in 1826 with a rare defeat on the battlefield, when an army led by Osei Tutu Kwame's successor Osei Yaw Akoto was routed at Katamanso on the Accra Plains, undone – depending on which interpretation of the calamity one follows – either by a lack of sufficient ritual protection or by the artillery rockets deployed by the British. The result was the loss of the empire's southern provinces, where, from the 1830s, Britain's colonial outpost, the so-called Gold Coast Forts and Settlements, fitfully evolved into a vaguely defined protectorate dedicated to the advance of 'legitimate commerce'. Yet a peace treaty with the British followed by the accession of Kwaku Dua Panin to the Golden Stool in 1834 enabled Asante to recover from these setbacks. Indeed, Kwaku Dua Panin's reign can be seen to represent the pinnacle of royal power. An autocratic, ruthless and, as Freeman observed, highly effective ruler, Kwaku Dua took forward the project of accumulation and increase not by further military adventures, but by encouraging commerce with the savannas to the north and the Gold Coast to the south. By his death in 1867, the dynasty was secure, trade was booming and the great chest was reported to be full.

Yet all this came with a cost. The system of wealth appropriation had begun to falter, as Kwaku Dua Panin broke the established understanding between state and society by imposing exploitative levels of taxation at a time when the growth of private trade with the Gold Coast provided ambitious entrepreneurs with an alternative commercial model based on free-market individualism. In his efforts to contain these pressures, the Asantehene became increasingly concerned with maintaining ideological conformity: the unauthorized introduction of any 'foreign fashion' – including Christianity and other religious innovations – was a capital offence. Dynastic power then broke down during the weak and divisive reigns of Kofi Kakari (r. 1867–1874) and his brother Mensa Bonsu (r. 1874–1883). Military defeat at the hands of a British expeditionary force in 1874 initiated a period of acute instability, as the northern Bono kingdoms rebelled against Kumasi overrule. Then, following the destoolment of Mensa Bonsu in 1883 by discontented so-called 'youngmen' chafing under his increasingly unjust rule, dynastic conflict escalated into a full-scale civil war, which ravaged the metropolitan heartland of the empire. The conflict was resolved in 1888 when the politically astute

Asantehemaa Yaa Kyaa secured the succession of her son Agyeman Prempeh, who sought to reach a modus vivendi with the new British crown colony of the Gold Coast. But by then it was too late: the European Scramble for Africa was in full swing, and in 1896 another British force marched unopposed to Kumasi, arrested Agyeman Prempeh, Yaa Kyaa and other members of the royal court and brought Asante under colonial rule. The sovereignty of the kingdom was terminated, its imperial domains dismantled and Komfo Anokye's prophecy that the power of the Golden Stool would wane after the reign of seven great kings (depending on how you count great kings) came to pass.

European imperial aggression was the decisive factor in the eclipse of the Asante kingdom. Yet internal division too played a role, undermining the ruling elite's ability to respond to the rising challenges of the late nineteenth century. An emergent class of aspirant businessmen was increasingly disenchanted with the authoritarianism and the exactions of the dynastic state. 'We do not want to hear the names of those down trodden degraded native African Kings and Chiefs', one group of dissident exiles on the Gold Coast wrote to the British governor in 1894. 'Down with native drums, native umbrellas, native swords and elephant tails: useless and good for nothing.'[51] For some, at least, a spell had been broken: the 'creativity of power' had faltered. Such sentiments – operating in tension with the nostalgic desire on the part of others for the renewal of past glories – would continue to shape Asante politics throughout the twentieth century and to the present day.

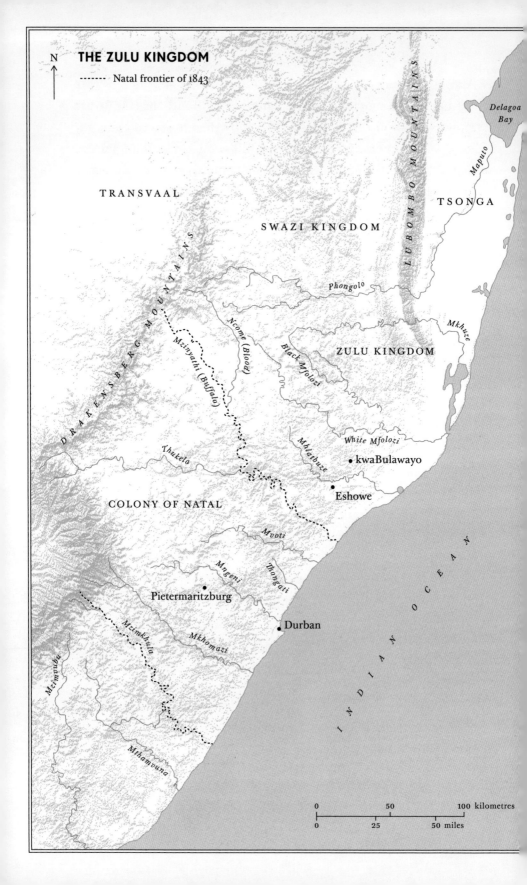

CHAPTER 9

THE ZULU KINGDOM

---- Natal frontier of 1843

N

TRANSVAAL

SWAZI KINGDOM

LUBOMBO MOUNTAINS

Delagoa
Bay

TSONGA

Maputo

DRAKENSBERG MOUNTAINS

Phongolo

Ncome (Blood)

Mzinyathi (Buffalo)

Black Mfolozi

ZULU KINGDOM

Mkhuze

Thukela

Mhlatuze

White Mfolozi

• kwaBulawayo

COLONY OF NATAL

• Eshowe

Mvoti

Mngeni

Thongati

Pietermaritzburg

Mzimkhula

Mkhomazi

• Durban

INDIAN OCEAN

Mzimvubu

Mthamvuna

0   50   100 kilometres

0   25   50 miles

THE ZULU KINGDOM

Wayne Dooling

The establishment of the Zulu kingdom between 1817 and 1828 is indelibly associated with the person of Shaka, the first-born son of Nandi and Senzangakhona, chief of the AmaZulu people. Senzangakhona's chiefdom, whose people took their name from an early ancestor called Zulu (meaning 'sky' or 'heavens'), was merely one of many small northern Nguni-speaking polities of that part of southeastern Africa that is today encompassed by the South African province of KwaZulu-Natal. The AmaZulus' neighbours included the AmaButhelezi, the AmaQungebe, the AmaChunu, the AmaMajola, the AmaXulu and the AmaSikakane (the Bantu-language prefix *ama* meaning 'the people of'). All lived in the vicinity of the AmaZulu royal capital and marriage between the different communities was not uncommon. The kingdom was thus diverse in origin, a fact recognized in the oral traditions passed down through the centuries.[1] Shaka's expansionist kingdom, however, would not only incorporate these neighbouring peoples but would ultimately occupy the entire region later known as Zululand, bounded by the Drakensberg mountain range in the west, the Indian Ocean in the east, and the Phongolo and Thukela rivers in the north and south respectively.

The Nguni of southeastern Africa constituted the southern edge of the expansion of Bantu-speaking farming peoples across the vast African savanna. Their entry into the region, which for several millennia had been occupied by hunter-gatherers, can be dated to at least the third century CE, while archaeologists have, with a reasonable degree

of precision, traced the ancestry of the Nguni polities that were ultimately brought within the AmaZulu orbit to around 1000 CE. These
communities were organized into chiefdoms comprising clans bound
by real or, in many cases, fictive ties of kinship, marriage and client-
ship, the latter constructed in order to justify certain claims, rights
and obligations. Settlements varied in scale from a few hundred to
several thousand individuals, and chiefdoms could occupy areas as
large as thousands of square miles. Most, however, tended towards
the smaller end of the spectrum. These were often fluid and unstable,
their boundaries shifting as ties of loyalty were tested and disrupted
by conflicts over access to resources. Although chiefdoms sometimes
coalesced into what can be called paramountcies, when one chief was
able to expand his clout by monopolizing resources by means of
warfare or other skillful methods, the resulting 'paramount chiefs'
were not possessed of especially great powers and mostly lacked the
coercive means to restrain dissidents or upstarts seeking to establish
new political units. Even paramount chiefs who had managed to
accumulate a greater-than-usual amount of wealth and power rarely
had the ability to force subordinate chiefdoms into complete submission, and if they did, it certainly did not continue over extended
periods of time. Although subordinate chiefdoms were compelled to
swear allegiance and make formal payments of tribute to paramount
chiefs, they were most often able to retain a degree of autonomy by
commanding their own military followings, making their own laws
and resisting those paramounts who wished to extract excessive payment of tribute. For this reason, such chiefdoms have been described
as being 'tributaries' rather than 'subjects' of paramount chiefs.[2]

ORIGINS

Shaka's outstanding achievement was to establish one of Africa's
most powerful kingdoms – its image of enduring power later immor-
talized by its famous victory over the British army at the Battle of

Isandlwana in 1879. He did this by transforming the established nature of political power in the region, by conquering and directly incorporating a large number of neighbouring chiefdoms into a single political entity under AmaZulu dominance. This feat was accomplished by a combination of diplomacy, novel methods of warfare and the deployment of a substantial amount of violence. Shaka's fearsome rule led to popular discontent and his ultimate undoing, but the kingdom itself survived his assassination in 1828 and the intrusion during the 1830s of *trekboers*, Afrikaans-speaking white farmers migrating north to escape British colonial rule in the Cape Colony. It was only at the end of the 1870s that the kingdom's dominance was eclipsed by British military power, after one of the iconic battles of the Victorian age.

A famous engraving of Shaka, from Nathaniel Isaacs, *Travels and Adventures in Eastern Africa* (London, 1836).

Although the Zulu kingdom has become virtually synonymous with the person of Shaka, most historians have long since abandoned the notion that complex historical processes can be simply ascribed to the actions of 'great men'. It is our task, therefore, to situate Shaka's achievements within their broader historical context. The AmaZulu kingdom was not the only example of political consolidation among the chiefdoms of southeastern Africa during the late eighteenth and early nineteenth centuries, and Shaka was only one of a number of powerful leaders in the region. Furthermore, it can no longer be asserted with certainty, as most earlier scholars did, that there were 'no large, centralised political units in the region until the end of the eighteenth century'.[3] Although the AmaZulu kingdom was a new state, it is not entirely clear that it was a new *kind* of state – it has been postulated that a large 'Zulu-type' state called Mbo, with its origins in the sixteenth century, may have existed in the Nguni region into the seventeenth or eighteenth centuries.[4] Be that as it may, among the most notable centralized chiefdoms to emerge more or less simultaneously from the late eighteenth century onwards were the Mabhudu chiefdom of present-day southern Mozambique, the AmaNdwandwe chiefdom in the region around Magudu, and the AmaMthethwa in the area between the lower Mfolozi and Mhlathuze rivers. The chiefs of these larger entities, such as Zwide of the AmaNdwandwe, Shaka's most powerful foe, and Matiwane of the AmaNgwane, were representative of a 'new kind of leader: men who owed their positions as much to their aggressiveness, powers of initiative, and ability to make quick decisions as they did to their diplomatic and organizational talents'.[5] What, then, was the broader context for such centralization of political power and consolidation of chiefdoms from the late eighteenth century onwards, and for the emergence of Zulu domination in particular?

Early European historical accounts of substantive political change among the northern Nguni placed the emphasis squarely on the influence and intervention of white settlers in the region. Based largely on the accounts of white settlers themselves, this narrative began to emerge in the nineteenth century but continued to hold sway in twentieth-century colonial South Africa. Such achievements, it argued, must have been the result of what it referred to as 'extraneous influences'; that is to say, they could not have come from developments within African societies. The settler narrative typically starts with the military innovations of Dingiswayo (r. *c.* 1795–1817), leader of the AmaMthethwa, who exerted considerable influence over the young Shaka. Rev. A. T. Bryant, a Catholic missionary who had spent much time among the AmaZulu, thought of Dingiswayo as a 'quite exceptional character, a decidedly capable man, observant, thoughtful, imaginative, pushful – and by no means wholly engrossed in wine and women'. But as a 'pure initiation of the Bantu mind and a product of purely Bantu training', Bryant believed, his 'progressive ideas and activities' would have been 'decidedly extraordinary'.[6] What were these 'extraneous influences'? The common thread that runs through several accounts is Dingiswayo's contact with Europeans in the Cape Colony to the southwest, founded by the Dutch East India Company in 1652 and taken over by the British in 1806. The narrative originated with Henry Francis Fynn, a trader who arrived in the neighbouring region of Natal in 1824, some years after Dingiswayo's death. Fynn claimed that during several years of exile following a failed attempt to usurp leadership of the chieftaincy, Dingiswayo came into contact with one Dr Cowan, a traveller from the Cape who introduced him to guns and horses, two of the essential elements of white colonial power. This account proved remarkably tenacious and was, in essence, adopted by several subsequent settler narratives. In 1875, Theophilus Shepstone, the British diplomatic agent in Natal since 1846, reiterated its main outlines:

> It seems that in his travels he [Dingiswayo] had reached the Cape Colony, and must have lived with or entered the service of some colonist .... It was during his stay in the Cape Colony that he acquired the information, or made the observations, which were to effect the great change in his native land and the

surrounding countries .... He learned the strength of standing armies, the value of discipline and training, as compared with the mobs called armies, in his own country. He saw that if he could gain possession of his tribe he could gratify his ambition. He had heard of or seen bodies of civilised soldiers. He had ascertained that they were divided into regiments and companies, with regularly appointed officers, and he thought that all soldiers were bachelors. He had no sooner got possession of power than he set to work to organize his tribe in accordance with these ideas.[7]

Fynn's original account, however, is blatantly inaccurate and he also altered dates to suit his narrative. Even if his story of the meeting with Cowan were true, recent research has demonstrated that Dingiswayo rose to prominence long before he was said to have come into contact with travellers from the Cape. Moreover, the 'innovations' most often ascribed to Dingiswayo, especially his building of something like a standing army, preceded his reign by some time.

We thus have to seek alternative explanations for the consolidation of Nguni chiefdoms at the end of the eighteenth century. Investigations into the relationship between political and environmental change have been especially fruitful. As far back as 1940, the anthropologist Max Gluckman suggested that the communities of southeastern Africa witnessed significant population growth from at least the sixteenth century onwards. Such growth, Gluckman argued, reached critical proportions in the last third of the eighteenth century. The result was what Gluckman described as a 'disequilibrium' between people and their environment. A 'land crisis' put a break on older processes, which had hitherto allowed communities to occupy free land and thus remain relatively small in size. According to Gluckman, the tensions between population and environmental limits were resolved by the centralized control assumed by especially strong lineage heads, who could more effectively allocate resources and mediate disputes.[8]

Gluckman's account does not stand up to scrutiny, however, and has been subjected to substantial criticism. First, there is little evidence to suggest anything like the existence of a 'land crisis' in the late eighteenth century or that population growth among the northern Nguni had reached a critical stage by 1775, the date he identified as the onset of political centralization. We lack precise demographic evidence for the period: Gluckman suggested a population density of 3.5 people per sq. mile (2.58 sq. km), but more recent studies have arrived at a much higher estimated figure of 12 people per sq. mile. Densities could be even higher in more favoured, well-watered regions: Portuguese records suggest that the coastal belt and lower river basins had substantial populations of people and cattle at least 250 years before Shaka's ascendancy and long before Gluckman thought densities in these areas reached critical levels. Second, much land remained unoccupied after 1775; it was only thirty years later, as far as we can tell, that pressure began to be felt on land and natural resources.[9]

Gluckman's hypothesis may not be entirely convincing, but the relationship between the environment and political change has remained an alluring avenue of exploration for historians, especially as it is clear that the process of state formation in southeastern Africa accelerated at a time of prolonged and severe drought. In order to understand these complex processes of change, we have to turn our attention to the nature of agricultural and pastoral production. The Bantu-speaking peoples of southern Africa planted crops and herded cattle, although hunting remained important. Production was centred on the homestead (*umuzi*), where the most basic division of labour was that between men and women. Homesteads varied in size and wealth, but the majority consisted of a male head, two or three wives and their children. Marriage involved the transfer of cattle from the homestead of the husband's family to that of the wife's family. The transaction was known as *lobola* and in essence represented the transfer of the labour power and reproductive capacities of women from one homestead to the other. Each wife had her own hut, its physical position in relation to that of her husband reflecting her status in the domestic realm. Women performed the great bulk of agricultural labour, cultivating staple crops that were well adapted to variable rainfall, such as sorghum (*amabele*), millet (*unyawothi*) and yams (*idumbe*). Sorghum was probably the most widely cultivated as it was especially well adapted to the environment.[10]

The region was also well suited to cattle-herding – overwhelmingly the domain of men – so long as the herders could move freely between the two dominant types of vegetation of the savanna: so-called sourveld and sweetveld. Sourveld was the characteristic grass cover of higher rainfall areas and provided grasses that were especially nutritious to herds during the spring and early summer months – indeed, it could only be utilized during four months of the year, after which the grasses lost their palatability. Sweetveld was characteristic of drier areas with scattered trees, and provided essential grazing during the dry winter months. Mixed veld made up the areas between the two dominant forms of vegetation and could be grazed from six to eight months of the year. The prevalence of these grasses depended on levels of precipitation, which varied substantially over short distances as rivers cut deep valleys into the landscape. In general, rainfall levels were higher on the coast where thick forests predominated, while the river valleys often received very little rainfall. These variations in vegetation and rainfall patterns meant that pastoralists had to be able to move freely in order to obtain optimum nutritional value for their herds throughout the year.[11]

It is not clear when maize was introduced to southeastern Africa from the Americas, but it was most likely cultivated by the mid-sixteenth century, and in Zululand from about 1700. Most sources agree that the crop was adopted only slowly and did not immediately displace indigenous staples until well into the nineteenth century. Compared to sorghum and millet, maize had several disadvantages. It required higher levels of rainfall and soil fertility and was especially susceptible to drought. Early varieties matured quickly, in about fifty to sixty days, but delivered low yields. In the wetter lowland regions, however, maize offered a number of distinct advantages: it required a shorter growing period, which allowed for the harvesting of multiple crops within a single agricultural season and thus delivered higher yields than sorghum; it required less looking after when growing; and its preparation for consumption was less labour intensive as it could be eaten roasted on the cob.[12]

As rainfall patterns changed from the mid-eighteenth century onwards, maize was able to spread from its lowland base to the upland interior. Dendro-climatological research (that is, based on the study of tree rings) has shown that the region experienced periods of wet and dry cycles with some regularity about every twenty years, and that three major shifts in climate occurred during the eighteenth and early nineteenth centuries. In the first period, from about 1700 to 1750, levels of rainfall declined, resulting in greater reliance upon drought-resistant crops, such as sorghum. The second phase, from around 1750, witnessed higher rainfall, which encouraged a significant expansion of maize production and increase in cattle numbers due to higher grass yield. These were years of plenty, and the northern Nguni were probably able to harvest substantially increased volumes of grain, milk and meat, which in turn allowed for rapid population growth. Growing herds also facilitated the ready transfer of cattle in the form of *lobola* payments, allowing young men to marry more easily and so establish their own homesteads.

The third phase, beginning around 1790, was characterized by significant climatic change; by this time, the northern Nguni region is believed to have been densely populated by people as well as livestock. Evidence from tree rings, recorded oral testimonies and eyewitness accounts by early travellers all point to a significant decline in rainfall throughout much of southeastern Africa. This can be related to worldwide changes in weather patterns, most likely stimulated by an increase in volcanic activity in the northern hemisphere between 1750 and the 1840s, which released vast amounts of ash and gases into the Earth's atmosphere. The effects were felt throughout the subcontinent, as the precipitous decline in rainfall led to drought and crop failures. In Cape Town, British authorities were compelled to import food in order to avert disaster; among the northern Nguni, the years of plenty gave way to famine.[13]

Two major droughts were recorded between 1800 and 1824. The first, which occurred between 1800 and 1806–7, was remembered among the northern Nguni as the *Madlathule* ('let one eat what he can and say naught' or 'let him eat and remain silent'). One inform-ant remembered that 'the sun on that occasion shone scorchingly for three years'.[14] Unlike previous periods of shortage, the *Madlathule* affected the entire region and caused much suffering. Memories of the famine lingered for a century. 'This famine was a general one .... People had to protect their gardens against human beings. For starv-ing people would make their way into a garden and eat raw the green mealies [maize] grown there.'[15] The period was associated with social breakdown, as homes were abandoned, settlement patterns upset and communities transformed into roaming marauders in search of food. 'There were cannibals. Famine caused these to exist. They appeared in Tshaka's time.'[16]

While there is no explicit evidence to link the *Madlathule* directly to the emergence of larger and more centralized political units, it does seem clear that the famine triggered a general subsistence crisis by preventing the free movement of cattle between different ecologi-cal zones. Moreover, maize had probably become the major staple in a number of areas by the early nineteenth century and increased dependence on the crop would have left communities especially vulnerable. It is in this context, therefore, that the drive to political consolidation must be understood. Additionally, a coincidence between the source and direction of the expansion of dominant chiefdoms and the most desirable grazing areas has been identified. Assuming political control over larger areas of land and over increased numbers of people, as happened under Dingiswayo and Shaka, would have given chiefdoms access to wider ecological zones, and thus to larger grazing and arable lands.[17]

There was a further relationship between the environment and the consolidation of political power in the early nineteenth century.

It is widely accepted that Shaka's kingdom owed much of its power to his successful construction and deployment of military regiments based on 'age-sets' or distinct generations of AmaZulu fighting men. These were called *amabutho* (sing. *ibutho*) and their members were prohibited from marrying until such time that they had spent much of their adult lives – perhaps fifteen or twenty years – working for the king, in both the productive and military spheres. Young women, too, were drawn into female age-set regiments and prevented from marrying until given permission by the king, which generally occurred when an associated male regiment of a matching age-grade had been released from service. The result was that women married several years after puberty, thus reducing the number of children they were likely to have, while the creation of new homesteads by young men was equally delayed. Though we cannot identify a causal relationship between the subsistence crisis and changes to the system of home-stead reproduction, it is inescapable that by delaying the age at which women and men got married, the Zulu king was able to influence the most fundamental processes of the kingdom – the process upon which its very existence was based. He could control to an important degree the intensity with which the environment was exploited, the rate of demographic increase, and the rate and direction in which the process of production could expand. The Zulu military system gave the king the means to control the process of reproduction and production within the Zulu kingdom.[18]

It should be remembered, however, that the *amabutho* system was not Shaka's innovation, and preceded his rule by some time. As noted earlier, the AmaMthethwa were among the most notable chiefdoms to emerge in the late eighteenth century. They rose to prominence under Dingiswayo, who successfully consolidated a large number of chiefdoms from the time that his reign commenced around 1795, a process that had been initiated by his father, Jobe. It seems likely, therefore, that the chiefdom was of considerable size before Dingiswayo's accession. Over the course of the following years, Dingiswayo was able to gain a significant advantage over his

neighbours. As one informant, Ndukwana, remembered several decades after the events:

> [The AmaMthethwa] made war over the whole country, and the
> Ndwandwe too. At first Dingiswayo defeated all the country.
> It was said he was sided with by womenkind, because his mode
> of conquest or warfare was to go, then halt, and so on by
> degrees, following or driving his enemy for many miles;
> in consequence of his perpetual pursuit the women would
> 'get tired' and return, whereupon the fleeing people, on account
> of their women, would be forced to surrender.[19]

Successful military campaigns thus brought many peoples under
Dingiswayo's sway, including the AmaZulu chiefdom of about two
thousand people.[20] By the time of his final campaign in 1816, Dingiswayo could count on the allegiance of no fewer than thirty chiefdoms, while his rule extended from the Mfolozi in the north to
the Thukela in the south, and about 80 miles (130 km) inland
from the Indian Ocean.[21] Fynn recorded Dingiswayo's conquests
in some detail:

> The wars which Dingiswayo began with his neighbours were not
> at first on a great scale. But they were successful, and spurred him
> on to more important movements. He assumed a despotic power
> hitherto unknown. In declaring war, being the first of the native
> chiefs in that part of South Africa that entered upon hostilities
> with other tribes in a regular warlike manner, he assigned as his
> reason that he wished to do away with the incessant quarrels that
> occurred amongst the tribes, because no supreme head was over
> them to say who was right and who was wrong .... The first tribe
> he conquered were the Qadi. He directed their cattle to be
> brought to his place of residence and there to be assorted. The
> oxen were distributed among his warriors, but he restored the
> cows to the defeated tribe, from which he exacted submission
> to his authority. On this principle he continued his conquests.[22]

Most sources agree that Dingiswayo did not completely annihilate the enemy and that he especially spared women and children. Ndukwana remembered that he 'made war everywhere, but refrained from killing the various chiefs', while Fynn noted that he 'gave his commanders strict orders not to allow the whole of the tribe's property to be plundered, and to destroy no more people than was absolutely necessary'.[23] Furthermore, Dingiswayo 'requested his people to promote intermarriages with the vanquished and so bring about a general union'.[24] The cost to subjugated chiefs who were allowed to remain in place was the regular payment of tribute; those who refused did so under pain of death.[25]

Although Dingiswayo's military strategies were clearly not adopted from white settlers, as Shepstone would have it, there can be little doubt that his success in battle stemmed from his efficient deployment of *amabutho*. Understanding their role is therefore crucial. The *amabutho* had their origins in circumcision schools long established among the Nguni of southern Africa. The schools assembled young men of a particular group and of about the same age around a chief or senior man of a ruling lineage for a period of ritual seclusion. Importantly, circumcision groups were organized primarily by place of origin and had their own names and insignia – all of which would contribute to the *amabutho*'s powerful and cohesive martial identity. The ritual isolation of the groups for three to four months served as the key marker in the transition from boyhood to manhood – after which the initiated were allowed to marry and establish their own homesteads – but the labour of the young men could also be utilized in services such as agricultural production, hunting or trade on behalf of the chief.

In the second half of the eighteenth century, however, the nature of circumcision schools changed: young men now found themselves more strictly controlled by chiefs and their labour was more commonly diverted to military ends. The periods of isolation associated with male circumcision was supplanted by longer periods of intensive training and practice in hunting and warfare. The evidence suggests that by the end of the eighteenth century, the practice of circumcision among the northern Nguni had fallen into widespread disuse: travellers' reports from the 1820s and 1830s noted that only the oldest men had passed through circumcision schools, and it is doubtful that Senzangakhona, Shaka's father, had been so initiated.[26] AmaMthethwa traditions suggest that circumcision schools lapsed before the reign of Dingiswayo and that *amabutho* had been established by his father, Jobe. According to Rev. A. T. Bryant, 'military regiments were the universal Nguni custom before either of them [Dingiswayo and Shaka] was king':

> The Nguni habit of banding together youths of a like age
> started with the old circumcision parties or guilds ....
> When, towards the end of the eighteenth century, circumcision
> fell into disuse, the practice of classifying the youth of the clan
> in separate groups according to age still continued, but now,
> not for circumcision, but for general state purposes. Each such
> band, still called by the old name *iButo* (a collected body),
> had also its own distinguishing appellation and separate
> headquarters; and since its principal occupation henceforth,
> as the clans grew in size, power and aggressiveness, was
> of a military nature, it may quite appropriately be termed
> a 'regiment'.[27]

Changes as profound as these could not have happened everywhere all at once. The timing of transformations suggests that environmental change alone cannot explain the emergence of *amabutho* and their deployment for purposes of political consolidation and centralization. Other factors were clearly at play too. A paucity of documentary evidence has led some scholars to minimize the significance of trade.[28] The importance of the ivory trade with Delagoa Bay (now Maputo Bay in present-day Mozmbique) cannot be overlooked, however, especially as significant changes in its scale and nature coincided with the transformation of the *amabutho* system. Although not much ivory was traded in the period up to 1750, European demand for tusks led to a marked change during the second half of the eighteenth century. Dingiswayo derived much wealth from delivering ivory to European traders at Delagoa Bay. Before he took control of the AmaMthethwa chieftaincy, institutional organization of trade was very limited, but as chief he introduced two important innovations that changed this. First, he organized a caravan, which comprised at least a hundred porters, to transport ivory and cattle to Delagoa Bay. Second, he claimed a monopoly over the trade, a restriction so important that those who breached it were put to death. By the time of Shaka's reign, the ivory trade was highly organized; on occasion Shaka deployed all of his *amabutho* to hunt elephants. By the 1820s, caravans of up to a thousand porters regularly carried elephant tusks to Delagoa Bay, while by 1834, Zululand was reported to be 'glutted' with beads obtained in exchange for the ivory.[29]

The ivory trade would not have escalated in such a way had the northern Nguni not attached real value to the commodities that were obtained in exchange with Europeans. Copper, brass and beads especially were greatly prized and used to maintain the dominance of ruling lineages. For Dingane, Shaka's successor, beads were closely tied to royal authority: he issued decrees limiting the type and colour of beads that members of his kingdom could wear and took great care in specifying the varieties he desired from traders. There is some evidence that doubled strings of large green beads (*izinhlalu*) some-times replaced cattle in the transfer of *lobola*. Since these foreign commodities were obtained in exchange for a product of the hunt, royal lineages were able to centralize much power by directing their *amabutho* in pursuit of elephants. Chiefs also provided young men's *lobola* requirements, which in turn could be offered as reward for participation in elephant hunting and the ivory trade. The lineages that were more successful in hunting were thus able to expand through the accumulation of wealth and power. At the end of the eighteenth century, however, there was a sharp decline in the trans-portation of ivory to Delagoa Bay. Ivory was now replaced by cattle as the region's main export commodity. Yet as the principal means to store wealth, cattle were far more highly valued within local society. There was, therefore, a great incentive to replace cattle lost in trade, but these could only be acquired through the raiding of neighbouring chiefdoms, carried out by the *amabutho*. The result was escalating militarization, conflict and instability.[30]

No single explanation can therefore be offered for the onset of political consolidation among the Nguni chiefdoms. Neither the strategic decisions of individual leaders, nor environmental change, nor the contradictions that emerged from the changing nature of the ivory trade with Delagoa Bay can, by themselves, explain the transformations at the end of the eighteenth century and the escalating violence and instability of the early nineteenth century, which resulted in the dramatic emergence of the Zulu kingdom.[31] Instead, these new factors combined in complex ways with an older cultural imperative to control nature and to maximize the size of households as safeguards against ecological uncertainty.

VIOLENCE, CONSENT AND RITUAL

As we have seen, the Zulu state was not the first large political unit to emerge in southeastern Africa, but it was the first to have the structural components and magnitude to be considered a kingdom by the 1820s. It was during Shaka's rule that the term *inkosi*, previously thought of as 'chief', came to refer to the highest political authority and be commonly thought of by Europeans at the time as meaning 'king'. According to most sources, Zulu and European, Shaka took control of the AmaZulu chiefdom not long before Dingiswayo's final campaign in 1816. He usurped power by arranging the murder of Sigujana, his own half-brother and more rightful heir to the chieftaincy, then secured his position by ordering the execution of all those he suspected might oppose his claims to be king, including a number of uncles and people associated with his father's rule.[32] Soon, Shaka became the ruler 'who overcame the chiefs', the 'bird which devours others', conquering neighbouring chiefdoms and fashioning a kingdom out of the relatively small AmaZulu chiefdom of which he took charge.[33] A key turning point came in 1821 with the decisive defeat of Zwide's AmaNdwandwe, a foe Shaka had failed to overcome when, in 1817, he sought to avenge their killing of Dingiswayo. Zwide's defeat led to the disintegration of the AmaNdwandwe chiefdom and the retreat of its remnants to the north of the Phongolo River. This moment, Elizabeth Eldredge has argued, 'marked the end of the old powerful chiefs' and established Shaka as the undisputed authority across the entire region.[34]

A strong military ethos infused the Zulu kingdom from the outset, for this was a state born of conquest, or as AmaZulu tradition has it, 'out of Shaka's spear'.[35] Unsurprisingly, therefore, much has been written about Shaka's military innovations. It was during his early years spent among the AmaMthethwa that he honed his military skills. He came to be known as a great warrior and earned the patronage of Dingiswayo, who placed him under the tutelage of his commander-in-chief, Ngomane kaMqomboli. All sources are clear, however, that Shaka invented neither the *amabutho* nor the *assegai*, the famous light stabbing spear, both of which are often attributed to his military success. As one informant remembered:

> Tshaka had the reputation of fighting fiercely (*hlabanaing*).
> In former times (*endulo*), before he came, people used to fight
> by hurling assegais at one another. He learnt the practice of
> stabbing from us Langeni; among us, people used to stab one
> another. This mode of fighting in our tribe began in Makedama's
> time, Makedama being about the same age as Tshaka.[36]

Another recounted:

> It was there at oYengweni that Tshaka learnt about war. When
> they went out to fight, the order was that they should hurl their
> assegais at the enemy with whom they were fighting. They
> fought, and the enemy fled. They were ordered to leave off, and

return, as the enemy had run away. The next day the enemy *impi*
[warriors] would return to fight again. Men were killed who had
survived the fighting of the previous day. Then Tshaka said,
'Wo! This is a bad way of fighting. No sooner had we routed the
enemy than we are ordered to leave off fighting. They then
return and kill our men. If we continued to pursue them, we
would finish them off.' He said, 'Wo! It would be better if we
did not let them go'. He said this to Dingiswayo's son.
Dingiswayo's son agreed with him. After this they would stab the
enemy; they would press the attack without withdrawing. With
this method of fighting they were always victorious. They caused
Dingiswayo to be a great chief who overcame the nations.[37]

If Shaka did not invent the *amabutho*, he certainly transformed
the institution into a centrepiece of royal authority, a function it
retained until the fall of the kingdom in the wake of the Anglo-Zulu
War of 1879. A great many regiments were established under his rule,
including the remnants of *amabutho* left behind by Dingiswayo and
Senzangakhona, as well as those of defeated chiefdoms. Each newly
created *ibutho* built a military village, or *ikanda*, to house its members
at a strategic location – Shaka's first wholly new *ibutho* was Fasimba,
established at present-day Eshowe. Within each *ibutho* and its *ikanda*
there were divisions, such as the *izigaba* and *amaviyo* (battalions and
companies), the latter typically comprising men who belonged to
the same locality. Each *ikanda* also served as a royal town. At its head
were the royal quarters of the king's female relatives, which served
as a visible reminder of the power of the ruling lineage.

From Shaka's time onwards, the formation of new *amabutho*
became the sole prerogative of the king, who prohibited subordinate
chiefs from assembling regiments of their own. Shaka recruited
young fighting men from across the expanding kingdom, assembling
them into regiments by age rather than by place of origin in order
to reinforce centralized royal power. This was a major innovation,
for it served to tie diverse communities directly to the person of the

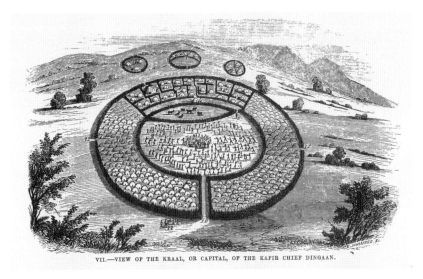

VII.—VIEW OF THE KRAAL, OR CAPITAL, OF THE KAFIR CHIEF DINGAAN.

The *isigodlo* or royal enclosure of Shaka's successor Dingane (r. 1828–1840) at UmGungundlovu, as depicted in Rev. William C. Holden, *History of the Colony of Natal, South Africa* (London, 1855). First built in 1829 and subsequently enlarged, the enclosure was designed according to the layout of the Zulu *ikanda* or military settlement.

king. Shaka established female regiments, too, and there is evidence that their members carried weapons, among other duties. Female regiment members could only marry once the king had given his permission, and only to men of *amabutho* permitted to wear the *isicoco*, a key indicator of adult manhood. The *isicoco* was a headring made from a combination of fibres and the wearer's own hair, which were wound together and then coated in resin or beeswax polished to a dark, high sheen. It was then sewn into the hair with sinews taken from cattle (see pl. XXII). Permission to wear the *isicoco* was granted not to individuals but to an entire *ibutho*, which had earned the right generally through long service. The *isicoco* predated Shaka, but, as John Laband has argued, he gave it special symbolic significance. 'From his reign until the fall of the kingdom the *isicoco* remained a quasi-sacred symbol of the monarch's absolute prerogative over every male married subject's life, for it was regarded as belonging not to the man who wore it, but to the king.'[38]

Among the Bantu-speaking societies of precolonial southern Africa, war was waged by foot soldiers, who carried *assegais* that were lobbed at the enemy from a distance. Shaka, however, favoured close-combat, hand-to-hand battle, and it was probably the centrality that he gave to this method of fighting that most distinguished him from his predecessors. One weapon favoured in close combat was the *iwisa*, a knobbed wooden stick, which could inflict much damage to an adversary. But it was the skilled use of the *isijula*, a long-bladed spear with a short shaft, that gave Shaka's warriors the greatest advantage. He compelled his warriors to carry one *isijula* only so as to force close combat. One informant noted how warriors were 'taught by Tshaka what true bravery was. He made them throw away many *assegais* and ordered that each man was to carry one *assegai*. Tshaka said that the old system of hurling *assegais* was bad; it caused cowardly behaviour.'[39] There was also a second type of spear, the *iklwa*, the use of which required great skill and involved much training beforehand. In battle, the warrior would stab the *iklwa* into the enemy's abdomen and rip upwards before withdrawing it. 'Undoubtedly, the *iklwa* evolved into the weapon of the hero, of the man who cultivated military honour, who proved his prowess in single combat, and who – as Shaka was said to have required – bore his own wounds only on his chest.'[40]

Under Shaka, the very purpose of warfare also changed. In a battle with the AmaMbata during his time with Dingiswayo, one informant remembered that 'Tshaka not only defeated the amaMbata but pursued them, killed them off and returned with their cattle etc. Dingiswayo, who had expected Tshaka to return sooner and had been waiting for him, reproved him for his drastic measures, it being against Dingiswayo's policy to exterminate any tribe.'[41] Once in power, however, Shaka was free to fight 'total war'. Evidence suggests that his *amabutho* spared few in battle: 'let no one remain alive', he ordered before battle, 'not even a dog or a child carried on its mother's back'.[42] Those exterminated often suffered cruel and lingering deaths. Crucially, contemporaries saw such violence as a deviation from earlier practice. As one informant, Ngidi, remembered, 'What is known as the *umradu* style of fighting began with Tshaka, which went to such extremes that children were impaled on posts and even the dogs of a kraal [i.e. enclosed homestead] were killed'.[43] Zwide's people appeared to suffer such fates. A number of other chiefdoms were also utterly destroyed by Shaka's armies, especially those who failed to recognize AmaZulu dominance. The period was commonly referred to as *izwekufa*, the 'killing of nations'.[44]

There can be little doubt that Shaka caused destruction over a very wide area. Thousands of people were killed, communities were displaced and many succumbed to famine in the aftermath of conflict. It is possible, however, to exaggerate the extent to which Shaka's *amabutho* pursued a policy of extermination, for he was set on enlarging his following by incorporating defeated chiefdoms into his domain. This was especially the case during his earliest military expeditions between 1817 and 1821, before the defeat of Zwide. There were occasions when incorporation was not accompanied by substantial violence: subdued chiefs were left with significant powers and free to conduct military campaigns on their own account. Although Shaka always insisted on subjecting incorporated chiefdoms to the dominant AmaZulu lineages as part of his drive to centralize royal power, he did not eliminate existing lineage hierarchies. Formal ties between the AmaZulu royal lineages and their subordinates were cemented by the transfer of daughters (*umdlunkulu* girls) to the king, who then controlled their marital arrangements. Such young women commanded very high *lobola* payments, typically one hundred cattle, and were most often married individually to selected men of advanced years on state occasions. Ordinary warriors were permitted to marry young women captured in battle, for whom no *lobola* was paid, while captured boys were made to serve *amabutho* on campaigns until they reached adulthood, after which they were incorporated as members.[45] Still, it has been estimated that mortality resulting from Shaka's military campaigns may have reached twenty thousand people – and many more would have died as a result of the destruction of communities and hunger in the aftermath of fighting.[46]

Those who were incorporated into the kingdom were never fully assimilated: the ruling house deliberately applied ethnic distinctions, of which the most visible were those between the favoured 'insider' and more distant 'outsider' chiefdoms. The former had come under Shaka's rule during the early years of his reign. Located in the AmaZulu heartland centred on the White Mfolozi River, their people were known as *amantungwa* after the *intungwu* grass that was used for thatching huts and weaving grain baskets. They filled the ranks of the *amabutho*, seeing themselves as being of common AmaZulu descent and ethnicity and the only true members of the kingdom. The *amantungwa* referred to the 'outsiders' as *iziyendane* (those with strange hairstyles) and *amalala*. The latter term originally meant 'menials' – the 'outsiders' typically worked as cattle-herds or guards – but in Shaka's time it became an ethnic slur applied to people regarded as inferior for having originated beyond the AmaZulu heartland.[47]

If Shaka was known for decimating foreign enemies, his reputation for violence against his own people was at least as great. Indeed, violence and the threat of violence underpinned Shaka's reign, and although historians have to tread carefully in their assessment of written accounts and traditions describing his excesses, this interpretation is confirmed by both AmaZulu and European sources. Crucially, these sources depict Shaka's reign as representing a sharp rupture with the past. In contrast to earlier practices and judicial processes, which required chiefs to respect life and property and adhere to notions of the rule of law, Shaka was widely thought to have secured AmaZulu domination by discarding ancient practices, acting illegally and exercising tyrannical power over both foreign and domestic enemies, so much so that during his reign he was known as 'the wrong-doer who knows no law'.[48] Cattle thieves, for example, faced execution, a practice that was not the case under Dingiswayo. In general, those who committed acts of disloyalty or disobedience ran the risk of incurring Shaka's wrath. Forms of punishment were so severe that they were remembered for several generations.

Disloyal or cowardly warriors often suffered extreme punishment. On one occasion, Shaka had an entire regiment killed (possibly as many as one or two thousand men) for withholding a greater share of cattle booty than what he had allocated; on another, he is said to have executed all the members of a regiment for resisting authority. Nor were political rivals spared. A particularly infamous mass killing occurred when Shaka survived an assassination attempt in 1824. The victims were AmaQwabe, a chiefdom incorporated six or seven years earlier and whose members he had identified as responsible for the plot. An African witness remembered that 'Tshaka said that the Qwabe people should be picked out and all put to death'.[49] Those rounded up were driven into the great cattle enclosure at kwaBulawayo, Shaka's capital, and killed, after which *amabutho* fanned out across the countryside in search of AmaQwabe. According to Fynn, Shaka dispatched a force of three thousand warriors with orders to spare no one.[50] There is evidence that the bodies filled mass graves and kwaBulawayo became known as a 'place of killing'.[51] Between ten thousand and twenty thousand people may have died as a consequence of domestic persecution, perhaps one in ten of the kingdom's estimated total population.

Like other African kings, however, those of the AmaZulu could not rule by fear and coercion alone. Ritual power was essential to *ukwesaba*, as the legitimate right to rule was known in Zululand. The fertility of the land and well-being of the people ultimately rested with the king. Among the Nguni peoples, the *umkhosi*, or first-fruits festival, was by far the most important ritual linking the *inkosi* to the agricultural cycle. Ceremonial styles differed from chiefdom to chiefdom – the differences were a sign of the distinctiveness of each royal house – but in every case the ritual took place at each of the major stages of crop production. The *umkhosi* invested the *inkosi* with decisive influence over planting, harvesting and consumption of the crop, and took place in two stages. The first, the 'little' *umkhosi*, was in late November or early December, the early summer months, which marked the beginning of the new year. In order to dispel evil, the king was ritually strengthened by 'black' *imithi* – a substance obtained from powerful and venomous animals, which no ordinary human was said to be capable of withstanding – which he sucked from his fingers and spat from his mouth at the time of the rising sun. Favoured cattle were sacrificed and the royal herd was driven to the graves of the king's ancestors, where the people chanted the great national anthems. The 'great' *umkhosi* then occupied much of January. Proceedings started with the assembly of *amabutho* at the king's *ikanda*, followed by the king's annual ritual hunt, after which he was again ritually purified with 'black' *imithi*. The purpose was to emphasize the sacred underpinning of royal power and the king was first to partake of the first fruits of the harvest.

There was a distinct hierarchy to these ritual processes. Once the king's status was reasserted, simpler ceremonies were held in the villages of other royal notables and then in ordinary communities. The consumption of new crops was made to follow this strict hierarchical procession, visibly demonstrating the line of authority descending downwards from the king. Those who contravened the designated order of planting, harvesting and consumption were deemed a threat to royal authority and risked heavy fines or even death. This close association between royal authority and the cycle of agricultural production served to buttress the former's ideological supremacy.[52]

By the early years of the nineteenth century, the *umkhosi* was closely associated with preparation for war and had become integrated with the ritual doctoring of the *amabutho*, which took place over the course of three days. The pattern was the same as that which preceded battle and served to bind the *amabutho* to the king. Proceedings involved the ritual vomiting by members of the *amabutho*. Some of the vomit was then added to the *inkatha yezwe yakwaZulu*, a circular grass coil, measuring about 3 ft (1 m) in diameter, wrapped in a python skin. This was the only ritual object that the Zulu specifically fashioned, and it was 'believed to possess the enormous mystical powers of rejuvenating and protecting the king and the nation, and of gathering the people together in loyalty to the king'.[53] The ritual strengthening of the *amabutho* was followed by much ritual feasting on sacrificed royal cattle. Ceremonies drew to a close as warriors formed a great crescent around the king while ordinary people sang his praises.

COLONIAL CONQUEST

Shaka's armies may have reigned supreme, but in the years following his death in 1828 his successors faced a new foe in the form of Europeans armed with superior weapons and increasingly motivated to assert control over the interior of present-day South Africa. European interest in the region had been transformed by the discovery of valuable minerals, first diamonds and then gold, in the interior during the last decades of the nineteenth century. In the British imperial mind, the continued existence of powerful African kingdoms (and independent Afrikaner republics) was incompatible with British interests and the demands of a dynamic capitalist economy.[54] While Africans from elsewhere on the subcontinent were drawn into the mining economy as migrant labourers, the AmaZulu were, up to the 1870s, able to resist this fate, an achievement of which they were proud. Although the kingdom by now had much greater contact with Europeans than in Shaka's time, and the land on its southern frontiers once traversed by AmaZulu armies was now under colonial rule, the fundamental social and political structures of earlier times were firmly intact. In short, on the eve of the Anglo-Zulu War of 1879, the 'vast majority of Zulu grew up, worked and died within the kingdom'.[55]

Thus, when in 1878, Sir Bartle Frere, the British High Commissioner for South Africa, issued an ultimatum to the Zulu king, Cetshwayo, he demanded nothing less than the destruction of the kingdom founded by Shaka. Frere mounted several arguments for this move, including the kingdom's failure to shed less blood in judicial proceedings, a demand imposed at the time of Cetshwayo's coronation.

Above all, the high commissioner wanted to see the end of the AmaZulu 'military system', which he denounced as a 'frightfully efficient manslaying war-machine'.[56] It was an ultimatum that Cetshwayo, who had acceded to the throne in 1872, could not possibly accept. When the ultimatum expired on 11 January 1879, three columns of British soldiers invaded Zululand, hoping for a quick and easy victory – as would-be empire-builders always did.

But the victory was neither quick nor easy. Rather than the invasion exposing divisions within the kingdom, as Frere had hoped, its subjects rallied around Cetshwayo. On 22 January, the day of the new moon, a force of some twenty thousand Zulu warriors under the command of Chief Ntshingwayo overran the central British column encamped at Isandlwana, annihilating nearly the entire force and leaving close to 1,300 British soldiers dead. It was the largest British military disaster since the Crimean War. The British defeat at Isandlwana looms large in the pantheon of colonial wars. 'That one engagement shook the military self-confidence of the world's largest empire and ensured the Zulu warrior a permanent place in the annals of military glory.'[57] But it also earned the Zulu a special place in the imperial mind; from this time on, 'the Zulus were Britain's favorite Africans'.[58]

According to much of the older literature on the Anglo-Zulu War, the British got their revenge on 4 July 1879, when they burned Ulundi, the royal residence, to the ground. Imperial authorities described this as a 'crushing military victory', but the outcome of the battle, which lasted for less than an hour, was not nearly as clear cut. The number of Zulu casualties at Ulundi is generally given at 1,500, but this was based on no more than the estimate of Lord Chelmsford, who had led the disastrous campaign at Isandlwana and had every incentive to inflate the number of enemy casualties. When Chelmsford's successor, Sir Garnet Wolseley, visited the field, he estimated the number at closer to four hundred.[59]

Both sides had an interest in bringing the conflict to an end. The British invasion of Zululand revealed the limits of the Zulu military system, which had remained largely unchanged since the days of Shaka, and, in the final analysis, it appears that the *amabutho* succumbed to British firepower. Despite the victory at Isandlwana, it had come at the cost of at least a thousand Zulu casualties – and the Zulu were certainly acutely aware of their losses. The army had been honed as a raiding and attacking force and could not effectively adapt to the defensive strategies required when Zululand was invaded in 1879. The *amabutho* had counted on plundering their enemies in order to obtain food, but this was not possible when they were attacked on their own soil by British forces. Zulu warriors well remembered the suffering caused by the resulting food shortages and hunger.[60] The British, for their part, were keen to portray the Battle of Ulundi as having removed the 'stain' of Isandlwana and use it as a basis for peace. Wolseley dropped many of the conditions specified in Frere's original ultimatum. In the weeks following the destruction of Ulundi, peace was attained on the promise that the Zulu would retain possession of their land if they laid down their arms. Although Cetshwayo was captured and sent into exile in Cape Town at the end of August 1879 (see pl. xxi), Zulu resistance during the war had been so fierce that the kingdom retained most of its land and avoided annexation.

In the aftermath of the war, Wolseley sought to refashion the kingdom. After detaining Cetshwayo, he informed the Zulu that they were henceforth to be ruled by thirteen independent chiefs appointed by the British; that the *amabutho* were to be abolished; that they would be forbidden to import firearms; and that although capital punishment without trial was to be abolished, they would be allowed to live according to what Wolseley described as their 'ancient laws and customs'. This so-called settlement effectively dismembered the monarchy as forged by Shaka. Motivated by the belief that most chiefs chafed at royal authority, Wolseley set about creating what he believed to be a pre-Shakan political order. The new chiefs owed their appointments to Wolseley's trust, the extent of their collaboration during the war and their opposition to the Zulu monarchy. One of Wolseley's newly appointed chiefs was John Dunn, Cetshwayo's former white advisor who sided with the British during the war and who was rewarded with the largest of the thirteen territories, his land clearly intended to serve as a buffer with the colony of Natal in the south. In northern Zululand, Prince Hamu kaNzibe, Cetshwayo's half-brother, was awarded a chiefdom after having defected to the British during the war, while Zibhebhu, who was given authority over a territory that included prominent members of Cetshwayo's family, emerged as the arch-enemy of the uSuthu, the supporters of the Zulu royal house. Thus, members of the old royal hierarchy who commanded large followings now found themselves ruled over by men whom they considered to be their inferiors and whose new status they refused to recognize. Other appointees were clearly alien – *amalala* – and commanded little loyalty.[61]

It is hardly surprising that civil war and disorder followed. One of the worst incidents occurred on 20 July 1883, when Zibhebhu and Hamu attacked Cetshwayo's homestead and massacred at least fifty-nine of the most notable uSuthu leaders – a slaughter that, John Laband and Paul Thompson have argued, 'marked the real end of the old order in Zululand'.[62] Desperate to bring an end to the disorder, Britain extended its 'protection' over the uSuthu leadership in February 1887, while formal annexation followed with the creation of the British Colony of Zululand on 19 May 1887. At Eshowe, the new British governor of the Zululand protectorate told Dinuzulu, Cetshwayo's son and heir, that 'Zululand is now a portion of the Queen [of England's] dominions, and the Zulu people, including Dinizulu [*sic*] ... and all other Chiefs are now British subjects, and are under the Queen's laws'. Although the AmaZulu were left in possession of their land, and although chiefs were not deprived of their titles, they were left in no doubt that there was 'now no sovereign in Zululand, except the Queen'.[63]

In 1897, Zululand was annexed to the British colony of Natal, after ten years of indirect imperial rule. Thus, much land was opened up to white settlement and African labour was more readily directed away from the homestead towards the colonial economy. But colonial authorities greatly underestimated the continued ideological sway of the Zulu monarchy. Allowed to return to Zululand in 1898 after eight years of exile on the island of Saint Helena, Dinuzulu was appointed as the *In Duna* or chief advisor to the British colonial government. To the vast majority of AmaZulu, however, Dinuzulu's return signalled the restoration of the royal house. Indeed, the term 'Zulu' now took on nationalist connotations that spilled beyond the borders of the old Zululand. When an uprising broke out in the colony of Natal in 1906 in opposition to colonial taxation, rebels drew on the name of Dinuzulu as the binding force of the nation, highlighting the monarchy's enduring power and appeal.[64] Though greatly diminished in power, the Zulu monarchy has effectively survived successive South African governments. To the present day, the imagery and historical legacy of a once-mighty kingdom continues to nourish the House of Shaka.

NOTES

———————————— INTRODUCTION ————————————

1. Michael A. Gomez, *African Dominion: A New History of Empire in Early and Medieval West Africa* (Princeton, 2018).
2. David Cannadine, 'Introduction: Divine Rites of Kings', in David Cannadine and Simon Price, eds, *Rituals of Royalty: Power and Ceremonial in Traditional Societies* (Cambridge, 1987), 19.
3. See Derek R. Peterson and Giacomo Macola, eds, *Recasting the Past: History Writing and Political Work in Modern Africa* (Athens, OH, 2009).
4. Aidan Southall, 'The Segmentary State in Africa and Asia', *Comparative Studies in Society and History* 30 (1988), 52.
5. M. Fortes and E. E. Evans-Pritchard, eds, *African Political Systems* (London, 1940), 16 and 21.
6. See T. O. Beidelman, 'Swazi Royal Ritual', *Africa* 36 (1966), and Gillian Feeley-Harnik, 'Issues in Divine Kingship', *Annual Review of Anthropology* 14 (1985), 278–80.
7. Ernst H. Kantorowicz, *The King's Two Bodies: A Study in Mediaeval Political Theology* (Princeton, 1957); Marc Bloch, *The Royal Touch: Sacred Monarchy and Scrofula in England and France*, translated by J. E. Anderson (London, 1973).
8. Marshall Sahlins, 'The Original Political Society', in David Graeber and Marshall Sahlins, *On Kings* (Chicago, 2017), 60; see too Lucy Mair, *African Kingdoms* (Oxford, 1977).
9. For a discussion of these misleading ideas, see Wyatt MacGaffey, 'Changing Representations in Central African History', *Journal of African History* 46 (2005).
10. John Lonsdale, 'States and Social Processes in Africa: A Historiographical Survey', *African Studies Review* 24 (1981), 139.
11. *Ibid.*, 171, citing John Beattie, *The Nyoro State* (Oxford, 1971).
12. Jan Vansina, *How Societies Are Born: Governance in West Central Africa before 1600* (Charlottesville, 2004), 243.
13. Quoted in John Iliffe, *Africans: The History of a Continent* (3rd edn, Cambridge, 2017), 161.
14. *Ibid.*, 22.
15. Paulo F. de Moraes Farias, *Arabic Medieval Inscriptions from the Republic of Mali: Epigraphy, Chronicles and Songhay-Tuareg History* (Oxford, 2003).
16. Neil Kodesh, *Beyond the Royal Gaze: Clanship and Public Healing in Buganda* (Charlottesville, 2010).

17. David Graeber, 'The People as Nursemaids of the King: Notes on Monarchs as Children, Women's Uprisings, and the Return of the Ancestral Dead in Central Madagascar', in Graeber and Sahlins, *On Kings*, 270.
18. Wyatt MacGaffey, 'A Central African Kingdom: Kongo in 1480', in Koen Bostoen and Inge Brinkman, eds, *The Kongo Kingdom: The Origins, Dynamics and Cosmopolitan Culture of an African Polity* (Cambridge, 2018), 55 and 57, emphasis added.
19. See W. Arens and Ivan Karp, eds, *Creativity of Power: Cosmology and Action in African Societies* (Washington, D.C., 1989).
20. See David C. Conrad, ed. and trans., *Sunjata: A New Prose Version* (Indianapolis, 2016); Ralph A. Austen, ed., *In Search of Sunjata: The Mande Epic as History, Literature and Performance* (Bloomington, 1999).
21. Gwyn Prins, *The Hidden Hippopotamus. Reappraisal in African History: The Early Colonial Experience in Western Zambia* (Cambridge, 1980).
22. For archaeological perspectives, see Susan Keech McIntosh, ed., *Beyond Chiefdoms: Pathways to Complexity in Africa* (Cambridge, 1999), and Graham Connah, *African Civilizations: An Archaeological Perspective* (3rd edn, Cambridge, 2016).
23. Elizabeth A. Eldredge, *Kingdoms and Chiefdoms of Southeastern Africa: Oral Traditions and History, 1400–1830* (Rochester, 2015), 1.
24. Vansina, *How Societies Are Born*, 101.
25. See too Suzanne Preston Blier, *Royal Arts of Africa: The Majesty of Form* (London, 1998).
26. See Mary Nooter Roberts and Allen F. Roberts, eds, *Memory: Luba Art and the Making of History* (New York, 1996).
27. Jacques Le Goff, *Must We Divide History into Periods?*, translated by M. B. DeBevoise (New York, 2015).
28. Christopher Ehret, *An African Classical Age: Eastern and Southern Africa in World History, 1000 BC to AD 400* (Charlottesville, 1998).
29. See François-Xavier Fauvelle, *The Golden Rhinoceros: Histories of the African Middle Ages*, translated by Troy Tice (Princeton, 2018).
30. See Toby Green, *A Fistful of Shells: West Africa from the Rise of the Slave Trade to the Age of Revolution* (London, 2019).

CHAPTER 1

1. Translation after Scott Morschauser, 'Approbation or Disapproval? The Conclusion of the Letter of Amenophis II to User-Satet, Viceroy of Kush (Urk. IV, 1344.10–20)', *Studien zur Altägyptischen Kultur* 24 (1997). Morschauser prefers the secular word 'flatterers' as a translation of the term more usually rendered as 'conjuror' or 'magician'. He denotes 'flatterers' as those with exceptional skills of oratory or persuasion, yet there seems no reason to see these skills as opposed to the use of sorcery or magic: in many parts of Africa, such capacities are associated precisely with people able to induce others to behave in ways they had otherwise never intended.

2. Simon Simonse, *Kings of Disaster: Dualism, Centralism, and the Scapegoat King in the Southeastern Sudan* (Leiden, 1992); David Graeber and Marshall Sahlins, *On Kings* (Chicago, 2017), 65–138.

3. Jeremy Pope, *The Double Kingdom under Taharqo: Studies in the History of Kush and Egypt, c. 690–664 BC* (Leiden, 2014); László Török, *The Kingdom of Kush: Handbook of the Napatan-Meroitic Civilization* (Leiden, 1997).

4. David N. Edwards, 'Meroe and the Sudanic Kingdoms', *Journal of African History* 39 (1998); David N. Edwards, 'Ancient Egypt in the Sudanese Middle Nile: A Case of Mistaken Identity?', and Dorian Fuller, 'Pharaonic or Sudanic? Models for Meroitic Society and Change', both in David O'Connor and Andrew Reid, eds, *Ancient Egypt in Africa* (London, 2003).

5. Jane Humphris and Thomas Scheibner, 'A New Radiocarbon Chronology for Ancient Iron Production in the Meroe Region of Sudan', *African Archaeological Review* 34 (2017).

6. Edwards, 'Meroe and the Sudanic Kingdoms'; David N. Edwards, *The Nubian Past: An Archaeology of the Sudan* (London, 2004), ch. 5–6; Gunnar Haaland and Randi Haaland, 'God of War, Worldly Ruler, and Craft Specialists in the Meroitic Kingdom of Sudan', *Journal of Social Archaeology* 7 (2007).

7. László Török, 'Ambulatory Kingship and Settlement History: A Study on the Contribution of Archaeology to History', in C. Bonnet, ed., *Études Nubiennes: Conférence du Genève I* (Geneva, 1992).

8. John Taylor, 'The Third Intermediate Period (1069–664 BC)', in Ian Shaw, ed., *The Oxford History of Ancient Egypt* (Oxford, 2000); Derek Welsby and Julie R. Anderson, eds, *Sudan: Ancient Treasures* (London, 2004), 132–85.

9. Angelika Lohwasser and Jacke Phillips, 'Women in Ancient Kush', in Geoff Emberling and Bruce Beyer Williams, eds, *The Oxford Handbook of Ancient Nubia* (Oxford, 2020).

10. Taylor, 'Third Intermediate Period', 360–62; Mariam F. Ayad, *God's Wife, God's Servant: The God's Wife of Amun (c. 740–525 BC)* (London, 2009).

11. Thomas Schneider, 'Periodizing Egyptian History: Manetho, Convention, and Beyond', in Klaus-Peter Adam, ed., *Historiographie in der Antike* (Berlin, 2008).

12. cf. Jan Assmann, *The Mind of Egypt: History and Meaning in the Time of the Pharaohs* (New York, 2003), ch. 23 'Memory and Renewal: The Ethiopian and Saite Renaissance'.

13. Dorian Fuller and Leilani Lucas, 'Savanna on the Nile: Long-term Agricultural Diversification and Intensification in Nubia', in Emberling and Williams, *Oxford Handbook of Ancient Nubia*.

14. Rudolph Kuper and Stefan Kröpelin, 'Climate-Controlled Holocene Occupation in the Sahara: Motor of Africa's Evolution', *Science* 313 (2006); Maria Carmela Gatto and Andrea Zerboni, 'Holocene Supra-Regional Environmental Changes as Trigger for Major Socio-Cultural Processes in Northeastern Africa and the Sahara', *African Archaeological Review* 32 (2015).

15. Sandro Salvatori and Donatella Usai, 'The Mesolithic and Neolithic in Sudan', in D. Raue, ed., *Handbook of Ancient Nubia* (Berlin, 2019).

16. David Wengrow, 'Landscapes of Knowledge, Idioms of Power: The African Foundations of Ancient Egyptian Civilisation Reconsidered', in O'Connor and Reid,

Ancient Egypt in Africa; David Wengrow, *The Archaeology of Early Egypt: Social Transformations in North-East Africa, 10,000 to 2650 BC* (Cambridge, 2006); David Wengrow, Michael Dee, Sarah Foster, Alice Stevenson and Christopher Bronk Ramsey, 'Cultural Convergence in the Neolithic of the Nile Valley: A Prehistoric Perspective on Egypt's Place in Africa', *Antiquity* 88 (2014); Maria Carmela Gatto, 'The Later Prehistory of Nubia in its Interregional Setting', in Raue, *Handbook of Ancient Nubia*.

17. Matthieu Honegger, 'Kerma et les debuts du Néolithique Africain', *Genava: revue d'histoire de l'art et d'archéologie* 53 (2005); cf. Wengrow et al., 'Cultural Convergence'.

18. Randi Haaland, 'The Meroitic Empire: Trade and Cultural Influences in an Indian Ocean Context', *African Archaeological Review* 31 (2014).

19. Ahmed M. Ali, 'Meroitic Settlement of the Butana (Central Sudan)', in Peter J. Ucko, Ruth Tringham and G. W. Dimbleby, eds, *Man, Settlement, and Urbanism* (London, 1972); Claudia Näser, 'The Great Hafir at Musawwarat es-Sufra: Fieldwork of the Archaeological Mission of Humboldt University Berlin in 2005 and 2006', in Włodzimierz Godlewski and Adam Łajtar, eds, *Between the Cataracts: Proceedings of the 11th Conference of Nubian Studies, Warsaw University, 27 August–2 September 2006, Part two, fascicule 1: Session papers* (Warsaw, 2010).

20. Derek Welsby, 'Human Adaptation to Environmental Change in the Northern Dongola Reach', in Emberling and Williams, *Oxford Handbook of Ancient Nubia*.

21. Maria Carmela Gatto, 'The A-Group and 4th millennium BC Nubia', in Emberling and Williams, *Oxford Handbook of Ancient Nubia*; László Török, *Between Two Worlds: The Frontier Region between Ancient Nubia and Egypt 3700 BC–AD 500* (Leiden, 2020).

22. For the significance of royal annals and the economic organization of the Egyptian state in the Old Kingdom, see Juan Carlos Moreno García, *The State in Ancient Egypt: Power, Challenges and Dynamics* (London, 2019).

23. Ellen Morris, 'Sacrifice for the State: First Dynasty Royal Funerals and the Rites at Macramallah's Triangle', in Nicola Laneri, ed., *Performing Death: Social Analysis of Funerary Traditions in the Ancient Near East and Mediterranean* (Chicago, 2007); and '(Un)dying Loyalty: Meditations on Retainer Sacrifice in Ancient Egypt and Elsewhere', in Roderick Campbell, ed., *Violence and Civilization: Studies of Social Violence in History and Prehistory* (Oxford, 2014).

24. Ann Macy Roth, 'The Meaning of Menial Labour: "Servant Statues" in Old Kingdom Serdabs', *Journal of the American Research Center in Egypt* 38 (2002).

25. Bruce Beyer Williams, 'Relations between Egypt and Nubia in the Naqada Period', in Emily Teeter, ed., *Before the Pyramids: The Origins of Egyptian Civilization* (Chicago, 2011).

26. Ellen Morris, *Ancient Egyptian Imperialism* (Hoboken, 2018).

27. Mark Lehner, 'Labor and the Pyramids: The Heit el-Ghurab "Workers Town" at Giza', in Piotr Steinkeller and Michael Hudson, eds, *Labor in the Ancient World* (Dresden, 2015).

28. Alice Stevenson, 'The Egyptian Predynastic and State Formation', *Journal of Archaeological Research* 24 (2016); Gatto, 'The A-Group'.

29. Renée F. Friedman, 'Excavating Egypt's Early Kings: Recent Discoveries in the Elite Cemetery at Hierakonpolis', in B. Midant-Reynes and Y. Tristant, eds, *Egypt at its*

Origins 2: Proceedings of the International Conference Origin of the State. Predynastic and Early Dynastic Egypt, Toulouse, 5th–8th September 2005 (Leuven, 2008).

30. Edwards, 'Ancient Egypt in the Sudanese Middle Nile'; Wengrow, *Archaeology of Early Egypt*, 158–73.

31. Richard Bussmann, 'Scaling the State: Egypt in the Third Millennium BC', *Archaeology International* 17 (2013).

32. Delwen Samuel, 'Brewing and Baking', in Paul Nicholson and Ian Shaw, eds, *Ancient Egyptian Materials and Technology* (Cambridge, 2000).

33. Ann Macy Roth, *Egyptian Phyles in the Old Kingdom: The Evolution of a System of Social Organization* (Chicago, 1991).

34. Stuart Tyson Smith, *Wretched Kush: Ethnic Identities and Boundaries in Egypt's Nubian Empire* (London, 2002); Morris, *Ancient Egyptian Imperialism*; see also Claudia Näser, 'Structures and Realities of the Egyptian Presence in Lower Nubia from the Middle Kingdom to the New Kingdom: The Egyptian Cemetery S/Sa at Aniba', in Neal Spencer, Anna Stevens and Michaela Binder, eds, *Nubia in the New Kingdom: Lived Experience, Pharaonic Control and Indigenous Traditions* (Leuven, 2017).

35. See Geoff Emberling, 'Pastoral States: Toward a Comparative Archaeology of Early Kush', *Origini* 36 (2004), 139; Elizabeth Joanna Minor, 'The Use of Egyptian and Egyptianizing Material Culture in Nubian Burials of the Classic Kerma Period', unpublished PhD thesis, University of California, Berkeley, 2012, 77; Welsby and Anderson, *Sudan*, 100–101, cat. 74.

36. Charles Bonnet, *The Black Kingdom on the Nile* (Cambridge, MA, 2019).

37. See Sandro Capo Chichi, 'On the Etymology of the Egyptian Word *Nehesi* "Nubian"', *New African Culture's Journal of African Cultures & Civilizations* 1 (2015) for consideration of alternative and still more widely accepted meanings.

38. Andrea Manzo, 'Architecture, Power, and Communication: Case Studies from Ancient Nubia', *African Archaeological Review* 34 (2017).

39. *Ibid.*; see also Charles Bonnet, 'Excavations at the Nubian Royal Town of Kerma: 1975–91', *Antiquity* 66 (1992).

40. Charles Bonnet and Matthieu Honegger, 'The Eastern Cemetery of Kerma', in Emberling and Williams, *Oxford Handbook of Ancient Nubia*.

41. Bonnet, *Black Kingdom*.

42. Elizabeth Joanna Minor, 'One More for the Road: Beer, Sacrifice and Commemoration in Ancient Nubian Burials of the Classic Kerma Period', in Ilaria Incordino et al., eds, *Current Research in Egyptology 2017* (Oxford, 2018).

43. Bonnet, 'Excavations'; Bonnet and Honegger, 'The Eastern Cemetery'.

44. J. Reinold, 'Kadruka and the Neolithic in the Northern Dongola Reach', *Sudan and Nubia* 5 (2001).

45. Henriette Hafsaas-Tsakos, 'Edges of Bronze and Expressions Masculinity: The Emergence of a Warrior Class at Kerma in Sudan', *Antiquity* 87 (2013).

46. See Charles Bonnet, 'The Kerma Culture', in Welsby and Anderson, *Sudan*, 70–77; Emberling, 'Pastoral States', 16; Welsby and Anderson, *Sudan*, 89, cat. 71.

47. Hafsaas-Tsakos, 'Edges of Bronze'.

48. Claudia Näser, 'Structures and Realities of Egyptian-Nubian Interactions from the Late Old Kingdom to the Early New Kingdom', in Dietrich Raue, Stephan Seidlmayer and Philipp Speiser, eds, *The First Cataract of the Nile: One Region, Diverse Perspectives* (Cairo, 2013); Morris, *Ancient Egyptian Imperialism*.

49. Emberling, 'Pastoral States', 17.

50. Bonnet, 'The Kerma Culture'; Bonnet and Honegger, 'The Eastern Cemetery'.

51. Henriette Hafsaas-Tsakos, 'The Kingdom of Kush: An African Centre on the Periphery of the Bronze Age World System', *Norwegian Archaeological Review* 42 (2009).

52. Bonnet, 'The Kerma Culture'; Brigette Gratien, 'Nouvelles empreintes de sceaux à Kerma: aperçus sur l'administration de Kouch au milieu du 2e millénaire av. J.-C.', *Genava: revue d'histoire de l'art et d'archéologie* 41 (1993), 39–44; Minor, 'Egyptian and Egyptianizing Material Culture'; Carl Walsh, 'Techniques for Egyptian Eyes: Diplomacy and the Transmission of Cosmetic Practices between Egypt and Kerma', *Journal of Egyptian History* 13 (2020).

53. Elizabeth Joanna Minor, 'Decolonizing Reisner: The Case Study of a Classic Kerma Female Burial for Reinterpreting Early Nubian Archaeological Collections through Digital Archival Resources', in M. Honegger, ed., *Nubian Archaeology in the XXIst Century: Proceedings of the Thirteenth International Conference for Nubian Studies, Neuchâtel, 1st–6th September 2014* (Leuven, 2018).

54. See Margaret Judd and Joel Irish, 'Dying to Serve: The Mass Burials at Kerma', *Antiquity* 83 (2009). A smaller number of subsidiary burials, placed within separate brick enclosures, were distributed around the tumulus mound, including a significant proportion of males armed with fancy copper daggers whose remains exhibit traces of injury consistent with their status as specialized warriors or bodyguards: see Hafsaas-Tsakos, 'Edges of Bronze'.

55. Ellen Morris, *The Architecture of Imperialism: Military Bases and the Evolution of Foreign Policy in Egypt's New Kingdom* (Leiden, 2005).

CHAPTER 2

1. Michael A. Gomez, *African Dominion: A New History of Empire in Early and Medieval West Africa* (Princeton, 2018).

2. See Michael A. Gomez, ed., 'Forum: The Imperial Tradition in the Sahel', *Journal of African History* 61 (2020).

3. Robert Cornevin, *Histoire de l'Afrique noire*, vol. 2 (Paris, 1966), 217.

4. Raymond Mauny, *Les siècles obscurs de l'Afrique noire: histoire et archéologie* (Paris, 1971).

5. Roderick J. McIntosh and Susan K. McIntosh, 'From *Siècles Obscurs* to Revolutionary Centuries in the Middle Niger', *World Archaeology* 20 (1988).

6. Paulo F. de Moraes Farias, *Arabic Medieval Inscriptions from the Republic of Mali: Epigraphy, Chronicles and Songhay-Tuareg History* (Oxford, 2003).

7. François-Xavier Fauvelle, 'Ghâna, Mâli, Songhay, royaumes courtiers du Sahel Occidental (VIIIe–XVIe siècle)', in François-Xavier Fauvelle, ed., *L'Afrique ancienne* (Paris, 2018).

8. See François-Xavier Fauvelle, *The Golden Rhinoceros: Histories of the African Middle Ages*, translated by Troy Tice (Princeton, 2018), 222–31.

9. Amy Niang, 'Reviving the Dormant Divine: Rituals as Political References in Moogo', *Journal of Ritual Studies* 28 (2014), 81.

10. Sources for Ghana, Mali and Songhay are collected in Nehemia Levtzion and J. F. P. Hopkins, eds, *Corpus of Early Arabic Sources for West African History* (Cambridge, 1981).

11. For this argument, see Roderick J. McIntosh, *The Peoples of the Middle Niger: The Island of Gold* (Oxford, 1998).

12. On the disputed evidence, see Fauvelle, *The Golden Rhinoceros,* 64–68.

13. D. T. Niane, *Sundiata: An Epic of Old Mali*, translated by G. D. Pickett (London, 1965); Camara Laye, *Le maître de la parole: kouma lafôlô kouma* (Paris, 1978); David C. Conrad, ed. and trans., *Sunjata: A New Prose Version* (Indianapolis, 2016).

14. See Ralph A. Austen, ed., *In Search of Sunjata: The Mande Epic as History, Literature and Performance* (Bloomington, 1999); and Thomas A. Hale, *Griots and Griottes: Masters of Words and Music* (Bloomington, 1998).

15. D. T. Niane, 'Mali and the Second Mandingo Expansion', in D. T. Niane, ed., *UNESCO General History of Africa, Vol. 4: Africa from the Twelfth to the Sixteenth Century* (Paris, 1984), 135; see also David C. Conrad and Barbara E. Frank, eds, *Status and Identity in West Africa: Nyamakalaw of Mande* (Bloomington, 1995).

16. See David C. Conrad, 'Mooning Armies and Mothering Heroes: Female Power in Mande Epic Tradition', in Austen, *In Search of Sunjata.*

17. David C. Conrad, 'A Town Called Dakajalan: The Sunjata Tradition and the Question of Ancient Mali's Capital', *Journal of African History* 35 (1994).

18. John Iliffe, *Africans: The History of a Continent* (3rd edn, Cambridge, 2017), 54.

19. Ibn al-Mukhtar, *Tarikh al-fattash*, edited and translated by O. Houdas and M. Delafosse (Paris, 1913), 67.

20. Paulo F. de Moraes Farias, 'Intellectual Innovation and Reinvention of the Sahel: The Seventeenth-Century Timbuktu Chronicles', in Shamil Jeppie and Souleymane Bachir Diagne, eds, *The Meanings of Timbuktu* (Cape Town, 2008), 104; see too John O. Hunwick, *Timbuktu and the Songhay Empire: Al-Sa'dī's Ta'rīkh al-sūdān down to 1613 and other Contemporary Documents* (Leiden, 1999).

21. J. O. Hunwick, 'Religion and State in the Songhay Empire, 1464–1591', in I. M. Lewis, ed., *Islam in Tropical Africa* (Oxford, 1966), 297.

22. My translation, from 'Épître d'al-Maghili à l'Askia Muhammad de Gao', in Joseph M. Cuoq, ed., *Recueil des sources arabes concernant l'Afrique occidentale du VIIIe au XVIe siècle (Bilad al-Sudan)* (Paris, 1985), 400.

23. Hunwick, 'Religion and State'; see too John O. Hunwick, 'Songhay, Borno and the Hausa States, 1450–1600', in J. F. Ade Ajayi and Michael Crowder, eds, *History of West Africa*, vol. 1 (3rd edn, Harlow, 1985).

24. Gomez, *African Dominion*, 310.

25. See Moussa Paré, 'L'Économie rurale dans le Bilad al-Sudan occidental (XVe-XVIe siècle)', *Études rurales* 193 (2014).

26. See Richard Roberts, *Warriors, Merchants and Slaves: The State and the Economy in the Middle Niger Valley, 1700–1914* (Stanford, 1987).

27. See, for example, Labelle Prussin, *Hatumere: Islamic Design in West Africa* (Berkeley, 1986); A. LaGamma, ed., *Sahel: Art and Empires on the Shores of the Sahara* (New York, 2020); O. Kane, *Beyond Timbuktu: An Intellectual History of Muslim West Africa* (Cambridge, MA, 2016).

CHAPTER 3

1. We have chosen to use the word 'Ethiopia' for both the polity and the geographical region, although neither have been static over time. Specifically, we use it to refer to the highlands of the present-day nations of Eritrea and Ethiopia, the region that has historically been known as Abyssinia and in which the Habasha people live. For ease of reading among a non-specialist audience, we have not used scholarly spelling conventions for the Ge'ez language.

2. For a survey of research on the origins of humanity, early agriculture and the birth of language, see Wendy Laura Belcher, *Abyssinia's Samuel Johnson: Ethiopian Thought in the Making of an English Author* (New York, 2012), 23–41.

3. Azeb Amha, 'On Loans and Additions to the Fidal (Ethiopic) Writing System', in Alex De Voogt and Irving Finkel, eds, *The Idea of Writing: Play and Complexity* (Leiden, 2010).

4. See Nadia Nurhussein, *Black Land: Imperial Ethiopianism and African America* (Princeton, 2019).

5. David W. Phillipson, *Ancient Ethiopia: Aksum; its Antecedents and Successors* (2nd edn, London, 2002).

6. See David W. Phillipson, *Foundations of an African Civilisation: Aksum and the Northern Horn, 1000 BC–AD 1300* (Woodbridge, 2012); Stuart Munro-Hay, *Aksum: An African Civilisation of Late Antiquity* (Edinburgh, 1991); George Hatke, *Migration Histories of the Medieval Afroeurasian Transition Zone* (Leiden, 2020), 291–326.

7. Quoted in Yuri M. Kobishchanov, ed., *Axum, Vol. 3* (University Park, Pennsylvania, 1980), 59.

8. G. W. Bowersock, *The Throne of Adulis: Red Sea Wars on the Eve of Islam* (New York, 2013).

9. Edward Ullendorff, *Ethiopia and the Bible* (London, 1968).

10. See Sergew Hable Selassie, *Ancient and Medieval Ethiopian History to 1270* (Addis Ababa, 1972); David W. Phillipson, *Ancient Churches of Ethiopia* (New Haven, 2009).

11. See especially Taddesse Tamrat, *Church and State in Ethiopia, 1270–1527* (Oxford, 1972).

12. Amsalu Tefera, '"Cycles of Zion" in Ethiopic Texts', in Alessandro Bausi, Alessandro Gori and Denis Nosnitsin, eds, *Essays in Ethiopian Manuscript Studies* (Hamburg, 2015); Gizachew Tiruneh, 'The Kebra Nagast: Can its Secrets be Revealed?', *International Journal of Ethiopian Studies* 8 (2014).

13. Wendy Laura Belcher and Michael Kleiner, trans. and eds, *The Kebra Nagast: A New English Translation of the Ancient Book About Glorious Monarchs, Including the Ethiopian Queen of Sheba, King Solomon, and their Son Menilek* (Princeton, forthcoming 2023).

14. Bairu Tafla and Heinrich Scholler, *Ser'ata Mangest: An Early Ethiopian Constitution* (Addis Ababa, 1976).

15. See Taddesse Tamrat, *Church and State*, 268–94, and 'Problems of Royal Succession in Fifteenth Century Ethiopia: A Presentation of the Documents', in *IV Congresso Internazionale di Studi Etiopici*, vol. 1 (Rome, 1974).

16. Donald Crummey, *Land and Society in the Christian Kingdom of Ethiopia from the Thirteenth to the Twentieth Century* (Oxford, 2000); Taddesse Tamrat, *Church and State*, 98–103.

17. Habtamu M. Tegegne, *Barara, Addis Ababa's Predecessor: Development, Destruction, and Refoundation and the Untold History of Ethiopia* [Amharic edition], ed. Bezza Tesfaw (Trenton, 2020).

18. Taddesse Tamrat, *Church and State*, 141–45; Deresse Ayenachew, 'Territorial Expansion and Administrative Evolution under the "Solomonic" Dynasty', in Samantha Kelly, ed., *A Companion to Medieval Ethiopia and Eritrea* (Leiden, 2021).

19. Habtamu M. Tegegne, 'The Edict of King Gälawdéwos Against the Illegal Slave Trade in Christians: Ethiopia, 1548', *The Medieval Globe* 2 (2016), 93.

20. Crummey, *Land and Society*, 29–35.

21. Habtamu Tegegne, *Barara*, 1–5.

22. See Taddesse Tamrat, *Church and State*; Marie-Laure Derat, *Le domaine des rois Éthiopiens (1270–1527): espace, pouvoir et monachisme* (Paris, 2003); Ephraim Isaac, *The Ethiopian Orthodox Täwahïdo Church* (Lawrenceville, NJ, 2012); John Binns, *The Orthodox Church of Ethiopia: A History* (London, 2016).

23. Kinefe-Rigb Zelleke, 'Bibliography of the Ethiopic Hagiographic Traditions', *Journal of Ethiopian Studies* 13 (1975); Taddesse Tamrat, 'Hagiographies and the Reconstruction of Medieval Ethiopian History', *Rural Africana* 11 (1970).

24. Taddesse Tamrat, *Church and State*, 206–40.

25. *Ibid.*, 206–31.

26. Taddesse Tamrat, 'Some Notes on Fifteenth Century Stephanite "Heresy" in the Ethiopian Church', *Rassegna di Studi Etiopici* 22 (1966); Getatchew Haile, 'Zämika'elites', in Siegbert Uhling, ed., *Encyclopedia Aethiopica: Supplementa, Addenda et Corrigenda*, vol. 5 (Wiesbaden, 2014), 131–33.

27. Zär'a Ya'qob, *The Mariology of Emperor Zär'a Ya'əqob of Ethiopia: Texts and Translations*, translated and edited by Getatchew Haile (Rome, 1992).

28. See Verena Krebs, *Medieval Ethiopian Kingship, Craft, and Diplomacy with Latin Europe* (Basingstoke, 2021); Denis Nosnitsin, 'Christian Manuscript Culture of the Ethiopian-Eritrean Highlands: Some Analytical Insights', in Kelly, *Companion to Medieval Ethiopia and Eritrea*; Marilyn E. Heldman, *The Marian Icons of the Painter Fr. Seyon: A Study in Fifteenth-Century Ethiopian Art, Patronage, and Spirituality* (Wiesbaden, 1994).

29. Judith McKenzie, Francis Watson and Michael Gervers, *The Garima Gospels: Early Illuminated Gospel Books from Ethiopia* (Oxford, 2016); Sergew Hable Selassie, *Bookmaking in Ethiopia* (Leiden, 1981).

30. The manuscript is documented in Stefan Bombeck, *Die Geschichte Der Heiligen Maria in Einer Altenäthiopischen Handschrift* (Dortmund, 2012), 161.

31. Stanisław Chojnacki, *Major Themes in Ethiopian Painting: Indigenous Developments, the Influence of Foreign Models, and Their Adaptation from the Thirteenth to the Nineteenth Century* (Wiesbaden, 1983), 59.

32. Carla Zanotti-Eman, 'Linear Decoration in Ethiopian Manuscripts', in Roderick Grierson, ed., *African Zion: The Sacred Art of Ethiopia* (New Haven, 1993).

33. Chojnacki, *Major Themes*, 22.

34. See Mattheus Immerzeel, 'Coptic-Ethiopian Artistic Interactions: The Issues of the Nursing Virgin and St George Slaying the Dragon', *Journal of the Canadian Society for Coptic Studies* 8 (2016).

35. Julien Loiseau, 'The Ḥaṭi and the Sultan: Letters and Embassies from Abyssinia to the Mamluk Court', in Frédéric Bauden and Malika Dekkiche, eds, *Mamluk Cairo, a Crossroads for Embassies: Studies on Diplomacy and Diplomatics* (Leiden, 2019).

36. Matteo Salvadore, *The African Prester John and the Birth of Ethiopian-European Relations, 1402–1555* (London, 2016); Samantha Kelly, 'The Curious Case of Ethiopic Chaldean: Fraud, Philology, and Cultural (Mis)understanding in European Conceptions of Ethiopia', *Renaissance Quarterly* 68 (2015).

37. Krebs, *Medieval Ethiopian Kingship*.

38. Samantha Kelly, 'Medieval Ethiopian Diasporas', in Kelly, *Companion to Medieval Ethiopia and Eritrea*.

39. Girma Beshah and Merid Wolde Aregay, *The Question of the Union of the Churches in Luso-Ethiopian Relations (1500–1632)* (Lisbon, 1964).

40. Šihāb ad-Dīn Aḥmad bin ʿAbd al-Qāder bin Sālem bin ʿUṯmān ʿArab Faqīh, *Futūḥ Al-Ḥabaša: The Conquest of Abyssinia (Sixteenth Century)*, translated by Paul Lester Stenhouse (Hollywood, 2005).

41. Jeffrey M. Shaw, *The Ethiopian-Adal War, 1529–1543: The Conquest of Abyssinia* (Warwick, 2021), 34–40 and 50–70.

42. An important source is Solomon Beyene Gebreyes, ed., *The Chronicle of Emperor Gälawdewos (1540–1559): A Source on Ethiopia's Mediaeval Historical Geography* (Louvain, 2019).

43. Crummey, *Land and Society*, 63–66.

44. Wendy Laura Belcher, 'Sisters Debating the Jesuits: The Role of African Women in Defeating Portuguese Cultural Colonialism in Seventeenth-Century Abyssinia', *Northeast African Studies* 12 (2013); Merid Wolde Aregay, 'The Legacy of Jesuit Missionary Activities in Ethiopia', in Getatchew Haile, Samuel Rubenson and Aasulv Lande, eds, *The Missionary Factor in Ethiopia: Papers from a Symposium on the Impact of European Missions on Ethiopian Society* (Frankfurt, 1998).

45. Habtamu Tegegne, 'Perpetrators: The Oromo Peoples and the Cultural Genocide of the Gafat People', in Igor Pérez Tostado, ed., *A Cultural History of Genocide*, vol. 3 (New York, 2021).

46. Habtamu M. Tegegne, *Rim and Zéga: The Origins of Elite Land Ownership and Peasant Dispossession in Ethiopia (1700–1974)* (forthcoming).

47. *Ibid.*

48. Bahru Zewde, *A History of Modern Ethiopia, 1855–1991* (Oxford, 2001), 27–30.

49. See Donald Crummey, 'Téwodros as Reformer and Modernizer', *Journal of African History* 10 (1969).

50. Bahru Zewde, *History*, 42–48 and 60–68; Crummey, *Land and Society*, 214–25.

——————————— CHAPTER 4 ———————————

1. See Jacob K. Olúpònà and Terry Ray, eds, *Òriṣà Devotion as World Religion: The Globalization of Yorùbá Religious Culture* (Madison, 2008). Yoruba is a tonal language with three pitch levels, low, middle and high. For the sake of simplicity, Yoruba names and words have been written without the accents indicating pitch or the subscript marks indicating pronunciation, except where they appear in source citations.

2. I. A. Akinjogbin, ed., *The Cradle of a Race: Ife from the Beginning to 1980* (Port Harcourt, 1992); Jacob K. Olúpònà, *City of 201 Gods: Ilé-Ifé in Time, Space, and the Imagination* (Berkeley, 2011).

3. Abiodun Adetugbo, 'The Yoruba Language in Western Nigeria: Its Major Dialect Areas', in S. O. Biobaku, ed., *Sources of Yoruba History* (Oxford, 1973).

4. Samuel Ajayi Crowther, *A Grammar and Vocabulary of the Yoruba Language* (London, 1852); Samuel Johnson, *The History of the Yorubas: From the Earliest Times to the Beginning of the British Protectorate* (Lagos, 1921).

5. On 'Yoruba' identity, see J. D. Y. Peel, 'The Cultural Work of Yoruba Ethnogenesis', in Toyin Falola, ed., *Pioneer, Patriot and Patriarch: Samuel Johnson and the Yoruba People* (Madison, 1993); Robin Law, 'Ethnicity and the Slave Trade: "Lucumi" and "Nago" as Ethnonyms in West Africa', *History in Africa* 24 (1997); and Henry Lovejoy and Olatunji Ojo, '"Lucumí" and "Terranova" and the Origins of the Yoruba Nation', *Journal of African History* 56 (2015).

6. See S. O. Biobaku, *The Origin of the Yoruba* (Lagos, 1955); Robert Smith, *Kingdoms of the Yoruba* (3rd edn, Madison, 1988), 13–28.

7. Gabriel O. I. Olomola, 'Ife Before Oduduwa', in Akinjogbin, *Cradle of a Race.*

8. See Robin Horton, 'Ancient Ife: A Reassessment', *Journal of the Historical Society of Nigeria* 9 (1979); S. A. Akintoye, *A History of the Yoruba People* (Dakar, 2010), 1–96; Akinwumi Ogundiran, *The Yorùbá: A New History* (Bloomington, 2020), 31–92.

9. Richard and John Lander, *Journal of an Expedition to Explore the Course and Termination of the Niger*, vol. 1 (London, 1832), 168 and 180.

10. Elizabeth Melville, *A Residence at Sierra Leone* (London, 1849), 257.

11. Ogundiran, *The Yorùbá*, 96–97.

12. John Pemberton III and Funso S. Afolayan, *Yoruba Sacred Kingship: 'A Power Like That of the Gods'* (Washington, D.C., 1996); Aribidesi Usman and Toyin Falola, *The Yoruba: From Prehistory to the Present* (Cambridge, 2019), 24.

13. Olúpònà, *City of 201 Gods*, 93–94.

14. Usman and Falola, *The Yoruba*, 24.
15. Pemberton and Afolayan, *Yoruba Sacred Kingship*, 73.
16. Ogundiran, *The Yorùbá*, 70.
17. Olúpònà, *City of 201 Gods*, 88.
18. Ogundiran, *The Yorùbá*, 138; see too William R. Bascom, *Ifá Divination: Communication between Gods and Men in West Africa* (Bloomington, 1969).
19. See Sandra T. Barnes, ed., *Africa's Ogun: Old World and New* (2nd edn, Bloomington, 1997); Joseph M. Murphy and Mei-Mei Sanford, eds, *Òṣun across the Waters: A Yoruba Goddess in Africa and the Americas* (Bloomington, 2001).
20. Frank Willett, *Ife in the History of West African Sculpture* (London, 1967); Suzanne Preston Blier, *Art and Risk in Ancient Yoruba: Ife History, Power, and Identity, c. 1300* (Cambridge, 2015).
21. Robin Horton, 'The Economy of Ife from *c.* AD 900 – *c.* AD 1700', in Akinjogbin, *Cradle of a Race*; Henry John Drewal and John Mason, *Beads, Body, and Soul: Art and Light in the Yorùbá Universe* (Los Angeles, 1997).
22. See Robin Law, *The Oyo Empire c. 1600–c. 1836: A West African Imperialism in the Era of the Atlantic Slave Trade* (Oxford, 1977).
23. J. F. A. Ajayi, 'The Aftermath of the Fall of Old Oyo', in J. F. Ade Ajayi and Michael Crowder, eds, *History of West Africa*, vol. 2 (2nd edn, Harlow, 1987), 178.
24. See Peter Morton-Williams, 'The Yoruba Kingdom of Oyo', in Daryll Forde and P. M. Kaberry, eds, *West African Kingdoms in the Nineteenth Century* (London, 1967).
25. Peter Morton-Williams, 'An Outline of the Cosmology and Cult Organization of the Oyo Yoruba', *Africa* 34 (1964).
26. Ajayi, 'Aftermath of the Fall of Old Oyo', 186; see too Robin Law, 'The Constitutional Troubles of Oyo in the Eighteenth Century', *Journal of African History* 12 (1971), 32.
27. Johnson, *History of the Yorubas*, 174–87, cited in Ajayi, 'Aftermath of the Fall of Old Oyo', 184.
28. Usman and Falola, *The Yoruba*, 77.
29. Ogundiran, *The Yorùbá*, 11.
30. Robin Law, 'The Heritage of Oduduwa: Traditional History and Political Propaganda among the Yoruba', *Journal of African History* 14 (1973); see too Ade M. Obayemi, 'The Yoruba and Edo-speaking Peoples and their Neighbours before 1600 AD', in J. F. Ade Ajayi and Michael Crowder, *History of West Africa*, vol. 1 (3rd edn, Harlow, 1985), 319.
31. Blier, *Art and Risk*, 59.
32. See Akin L. Mabogunje, *Yoruba Towns* (Ibadan, 1962); G. J. Afolabi Ojo, *Yoruba Palaces: A Study of Afins of Yorubaland* (London, 1967); J. D. Y. Peel, *Ijeshas and Nigerians: The Incorporation of a Yoruba Kingdom, 1890s–1970s* (Cambridge, 1983), 31–75.
33. Quoted in Usman and Falola, *The Yoruba*, 123.
34. Ajayi, 'The Aftermath of the Fall of Old Oyo', 184.
35. Andrew Apter, 'Discourse and its Disclosures: Yoruba Women and the Sanctity of Abuse', *Africa* 68 (1998); Judith Byfield, 'Dress and Politics in Post-World War II Abeokuta (Western Nigeria)', in Jean Allman, ed., *Fashioning Africa: Power and the Politics of Dress* (Bloomington, 2004).

36. Toyin Falola, *The Political Economy of a Pre-Colonial African State: Ibadan, 1830–1900* (Ile-Ife, 1984), 146–52; Ann O'Hear, 'Political and Commercial Clientage in Nineteenth-Century Ilorin', *African Economic History* 15 (1986).

37. A. K. Ajisafe, *A History of Abeokuta* (Bungay, 1924), 20; S. O. Biobaku, *The Egba and their Neighbours, 1842–72* (Oxford, 1957), 4–15.

38. J. O. Atandare, *Iwe Itan Akure* (Akure, n.d.); A. O. Oguntuyi, *A Short History of Ado-Ekiti Part II* (Ado-Ekiti, 1978).

39. See Kristin Mann, *Slavery and the Birth of an African City: Lagos, 1760–1900* (Bloomington, 2007), 22–50; Kunle Lawal, 'The Coastal Scene: The Yoruba of Lagos Society Before 1900', in D. Ogunremi and B. Adediran, eds, *Culture and Society in Yorubaland* (Ibadan, 1998).

40. See J. U. Egharevba, *A Short History of Benin* (3rd edn, Ibadan, 1960 [orig. 1934]), 6–8; R. E. Bradbury, 'The Kingdom of Benin', in Forde and Kaberry, *West African Kingdoms*; G. A. Akinola, 'The Origin of the Eweka Dynasty of Benin: A Study of the Use and Abuse of Oral Traditions', *Journal of the Historical Society of Nigeria* 8 (1976); E. B. Eweka, *The Benin Monarchy: Origin and Development* (Benin City, 1989).

41. Olúpònà, *City of 201 Gods*, 61.

42. Obayemi, 'The Yoruba and Edo-speaking Peoples'.

43. Suzanne Preston Blier, *Royal Arts of Africa: The Majesty of Form* (London, 1998), 53.

44. See A. F. C. Ryder, *Benin and the Europeans, 1485–1897* (London, 1969).

45. Olfert Dapper, *Description de l'Afrique* (Amsterdam, 1686), quoted in Thomas Hodgkin, ed., *Nigerian Perspectives: An Historical Anthology* (London, 1960), 123–24.

46. Paula Girshick Ben-Amos, *Art, Innovation, and Politics in Eighteenth-Century Benin* (Bloomington, 1999), 31 and 54.

47. Paula Girshick Ben-Amos and John Thornton, 'Civil War in the Kingdom of Benin, 1689–1721: Continuity or Political Change?', *Journal of African History* 42 (2001).

48. Ben-Amos, *Art, Innovation, and Politics*, 137.

49. Ogundiran, *The Yorùbá*, 357.

50. Ajayi, 'The Aftermath of the Fall of Old Oyo', 190.

51. S. A. Akintoye, *Revolution and Power Politics in Yorubaland, 1840–1893* (London, 1971); Toyin Falola and Dare Oguntomisin, *Yoruba Warlords of the Nineteenth Century* (Trenton, 2001).

52. See J. F. A. Ajayi, *Christian Missions in Nigeria, 1841–1891* (Evanston, 1965), and J. D. Y. Peel, *Religious Encounter and the Making of the Yoruba* (Bloomington, 2000).

53. Ajayi, 'The Aftermath of the Fall of Old Oyo', 214.

———————————————— **CHAPTER 5** ————————————————

My thanks to Thiago Sapede and John Thornton for their comments on early drafts of this chapter.

1. For the correspondence of Afonso, see António Brásio, *Monumenta missionária africana: África ocidental*, vol. 1 (Lisbon, 1952).

2. Jan Vansina, *Kingdoms of the Savanna: A History of Central African States until European Occupation* (Madison, 1966).

3. On Afonso's erudition, see the letter from Rui de Aguiar to King Manuel of Portugal, 25 May 1516, in Brásio, *Monumenta missionaria africana: África ocidental*, vol. 1, 361.

4. Luc de Heusch, *Le roi de Kongo et les monstres sacrés* (Paris, 2000).

5. Cécile Fromont, *The Art of Conversion: Christian Visual Culture in the Kingdom of Kongo* (Chapel Hill, 2014), 36, note 21.

6. Koen Bosteen and Inge Brinkman, 'Introduction: Cross-Disciplinary Approaches to Kongo History', in Koen Boeston and Inga Brinkman, eds, *The Kongo Kingdom: The Origins, Dynamics and Cosmopolitan Culture of an African Polity* (Cambridge, 2018), 1.

7. See Vansina, *Kingdoms of the Savanna*.

8. Luc de Heusch, *The Drunken King, or The Origin of the State*, translated by Roy Willis (Bloomington, 1982), and *Le roi de Kongo*.

9. Marshall Sahlins, 'The Atemporal Dimensions of History: In the Old Kongo Kingdom, for Example', in David Graeber and Marshall Sahlins, *On Kings* (Chicago, 2017), 210.

10. Bosteen and Brinkman, 'Cross-Disciplinary Approaches', 12; see too Koen Bosteen, Odjas Ndonda Tshiyayi and Gilles-Maurice de Schryver, 'On the Origin of the Royal Kongo Title *Ngangula*', *Africana Linguistica* 19 (2013), and on the region of Angola to the south of Kongo, Jan Vansina, *How Societies Are Born: Governance in West Central Africa before 1600* (Charlottesville, 2004).

11. Wyatt MacGaffey, 'A Central African Kingdom: Kongo in 1480', in Bosteen and Brinkman, *The Kongo Kingdom*; see too Wyatt MacGaffey, 'Dialogues of the Deaf: Europeans on the Atlantic Coast of Africa', in Stuart B. Schwartz, ed., *Implicit Understandings: Observing, Reporting, and Reflecting on the Encounters Between Europeans and Other Peoples in the Early Modern Era* (Cambridge, 1994).

12. John K. Thornton, 'The Origins of Kongo: A Revised Vision', in Bosteen and Brinkman, *The Kongo Kingdom*, 40.

13. John K. Thornton, *A History of West Central Africa to 1850* (Cambridge, 2020), 33.

14. John K. Thornton, *The Kingdom of Kongo: Civil War and Transition, 1641–1718* (Madison, 1983), 3–14; Anne Hilton, *The Kingdom of Kongo* (Oxford, 1985); Jan Vansina, 'Raffia Cloth in West Central Africa, 1500–1800', in Maureen Fennell Mazzaoui, ed., *Textiles: Production, Trade and Demand* (Aldershot, 1998).

15. See António Custódio Gonçalves, *A historia revisitada do Kongo e de Angola* (Lisbon, 2005).

16. Thiago Clemencio Sapede, 'Le roi et le temps, le Kongo et le monde: une histoire globale des transformations politiques du Royaume du Kongo (1780–1860)', unpublished PhD thesis, Paris, EHESS (2020), 78–82.

17. See, for example, Cristóvao Ribeiro, quoted in António Brásio, *Monumenta missionária africana: África ocidental*, vol. 15 (Lisbon, 1988), 161–63.

18. Wyatt MacGaffey, 'Changing Representations in Central African History', *Journal of African History* 46 (2005), 204–5.

19. MacGaffey, 'A Central African Kingdom', 55; see too Wyatt MacGaffey, *Art and Healing of the Bakongo, Commented by Themselves: Minkisi from the Laman Collection* (Stockholm, 1991).

20. For the broader context, see John Thornton, *Africa and Africans in the Making of the Atlantic World, 1400–1800* (2nd edn, Cambridge, 1998), and Toby Green, *A Fistful of Shells: West Africa from the Rise of the Slave Trade to the Age of Revolution* (London, 2019).

21. See Cécile Fromont, *Images on a Mission in Early Modern Kongo and Angola* (University Park, PA, 2022).

22. Cécile Fromont, 'Dance, Image, Myth, and Conversion in the Kingdom of Kongo: 1500–1800', *African Arts* 44 (2011).

23. Inge Brinkman, 'Kongo Interpreters, Travelling Priests and Political Leaders in the Kongo Kingdom (15th–19th century)', *International Journal of African Historical Studies* 49 (2016).

24. Louis Jadin, 'Le clergé séculier et les capucins du Congo et d'Angola aux XVIe et XVIIe siècles: conflits de juridiction, 1700–1726', *Bulletin de l'Institut Historique Belge de Rome* 36 (1964).

25. Fromont, *Art of Conversion*, 5–6.

26. See Bernard-Olivier Clist et al., 'Fouilles et prospections à l'ouest de l'Inkisi, région de Ngongo Mbata', in B. Clist, P. de Maret and K. Bostoen, eds, *Une archéologie des provinces septentrionales du royaume Kongo* (Oxford, 2018).

27. Olfert Dapper, *Naukeurige beschrijvinge der afrikaensche gewesten* (Amsterdam, 1668).

28. Michiel van Groesen, 'Abraham Willaerts: Marine Painter of Dutch Brazil and the Atlantic World', *Oud Holland: Journal for Art of the Low Countries* 132 (2019).

29. For a description of a coronation and its regalia, see Brásio, *Monumenta missionária africana: África ocidental*, vol. 15, 482–97.

30. 'Mbanza Kongo, Vestiges of the Capital of the former Kingdom of Kongo', UNESCO, https://whc.unesco.org/en/list/1511/, accessed 25 June 2022.

31. For recent archaeological findings, see Clist, de Maret and Bostoen, *Une archéologie des provinces septentrionales*.

32. John K. Thornton and Andrea Mosterman, 'A Re-interpretation of the Kongo-Portuguese War of 1622 According to New Documentary Evidence', *Journal of African History* 51 (2010).

33. Quoted in Linda M. Heywood, 'Slavery and its Transformation in the Kingdom of Kongo: 1491–1800', *Journal of African History* 50 (2009).

34. Cécile Fromont, 'Common Threads: Cloth, Colour, and the Slave Trade in Early Modern Kongo and Angola', *Art History* 41 (2018).

35. Sapede, 'Le roi et le temps'.

36. Heywood, 'Slavery and its Transformation', 136–39; Sapede, 'Le roi et le temps'.

37. On the disputed identity of the Jaga, see Paulo Jorge Sousa Pinto, 'Em torno de um problema de identidade: os «Jagas» na história de Congo e Angola', *Mare Liberum* 18–19 (2000).

38. John K. Thornton, *The Kongolese Saint Anthony: Dona Beatriz Kimpa Vita and the Antonian Movement, 1684–1706* (Cambridge, 1998).

39. António Custódio Gonçalves, *Le lignage contre l'etat: dynamique politique Kongo du XVIème au XVIIIème siècle* (Lisbon, 1985).

40. Sapede, 'Le roi et le temps'.

41. See Adolf Bastian, *Ein Besuch in São Salvador in 1858* (Bremen, 1859), and the account by Mpetelo Boka recorded in Jean Cuvelier, *Nkutama a Mvila za Makanda* (Tumba, 1934).

42. MacGaffey, 'A Central African Kingdom', 58; and see Susan Herlin Broadhead, 'Beyond Decline: The Kingdom of the Kongo in the Eighteenth and Nineteenth Centuries', *International Journal of African Historical Studies* 12 (1979).

43. Cécile Fromont, ed., *Afro-Catholic Festivals in the Americas: Performance, Representation, and the Making of Black Atlantic Tradition* (University Park, PA, 2019).

44. Jeroen Dewulf, 'Pinkster: An Atlantic Creole Festival in a Dutch-American Context', *Journal of American Folklore* 126 (2013).

45. See John K. Thornton, 'I Am a Subject of the King of Kongo: African Political Ideology and the Haitian Revolution', *Journal of World History* 4 (1993).

46. See Marina de Mello e Souza, *Reis negros no Brasil escravista: história da festa de coroação de rei congo* (Belo Horizonte, 2002).

47. Thornton, *History of West Central Africa*, 342–44.

48. Broadhead, 'Beyond Decline'; Jelmer Vos, *Kongo in the Age of Empire, 1860–1913: The Breakdown of a Moral Order* (Madison, 2015).

49. Seal of the King of Kongo, 1859, in Additional Manuscripts 29960 D, fol. 22, British Library, London.

50. Secretaria do Estado da Marinha e do Ultramar, Direçao Geral do Ultramar, box 628, 1860, Arquivo Histórico Ultramarino, Lisbon.

51. Wyatt MacGaffey, 'Constructing a Kongo Identity: Scholarship and Mythopoesis', *Comparative Studies in Society and History* 58 (2016).

52. Yolanda Covington-Ward, 'Joseph Kasa-Vubu, ABAKO, and Performances of Kongo Nationalism in the Independence of Congo', *Journal of Black Studies* 43 (2012).

53. Zana Etambala, 'Comment nous avons retrouvé Ambroise Boimbo le voleur du sabre du Roi Baudouin le 29 juin 1960', *L'Africain: Revue des Étudiants Africains en Belgique* 255 (2012).

--- **CHAPTER 6** ---

1. Jean-Pierre Chrétien, *The Great Lakes of Africa: Two Thousand Years of History*, translated by Scott Straus (New York, 2006), 27.

2. In the Bantu languages, nouns have prefixes that alter the meaning of the stem. According to standard convention, I have retained the prefixes in the words for states (Buganda, Bunyoro, etc.) and languages (Luganda), but have otherwise used only the stem: Ganda.

3. Richard J. Reid, *A History of Modern Uganda* (Cambridge, 2017).

4. David L. Schoenbrun, *A Green Place, A Good Place: Agrarian Change, Gender, and Social Identity in the Great Lakes Region to the 15th Century* (Portsmouth, NH, 1998).

5. Chrétien, *The Great Lakes*, 157.

6. David L. Schoenbrun, 'The (In)visible Roots of Bunyoro-Kitara and Buganda in the Lakes Region: AD 800–1300', in Susan Keech McIntosh, ed., *Beyond Chiefdoms: Pathways to Complexity in Africa* (Cambridge, 1999), 136–37.

7. Rhiannon Stephens, *A History of African Motherhood: The Case of Uganda, 700–1900* (Cambridge, 2013).

8. Sir Apolo Kaggwa, *The Kings of Buganda*, translated and edited by M. S. M. Kiwanuka (Nairobi, 1971); M. S. M. Semakula Kiwanuka, *A History of Buganda: From the Foundation of the Kingdom to 1900* (London, 1971).

9. See Michael Twaddle, 'On Ganda Historiography', *History in Africa* 1 (1974).

10. Christopher Wrigley, *Kingship and State: The Buganda Dynasty* (Cambridge, 1996), 8.

11. Benjamin C. Ray, *Myth, Ritual, and Kingship in Buganda* (New York, 1991), 22–53, quote from 53.

12. Kaggwa, *The Kings of Buganda*, 162.

13. Wrigley, *Kingship and State*, 170.

14. Jan Vansina, *Antecedents to Modern Rwanda: The Nyiginya Kingdom* (Madison, 2004).

15. See Kaggwa, *The Kings of Buganda*, appendix 3: 'List of the jawbone shrines', 225–28.

16. Ray, *Myth, Ritual, and Kingship*, 74.

17. Schoenbrun, *A Green Place*, 185–95; see too Stephens, *History of African Motherhood*, 61–62.

18. Neil Kodesh, *Beyond the Royal Gaze: Clanship and Healing in Buganda* (Charlottesville, 2010), 27–48.

19. See Iris Berger, 'Deities, Dynasties, and Oral Tradition: The History and Legend of the Abacwezi', in Joseph C. Miller, ed., *The African Past Speaks: Essays on Oral Tradition and History* (Folkestone, 1980).

20. See John W. Nyakatura, *Anatomy of an African Kingdom: A History of Bunyoro-Kitara*, edited and translated by G. N. Uzoigwe (Garden City, NY, 1973).

21. Reid, *History of Modern Uganda*, 116.

22. David Henige, '"The Disease of Writing": Ganda and Nyoro Kinglists in a Newly Literate World', in Miller, *The African Past Speaks*.

23. Holly Elizabeth Hanson, *Landed Obligation: The Practice of Power in Buganda* (Portsmouth, NH, 2003), 32.

24. *Ibid.*, 44.

25. Stephens, *History of African Motherhood*, 107–11; and see Kaggwa, *The Kings of Buganda*, appendix 3: 'List of royal wives, their families, clans and offspring', 203–21.

26. Ray, *Myth, Ritual, and Kingship*, 82, citing Bartolomayo M. Zimbe, *Buganda ne Kabaka* (Mengo, 1939).

27. Wrigley, *Kingship and State*, 170.

28. John Iliffe, *Africans: The History of a Continent* (3rd edn, Cambridge, 2017), 114.

29. Kodesh, *Beyond the Royal Gaze*, 131–58, quote from 158.

30. David Graeber, 'The Divine Kingship of the Shilluk: On Violence, Utopia, and the Human Condition', in David Graeber and Marshall Sahlins, *On Kings* (Chicago, 2017), 66.

31. Graeber and Sahlins, 'Introduction: Theses on Kingship', in *On Kings*, 6.

32. Hanson, *Landed Obligation*, 1.

33. Ray, *Myth, Ritual, and Kingship*, 162.

34. Wrigley, *Kingship and State*, 23 and 220.

35. *Ibid.*, 228.

36. Ray, *Myth, Ritual, and Kingship*, 162; see too Hanson, *Landed Obligation*, 76.

37. Reid, *History of Modern Uganda*, 129.

38. Vansina, *Antecedents to Modern Rwanda*, 164.

39. Ray, *Myth, Ritual, and Kingship*, 48.

40. Hanson, *Landed Obligation*, 85; see too Richard Reid, 'Human Booty in Buganda: Some Observations on the Seizure of People in War', in Henri Médard and Shane Doyle, eds, *Slavery in the Great Lakes Region of Africa* (Oxford, 2007).

41. Chrétien, *The Great Lakes*, 201.

42. Kaggwa, *The Kings of Buganda*, 100–101, 110–11 and 119; Ray, *Myth, Ritual, and Kingship*, 44–45 and 164–65.

43. Iliffe, *Africans*, 193.

44. *Ibid.*, 196.

45. Hanson, *Landed Obligation*, 93.

46. Iliffe, *Africans*, 197; Vansina, *Antecedents to Modern Rwanda*.

47. Chrétien, *The Great Lakes*, 225.

48. L. A. Fallers, ed., *The King's Men: Leadership and Status in Buganda on the Eve of Independence* (London, 1964).

49. Chrétien, *The Great Lakes*, 298.

-------------------------------- **CHAPTER 7** --------------------------------

1. Anne Haour and Benedetta Rossi, 'Hausa Identity: Language, History and Religion', in Anne Haour and Benedetta Rossi, eds, *Being and Becoming Hausa: Interdisciplinary Perspectives* (Leiden, 2010), 1.

2. For authoritative historical overviews, see J. O. Hunwick, 'Songhay, Borno and the Hausa States, 1450–1600', and R. A. Adeleye, 'Hausaland and Borno, 1600–1800', both in J. F. Ade Ajayi and Michael Crowder, eds, *History of West Africa*, vol. 1 (3rd edn, Harlow, 1985).

3. David Robinson, 'Revolutions in the Western Sudan', in Nehemia Levtzion and Randall L. Pouwels, eds, *The History of Islam in Africa* (Athens, OH, 2000), 138; see too Murray Last, 'The Book in the Sokoto Caliphate', in Shamil Jeppie and Soulemane Bachir Diagne, eds, *The Meanings of Timbuktu* (Cape Town, 2008).

4. The writings of 'Uthman Dan Fodio, Muhammad Bello and others are available in their original Arabic form and in translated versions in various libraries in Nigeria: the Waziri Junaidu History and Culture Bureau, in Sokoto; the library of Ahmadu Bello University, Zaria, which houses the papers of the Northern History Research Scheme; and the Arewa House Centre of Documentation and Historical Research, in Kaduna. Much published and unpublished research has been conducted in the history

departments of Usman Danfodio University, Sokoto; Ahmadu Bello University, Zaria; and Bayero University, Kano.

5. Murray Last, 'Reform in West Africa: The *Jihad* Movements of the Nineteenth Century', in J. F. Ade Ajayi and Michael Crowder, eds, *History of West Africa*, vol. 2 (2nd edn, Harlow, 1987), 1. For a recent analysis of the movement as an integral part of the global 'age of revolution', see Paul E. Lovejoy, *Jihad in West Africa during the Age of Revolutions* (Athens, OH, 2016).

6. Key studies include Mahdi Adamu, *The Hausa Factor in West Africa* (Zaria, 1978); Y. B. Usman, *The Transformation of Katsina, 1400–1883: The Emergence and Overthrow of the 'Sarauta' System and the Establishment of the Emirate* (Zaria, 1981); M. G. Smith, *Government in Zazzau, 1800–1950* (London, 1960) and *Government in Kano, 1350–1950* (Boulder, 1997); G. Na-Dama, 'The Rise and Collapse of a Hausa Kingdom: A Political History of Zamfara', unpublished PhD thesis, Ahmadu Bello University, Zaria, 1977.

7. John Iliffe, *Africans: The History of a Continent* (3rd edn, Cambridge, 2017), 77.

8. For this hypothesis, see Murray Last, 'The Early Kingdoms of the Nigerian Savanna', in Ajayi and Crowder, *History of West Africa*, vol. 1, and Abdullahi Smith, 'Some Considerations Relating to the Formation of States in Hausaland', in *A Little New Light: Selected Historical Writings of Abdullahi Smith* (Zaria, 1987); for a recent critique, see John E. G. Sutton, 'Hausa as a Process in Time and Space', in Haour and Rossi, *Being and Becoming Hausa*.

9. Last, 'Early Kingdoms', 176.

10. The *Kano Chronicle* was translated by the British colonial administrator H. R. Palmer in his *Sudanese Memoirs*, vol. 3 (Lagos, 1928; 2nd edn, London, 1967); see Paul E. Lovejoy, 'The *Kano Chronicle* Revisited', in Toby Green and Benedetta Rossi, eds, *Landscapes, Sources and Intellectual Projects of the West African Past* (Leiden, 2018).

11. For a version of the legend recorded in Daura and included in Palmer's *Sudanese Memoirs*, see Thomas Hodgkin, *Nigerian Perspectives: An Historical Anthology* (London, 1960), 54–56; also W. K. R. Hallam, 'The Bayajida Legend in Hausa Folklore', *Journal of African History* 7 (1966).

12. Last, 'Early Kingdoms', 193; see too Hunwick, 'Songhay, Borno and the Hausa States', 329–30.

13. Iliffe, *Africans*, 78; see too Usman, *Transformation of Katsina*, and A. Mahadi, 'The State and the Economy: The Sarauta System and its Roles in Shaping the Society and Economy of Kano', unpublished PhD thesis, Ahmadu Bello University, Zaria, 1982.

14. Hunwick, 'Songhay, Borno and the Hausa States', 353.

15. *Ibid.*, 331.

16. *Kano Chronicle*, in Hodgkin, *Nigerian Perspectives*, 89–90.

17. David Robinson, *Muslim Societies in African History* (Cambridge, 2004), 141.

18. Hunwick, 'Songhay, Borno and the Hausa States', 338.

19. *Ibid.*, 334.

20. Last, 'Early Kingdoms', 220.

21. Smith, *Government in Kano*; Murray Last, 'From Sultanate to Caliphate: Kano, 1550–1800', in B. M. Barkindo, ed., *Studies in the History of Kano* (Ibadan, 1983).

22. Adeleye, 'Hausaland and Borno', 583.

23. M. Aliyu, 'The History of Birnin Zaria: A Study into the Socio-Economic and Political History of Zaria, *c.* 1492–1808', unpublished MA dissertation, Ahmadu Bello University, Zaria, 2000, 17.

24. M. Adamu, 'The Economy of Hausa Capitals: Zaria in the 18th and 19th Centuries', in M. A. Mamman, ed., *History Department Seminar Series*, vol. 4 (Ahmadu Bello University, Zaria, 2012), 49.

25. See A. R. Augi, 'The Sokoto-Rima Basin Area: A Preliminary View of its Political History in the 18th Century', in Mamman, *Seminar Series*; S. S. Gusau, 'A History of Zamfara 1764–2013', unpublished PhD thesis, Usman Danfodio University, Sokoto, 169–71; Adeleye, 'Hausaland and Borno', 586–90 and 605–8.

26. Quoted in *ibid.*, 614.

27. Landmark studies include: Murray Last, *The Sokoto Caliphate* (London, 1967); R. A. Adeleye, *Power and Diplomacy in Northern Nigeria, 1804–1906: The Sokoto Caliphate and its Enemies* (London, 1971); R. A. Adeleye and C. C. Stewart, 'The Sokoto Caliphate in the Nineteenth Century', in Ajayi and Crowder, *History of West Africa*, vol. 2; Y. B. Usman, ed., *Studies in the History of the Sokoto Caliphate* (Lagos, 1979); H. I. Sa'id, *Revolution and Reaction: The Fulani Jihad in Kano and its Aftermath, 1807–1919* (Zaria, 2012); and a collection marking the bicentenary of the *jihad*, H. Bobboyi and A. M. Yakubu, eds, *The Sokoto Caliphate: History and Legacies, 1804–2004*, 2 vols (Kaduna, 2006).

28. Kabiru S. Chafe, 'Remarks on the Historiography of the Sokoto Caliphate', in *ibid.*, vol. 2, 325.

29. For useful overviews, see Robinson, 'Revolutions in the Western Sudan', and *Muslim Societies*, 42–59.

30. Last, 'Reform in West Africa', 14.

31. A. M. Kani, 'The Political and Social Basis of the Sokoto Jihad', in Mamman, *History Department Seminar Series*.

32. Na-Dama, 'Political History of Zamfara', 170–72.

33. For a biography, see Mervyn Hiskett, *The Sword of Truth: The Life and Times of the Shehu Usuman dan Fodio* (Oxford, 1973).

34. Last, 'Reform in West Africa', 18.

35. 'Uthman Dan Fodio, 'Tanbikhu'l-Ikhwan', in Hodgkin, *Nigerian Perspectives*, 192.

36. Ibrahim Ado-Kurawa, 'The *Jihad* and the Consolidation of Sudanic Intellectual Tradition', in Bobboyi and Yakubu, *The Sokoto Caliphate*, vol. 2.

37. Robinson, *Muslim Societies*, 146; see further Louis Brenner, 'The *Jihad* Debate between Sokoto and Borno: An Historical Analysis of Islamic Political Discourse in Nigeria', in J. F. Ade Ajayi and J. D. Y. Peel, eds, *Peoples and Empires in African History: Essays in Memory of Michael Crowder* (Harlow, 1992).

38. Last, 'Reform in West Africa', 20 and 24.

39. Iliffe, *Africans*, 181.

40. *Ibid.*

41. Hamid Bobboyi, '*Ajami* Literature and the Study of the Sokoto Caliphate', in Jeppie and Diagne, *The Meanings of Timbuktu*.

42. Robinson, *Muslim Societies*, 150; see too Jean Boyd and Beverly Mack, *One Woman's Jihad: Nana Asma'u, Scholar and Scribe* (Bloomington, 2000).

43. See Chafe, 'Historiography of the Sokoto Caliphate'.

44. Heinrich Barth, *Travels and Discoveries in North and Central Africa, 1849–1855*, vol. 1 (London, 1857–59), 488, quoted in Haour and Rossi, 'Hausa Identity', 11.

45. See Paul E. Lovejoy and Jan S. Hogendorn, *Slow Death for Slavery: The Course of Abolition in Northern Nigeria, 1897–1936* (Cambridge, 1993).

46. Iliffe, *Africans*, 180.

47. Adeleye, 'Hausaland and Borno', 617.

48. William F. S. Miles, 'Religious Pluralism in Northern Nigeria', in Levtzion and Pouwels, *History of Islam in Africa*, 210–11.

49. Quoted in Iliffe, *Africans*, 215.

CHAPTER 8

---

1. T. Edward Bowdich, *Mission from Cape Coast Castle to Ashantee* (London, 1819; 3rd edn, 1966), 28.

2. *Ibid.*, 31–37.

3. *Ibid.*, 38–39.

4. Toby Green, *A Fistful of Shells: West Africa from the Rise of the Slave Trade to the Age of Revolution* (London, 2019), ch. 7.

5. David Graeber and Marshall Sahlins, *On Kings* (Chicago, 2017).

6. See Ivor Wilks, *Asante in the Nineteenth Century: The Structure and Evolution of a Political Order* (Cambridge, 1975).

7. See T. C. McCaskie, *State and Society in Pre-colonial Asante* (Cambridge, 1995).

8. See W. Arens and Ivan Karp, eds, *Creativity of Power: Cosmology and Action in African Societies* (Washington, D.C., 1989).

9. A. Adu Boahen, Emmanuel Akyeampong, Nancy Lawler, T. C. McCaskie and Ivor Wilks, eds, *'The History of Ashanti Kings and the Whole Country Itself' and Other Writings by Otumfuo, Nana Agyeman Prempeh I* (Oxford, 2003), 86.

10. Ivor Wilks, *Forests of Gold: Essays on the Akan and the Kingdom of Asante* (Athens, OH, 1993), 66.

11. On Akan origins, see Wilks, *Forests of Gold*, chs 1–3.

12. See Gérard L. Chouin and Christopher R. DeCorse, 'Prelude to the Atlantic Trade: New Perspectives on Southern Ghana's Pre-Atlantic History (800–1500)', *Journal of African History* 51 (2010).

13. Green, *Fistful of Shells*, 33.

14. Rev. C. C. Reindorf, *History of the Gold Coast and Asante* (Basel, 1895), 49; see too T. C. McCaskie, 'Denkyira and the Making of Asante, c. 1660–1720', *Journal of African History* 48 (2007).

15. Boahen et al., *History of Ashanti Kings*, 108–9.

16. Wilks, *Forests of Gold*, 111; William Bosman, *A New and Accurate Description of the Coast of Guinea* (London, 1705, 4th edn, 1967), 76–77.

17. R. S. Rattray, *Ashanti* (Oxford, 1923), 289–90.

18. R. S. Rattray, *Ashanti Law and Constitution* (Oxford, 1929), 276.

19. *Ibid.*, 277.

20. Boahen et al., *History of Ashanti Kings*, 119.

21. Ivor Wilks, 'Ashanti Government', in Daryll Forde and P. M. Kaberry, eds, *West African Kingdoms in the Nineteenth Century* (Oxford, 1967), 211.

22. Kwame Arhin, 'The Structure of Greater Ashanti (1700–1824)', *Journal of African History* 8 (1967).

23. See John Parker, *In My Time of Dying: A History of Death and the Dead in West Africa* (Princeton, 2021), 107–23.

24. Joseph Dupuis, *Journal of a Residence in Ashantee* (London, 1824; 2nd edn, 1966), 161.

25. *Ibid.*, 245; on this episode, see Parker, *In My Time of Dying*, 148–51.

26. Wilks, 'Ashanti Government', 213.

27. *Ibid.*

28. Ivor Wilks, *One Nation, Many Histories: Ghana Past and Present* (Accra, 1996), 32; see too *Forests of Gold*, 193.

29. Robin Law, 'Human Sacrifice in Pre-colonial West Africa', *African Affairs* 84 (1985), 55.

30. John Iliffe, *Africans: The History of a Continent* (3rd edn, Cambridge, 2017), 152.

31. Law, 'Human Sacrifice', 55; see too Parker, *In My Time of Dying*, 139–54.

32. McCaskie, *State and Society*, 16.

33. Lucy Mair, *African Kingdoms* (Oxford, 1977), 21.

34. Marshall Sahlins, 'The Original Political Society', in Graeber and Sahlins, *On Kings*, 60.

35. See the collection of essays in Tom McCaskie, *Asante, Kingdom of Gold: Essays in the History of an African Culture* (Durham, NC, 2015).

36. Marshall Sahlins, 'The Cultural Politics of Core-Periphery Relations' in Graeber and Sahlins, *On Kings*, 348.

37. See Michelle Gilbert, 'The Person of the King: Ritual and Power in a Ghanaian State', in David Cannadine and Simon Price, eds, *Rituals of Royalty: Power and Ceremonial in Traditional Societies* (Cambridge, 1987).

38. Eva L. R. Meyerowitz, *The Sacred State of the Akan* (London, 1951), 55.

39. Dupuis, *Journal*, 245.

40. Bowdich, *Mission*, 71.

41. McCaskie, *State and Society*, 261.

42. Iliffe, *Africans*, 141.

43. SOAS University of London, Wesleyan Methodist Missionary Archives, 'Reminiscences and Incidents of Travels and Historical and Political Sketches in and of the Countries Bordering on the Gold Coast and Slave Coast and in Ashantee, Dahomey, etc', by T. B. Freeman [no date, but 1859–69], 41.

44. *Ibid.*, 154–55.

45. T. C. McCaskie, *Asante Identities: History and Modernity in an African Village, 1850–1950* (Edinburgh, 2000), 29–30.

46. Tom McCaskie, 'Kwaduenya: Three Hundred Years of Land Tenure in Asante', *International Journal of African Historical Studies* 50 (2017), 193.

47. Freeman, 'Reminiscences', 108; Bowdich, *Mission*, 306.

48. McCaskie, *State and Society*, 438.

49. Bowdich, *Mission*, 279.

50. McCaskie, *State and Society*, 144–242, quote from 204.

51. Quoted in Wilks, *Forests of Gold*, 180.

CHAPTER 9

1. Elizabeth A. Eldredge, *The Creation of the Zulu Kingdom, 1815–1828: War, Shaka, and the Consolidation of Power* (New York, 2014), 1.

2. John Wright and Carolyn Hamilton, 'The Phongolo-Mzimkhulu Region in the Late Eighteenth and Early Nineteenth Centuries', in Andew Duminy and Bill Guest, eds, *Natal and Zululand from Earliest Times to 1910: A New History* (Pietermaritzburg, 1989), 57–59.

3. John Laband, *The Rise and Fall of the Zulu Nation* (London, 1997), 13.

4. Norman Etherington, 'Were There Large States in the Coastal Regions of Southeast Africa Before the Rise of the Zulu Kingdom?', *History in Africa* 31 (2004), 158; Norman Etherington, *The Great Treks: The Transformation of Southern Africa, 1815–1854* (Harlow, 2001), xx–xxi.

5. Wright and Hamilton, 'Phongolo-Mzimkhulu Region', 68.

6. A. T. Bryant, *Olden Times in Zululand and Natal: Containing Earlier Political History of the Eastern-Nguni Clans* (London, 1929), 94 and 96.

7. Cited in Leonard Thompson, 'Co-operation and Conflict: The Zulu Kingdom and Natal', in Monica Wilson and Leonard Thompson, eds, *A History of South Africa to 1870* (Cape Town and Johannesburg, 1982), 339.

8. See Max Gluckman, 'The Rise of the Zulu Empire', *Scientific American* (1963), and 'The Individual in a Social Framework: The Rise of King Shaka of Zululand', *Journal of African Studies* 1 (1974).

9. David W. Hedges, 'Trade and Politics in Southern Mozambique and Zululand in the Eighteenth and Early Nineteenth Centuries', unpublished PhD thesis, SOAS University of London, 1978, 6–8.

10. Jeff Guy, 'Ecological Factors in the Rise of Shaka and the Zulu Kingdom', in Shula Marks and Anthony Atmore, eds, *Economy and Society in Pre-industrial South Africa* (Harlow, 1980), 113–14; Hedges, 'Trade and Politics', 36; Charles Ballard, 'Drought and Economic Distress: South Africa in the 1800s', *Journal of Interdisciplinary History* 17 (1986), 369; Jeff Guy, 'Analysing Pre-capitalist Societies in Southern Africa', *Journal of Southern African Studies* 14 (1987), 21–22.

11. Guy, 'Ecological Factors', 105–9; Ballard, 'Drought and Economic Distress', 365.

12. Hedges, 'Trade and Politics', 39–41; Jeff Guy, *The Destruction of the Zulu Kingdom: The Civil War in Zululand, 1879–1884* (London, 1979), 7; Neil Parsons, 'Prelude to the Difaqane in

the Interior of Southern Africa, *c.* 1600–*c.* 1822' in Carolyn Hamilton, ed., *Mfecane Aftermath: Reconstructive Debates in Southern African History* (Johannesburg, 1995), 338.

13. Ballard, 'Drought and Economic Distress', 360–69.

14. Mahaya ka Nongqabana, cited in Ballard, 'Drought and Economic Distress', 370.

15. C. de B. Webb and J. B. Wright, eds, *The James Stuart Archive of Recorded Oral Evidence Relating to the History of the Zulu and Neighbouring Peoples*, vol. 1 (Pietermaritzburg, 1976–2001), 201; Ballard, 'Drought and Economic Distress', 370–71; Wright and Hamilton, 'Phongolo-Mzimkhulu Region', 66.

16. *James Stuart Archive*, vol. 1, 201.

17. Guy, 'Ecological Factors', 111; Ballard, 'Drought and Economic Distress', 373.

18. Guy, 'Ecological Factors', 117.

19. *James Stuart Archive*, vol. 4, 289; Eldredge, *Creation of the Zulu Kingdom*, 32.

20. The estimate is that of H. F. Fynn, *The Diary of Henry Francis Fynn*, compiled and edited by James Stuart (Pietermaritzburg, 1950), 12.

21. Edgar H. Brookes and Colin de B. Webb, *A History of Natal* (Pietermaritzburg, 1987), 10; Thompson, 'Co-operation and Conflict', 342.

22. *Ibid.*, 9.

23. *James Stuart Archive*, vol. 4, 361; Fynn, *Diary*, 9.

24. *Ibid.*, 10.

25. Eldredge, *Creation of the Zulu Kingdom*, 33.

26. Hedges, 'Trade and Politics', 195–96; Wright and Hamilton, 'Phongolo-Mzimkhulu Region', 62–63; John Wright, 'Turbulent Times: Political Transformations in the North and East, 1760s–1830s', in Carolyn Hamilton, Bernard K. Mbenga and Robert Ross, eds, *The Cambridge History of South Africa, Volume 1: From Early Times to 1885* (Cambridge, 2009), 221; James Gump, 'Origins of the Zulu Kingdom', *The Historian* 50 (1988), 524.

27. Bryant, *Olden Times*, 641–42; Gump, 'Origins of the Zulu Kingdom', 529–30.

28. For example, Thompson, 'Co-operation and Conflict', 340; Gump, 'Origins of the Zulu Kingdom', 525–27.

29. Hedges, 'Trade and Politics', 186–96; Alan Smith, 'The Trade of Delagoa Bay as a Factor in Nguni Politics', in Leonard Thompson, ed., *African Societies in Southern Africa* (London, 1969), 187–88.

30. Hedges, 'Trade and Politics', 197–98 and 241.

31. The strongest case for a multicausal explanation has been made by Elizabeth Eldredge, 'Sources of Conflict in Southern Africa, ca. 1830: The Mfecane Reconsidered', *Journal of African History* 33 (1992).

32. John Laband, *The Eight Zulu Kings* (Jeppestown, 2018), 27–29.

33. Cited in Eldredge, *Creation of the Zulu Kingdom*, 76.

34. *Ibid.*, 121.

35. Laband, *Eight Zulu Kings*, 16.

36. Cited in Eldredge, *Creation of the Zulu Kingdom*, 61.

37. *Ibid.*

38. Laband, *Eight Zulu Kings*, 33.

39. Cited in Eldredge, *Creation of the Zulu Kingdom*, 81.

40. Laband, *Eight Zulu Kings*, 38.

41. Cited in Eldredge, *Creation of the Zulu Kingdom*, 62.

42. Cited in Laband, *Eight Zulu Kings*, 39.

43. Testimony of Ngidi, *James Stuart Archive*, vol. 5, 60.

44. Eldredge, *Creation of the Zulu Kingdom*, 92.

45. Hedges, 'Trade and Politics', 208.

46. Eldredge, *Creation of the Zulu Kingdom*, 293.

47. Laband, *Eight Zulu Kings*, 46; see also Carolyn Hamilton and John Wright, 'The Making of the AmaLala: Ethnicity, Ideology and Relations of Subordination in a Precolonial Context', *South African Historical Journal* 22 (1990).

48. Cited in Eldredge, *Creation of the Zulu Kingdom*, 7.

49. Testimony of Baleka, *James Stuart Archive*, vol. 1, 8.

50. John Laband, *The Assassination of King Shaka* (Johannesburg, 2017), 49.

51. Cited in Eldredge, *Creation of the Zulu Kingdom*, 248.

52. Hedges, 'Trade and Politics', 80–83.

53. Laband, *Eight Zulu Kings*, 50.

54. The classic statement in this regard was made nearly five decades ago: Anthony Atmore and Shula Marks, 'The Imperial Factor in South Africa in the Nineteenth Century', *Journal of Imperial and Commonwealth History* 3 (1974).

55. Guy, *Destruction of the Zulu Kingdom*, 18.

56. Cited in Laband, *Rise and Fall*, 189–90.

57. Norman Etherington, Patrick Harries and Bernard Mbenga, 'From Colonial Hegemonies to Imperial Conquest, 1840–1880', in Hamilton et al., eds, *Cambridge History*, vol. 1, 384.

58. Richard Price, *Making Empire: Colonial Encounters and the Creation of Imperial Rule in Nineteenth-Century Africa* (Cambridge, 2008), 3.

59. Guy, *Destruction of the Zulu Kingdom*, 59–61.

60. *Ibid.*, 61; Laband, *Rise and Fall*, 229.

61. John Laband and Paul Thompson, 'The Reduction of Zululand, 1878–1904', in Duminy and Guest, *Natal and Zululand*, 203–6; Guy, *Destruction of the Zulu Kingdom*, 239–40.

62. Laband and Thompson, 'Reduction of Zululand', 212.

63. British Parliamentary Papers, C. 5331, *Further Correspondence Respecting the Affairs of Zululand and Adjacent Territories*, Memorandum by the Governor, A. E. Havelock, 15 Nov. 1887.

64. Shula Marks, *Reluctant Rebellion: The 1906–08 Disturbances in Natal* (Oxford, 1970), 110.

SOURCES OF ILLUSTRATIONS

a = above; b = below; l = left; r = right

Colour plates
I Photo AGF Srl / Alamy Stock Photo; II Photo courtesy I.T.C. Sudan; III Photo oversnap / Getty Images; IV Bibliothèque nationale de France, Paris; V Photo courtesy Matthieu Honegger, Mission Archéologique Suisse à Kerma; VI Princeton University Library Special Collections; VII Photo Meinzahn / Dreamstime; VIII The British Museum, London. Photo The Trustees of the British Museum; IX National Museum of Ife. Photo Andrea Jemolo / Scala, Florence; X Minneapolis Institute of Art. The Ethel Morrison Van Derlip Fund; XI Biblioteca Nacional, Rio de Janeiro. Photo Archives of the National Library Foundation, Brazil; XII Biblioteca Civica Centrale, Turin; XIII Photo The Reading Room / Alamy Stock Photo; XIV Photo Janusz Gniadek / Alamy Stock Photo; XV Photo courtesy Olusola Bakhita; XVI Photo Werner Forman Archive / Shutterstock; XVII The British Library, London; XVIII The British Library, London; XIX Fowler Museum at UCLA, Los Angeles. Photo Don Cole / Fowler Museum at UCLA, Los Angeles; XX The British Library, London. Photo Bridgeman Images; XXI Veneranda Biblioteca Ambrosiana, Milan. Photo De Agostini / Biblioteca Ambrosiana / agefotostock; XXII Royal Collection Trust, London. Photo Royal Collection Trust, London

Black and white illustrations, listed by page
44a The Oriental Institute of the University of Chicago. Photo CPA Media Pte Ltd / Alamy Stock Photo; 44b Photo Courtesy The Oriental Institute of the University of Chicago; 51 Museum of Fine Arts, Boston. Photo Museum of Fine Arts, Boston / Harvard University—Boston Museum of Fine Arts Expedition / Bridgeman Images; 52 Photo P. Rummler. Courtesy Charles Bonnet, Swiss-Franco-Sudanese Archaeological Mission of Kerma-Dukki Gel; 70 Photo Edmond Fortier; 75 Smithsonian National Museum of African Art, Washington. Museum purchase; 91 Photo Matyas Rehak / Shutterstock; 108 Photo Rudi Ernst / Shutterstock; 112 Photo Scherl / Süddeutsche Zeitung Photo / Alamy Stock Photo; 121 Collection of Arthur F. Humphrey III; 136 KB, National Library of the Netherlands, The Hague; 140 The British Museum, London. Photo The Trustees of the British Museum; 155 Photo DeAgostini / Alfredo Dagli Orti / Diomedia; 156l, 156r The Metropolitan Museum of Art, New York. Gift of Ernst Anspach, 1999; 158 Photo Rev. Fr. Jan Vissers. Royal Museum for Central Africa, Tervuren, E.P.o.o.13505; 166 Photo Robert Lebeck. © Archiv Robert Lebeck; 172 Photo Pictorial Press Ltd / Alamy Stock Photo; 174 Photo Prisma Archivo / Alamy Stock Photo; 193 Photo Mary Evans / Grenville Collins Postcard Collection / Diomedia; 207 Photo George Rodger / Magnum Photos; 218 The Cleveland Museum of Art. Alma Kroeger Fund 2013.6; 219 Bibliothèque nationale de France, Paris. Photo Archives Charmet / Bridgeman Images; 231 The National Archives, Kew; 245 Photo Sepia Times / Universal Images Group via Getty Images; 255 From Nathaniel Isaacs, *Travels and Adventures in Eastern Africa*, London, 1836; 271 From Rev. William C. Holden, *History of the Colony of Natal, South Africa*, London, 1855

CONTRIBUTORS

Wendy Laura Belcher is a professor of African literature in Princeton University's departments of Comparative Literature and African American Studies. Her work seeks to bring attention to early African literature and how African thought has shaped global history. She is the author of *Abyssinia's Samuel Johnson: Ethiopian Thought in the Making of an English Author* (Oxford, 2012) and the translator and editor, with Michael Kleiner, of *The Life and Struggles of Our Mother Walatta Petros: A Seventeenth-Century African Biography of an Ethiopian Woman* (Princeton, 2015).

Wayne Dooling is Senior Lecturer in African History at SOAS University of London. His research interests are primarily in the history of colonial South Africa. He is the author of *Slavery, Emancipation and Colonial Rule in South Africa* (Pietermaritzburg, 2007).

Cécile Fromont is an art historian at Yale University whose writing and teaching focus on the visual, material and religious culture of Africa and Latin America in the period from 1500 to 1800, on the Portuguese-speaking Atlantic Ocean world and on the slave trade. She is the author of *The Art of Conversion: Christian Visual Culture in the Kingdom of Kongo* (Chapel Hill, 2014) and *Images on a Mission in Early Modern Kongo and Angola* (University Park, Pennsylvania, 2022).

Muhammadu Mustapha Gwadabe is a professor of political history at Ahmadu Bello University, Nigeria, whose present research is on inter- and intra-religious discord in northern Nigeria. He is a contributor to *Transnational Islam: Circulation of Religious Ideas, Actors and Practices between Niger and Nigeria*, edited by Elodie Apard (Ibadan, 2020).

Habtamu Mengistu Tegegne is Assistant Professor of History at Rutgers University, Newark. His research focuses on a critical understanding of the social and economic history of Ethiopia, and he is the author of *Barara,*

Addis Ababa's Predecessor: Development, Destruction, and Refoundation and the Untold History of Ethiopia [Amharic edition], edited by Beza Tesfaw (Trenton, 2020).

Rahmane Idrissa is a senior researcher at Leiden University's Africa Studies Centre and at LASDEL, a social science research institute in Niamey, Niger. He is currently at work on a history of the Songhay Empire and the dawn of modernity.

Olatunji Ojo teaches African history at Brock University, Ontario. His research focuses on social and economic change in West Africa since the eighteenth century, particularly on the themes of slavery, identity, religion and gender. His recent publications include 'The Yoruba Church Missionary Society Slavery Conference 1880', *African Economic History* 49 (2021), and 'Performing Trauma: The Ghosts of Slavery in Yoruba Music and Ritual Dance', *Journal of West African History* 5 (2019).

John Parker taught the history of Africa at SOAS University of London from 1998 to 2020. His most recent book is *In My Time of Dying: A History of Death and the Dead in West Africa* (Princeton, 2021).

David Wengrow is Professor of Comparative Archaeology at the Institute of Archaeology, University College London, and has been a visiting professor at New York University, the University of Auckland and the University of Freiburg. He has conducted archaeological fieldwork in Africa and the Middle East and is the author of *The Archaeology of Early Egypt: Social Transformations in North-East Africa, c. 10,000 to 2650 bc* (Cambridge, 2006), *What Makes Civilization? The Ancient Near East and the Future of the West* (Oxford, 2010) and co-author, with David Graeber, of *The Dawn of Everything: A New History of Humanity* (London, 2021).

INDEX

Page references in *italics* refer to illustrations; roman numerals refer to colour plates.